I0887378

CULTURAL VALUES IN THE SOUTHERN SPORTING NARRATIVE

CULTURAL VALUES IN THE SOUTHERN SPORTING NARRATIVE

JACOB F. RIVERS III

University of South Carolina Press

© 2002 University of South Carolina

Published in Columbia, South Carolina,
by the University of South Carolina Press

Manufactured in the United States of America

06 05 04 03 02 5 4 3 2 1

Library of Congress Cataloging-in-Publication Data

Rivers, Jacob F., 1951–
Cultural values in the Southern sporting narrative / Jacob F. Rivers, III.
p. cm.
Includes bibliographical references and index.
ISBN 1-57003-483-4 (alk. paper)
1. American fiction—Southern States—History and criticism. 2. Hunting stories, American—History and criticism. 3. Fishing stories, American—History and criticism. 4. Sports stories, American—History and criticism. 5. Southern States—In literature. 6. Culture in literature. 7. Narration (Rhetoric) I. Title.
PS261 .R48 2002
813'.008'0355—dc21 2002007875

A spirit broods here that is autumnal;
it is rich and sad, full of haunting pathos
and romantic charm.

Archibald Rutledge
Plantation Game Trails

CONTENTS

PREFACE

This book examines artistic expressions of cultural values as they appear in leading examples of the southern sporting narrative, a subgenre within the larger corpus of imaginative southern writing that employs imagery from the field arts of hunting and fishing as the vehicle for narrative development. As we examine the philosophical and historical underpinnings of sporting literature by both non-canonical and mainstream southern authors, we find that an important continuity of cultural and environmental assumptions underlies these classic sporting yarns and grounds them solidly in the moral consciousness of the American South. That these dimensions should have been largely overlooked is not surprising, for the intricate system of communal beliefs we find within their pages is often expressed in a deceptively simply yet highly figurative language, a deliberate, narrative pose that masks the artistry of its creators and causes them to appear unconscious of their linguistic and rhetorical subtlety. Viewed in this light, a great deal of what has been dismissed by the scholarly community as simplistic narratives lacking the imaginative complexity required of serious art can now be approached differently—as texts that reveal an important continuity of values and beliefs exemplified by much of Faulkner's best work and most artfully developed in *Go Down, Moses*. The moral continuities of honor, fair play, and noblesse oblige are their major themes throughout, and they sternly evaluate their sporting characters by how well they adhere to an aristocratic code that consistently demands the highest standards of ethical, responsible conduct toward both society and the natural world. What changes as we move along our literary and cultural continuum is the authors' growing awareness that the codes of morality they admire are becoming as threatened as the natural world in which they live and hunt. Their celebration of the aristocratic principles that inform the code of proper sporting etiquette therefore develops over time into a profound sense of cultural and environmental loss, a special kind of backward-looking lament that gains in intensity and broadens in scope, ultimately evolving into the stark realization that survival depends, as it did for primitive man, on a proper respect for the natural world and the human society of which he is a part.

The period of southern literary history examined herein begins in 1846, when the Harvard-educated plantation owner William Elliott wrote about his encounters with the natural world through hunting and fishing, and it continues through 1985, when the University of Georgia English professor James Kilgo wrote about how his experiences as a sportsman helped him to reestablish his ties both to nature and to his family's involvement with the land of the South Carolina lowcountry. Though separated by nearly a century and a half, both writers were drawn into the mysteries of nature through the hunt, and both used its imagery to comment critically on the cultures in which they lived. Their narrative styles and authorial intents were, of course, quite different: Elliott the aristocrat was writing for men of his own class, aiming to celebrate the virtues and experiences they shared and admired, while Kilgo deliberately crafted his prose to the highest critical and thematic standards demanded by the intellectual community of which he was a part. The truly remarkable thing about these authors whose work brackets the chronological scope of our study is that they came to the same fundamental conclusion: In the course of their life's experiences while hunting and fishing in the South, the principles underlying the aristocratic code of southern sportsmanship provided an excellent cultural framework within which to think about and to articulate the negative changes they saw in their respective societies. When the exploitation of the land and the sense of social breakdown and moral decay gains momentum, so does the intensity of their outcry against it. As the authors responded to these multiple and interrelated facets of southern society through the lens of southern sportsmanship, they chose imaginatively to articulate their critical responses from a particular kind of dual perspective. Their characteristically southern concern with the problematic realities of the here and now resonates within the older, more universal mysteries of the hunt, and it is this larger, indelibly Paleolithic reality that accounts in large part for much of the continuity in their work.

In order to understand why this is so, we have to remember the 140 years that their writing spans as it is situated on the time line of human evolution. Without dredging up too much of the accepted anthropological framework of human evolutionary history, it is fairly safe to say that man as we now know him had developed into an anatomically modern form of Homo sapiens about one hundred thousand years ago. For about ninety thousand of those years, he was dependent entirely on natural food supplies, especially on the meat of the large game that his fully developed brain enabled him to outwit and to kill. He had, moreover, a rich and a varied culture and an increasingly symbolic system of ceremonial activities through which he paid tribute to the natural deities that he felt surrounded him (Haviland, *Human Evolution,* 205). Because his central activity was hunting, and because all of the major characteristics that defined him as uniquely human (size, metabolism, sexual and reproductive behavior, intuition, intelligence) had come into existence and were oriented to the hunting life, it was only natural that his culture, in both its technology and its philosophy, should have developed and celebrated the qualities, characteristics, and modes of thought that were most conducive to success in the single activity that was most important to his survival (Shepard, *The Tender Carnivore,* 7). Because of the permanence of these developments, the orientation toward the hunt remains an enduring, if often muted, part of our identities. With the advent of the food-producing revolution that occurred approximately ten thousand years ago, man found himself in somewhat of a philosophical bind. That does not suggest that this new way of doing things occurred overnight, only that, as Paul Shepard points out, "the mental, social, and ecological complex based on hunting" had to be adapted gradually to a relatively sedentary, acquisitive type of existence (6). The important point is that the Neolithic revolution in food producing demanded that man's preexisting view of himself as totally dependent on nature be adjusted in order to accommodate the agricultural and urban way of life.

In *The Primitive World and Its Transformations*, the anthropologist Robert Redfield pinpoints the essence of that adaptation. Paleolithic hunters lived within a *self-imposed moral order* that posited a universe of which man not only was a part, but one toward which he was obligated to conduct himself responsibly if he meant to survive. With convincing evidence collected through documented studies of primitive peoples who remain food foragers instead of food producers, Redfield argues that "in the primary world, man and Not-Man are bound together in one moral order. . . . What man sees out there, that which is not himself and yet in which he somehow participates, is a great drama of conduct . . . spun of duty and ethical judgement" (Redfield, *The Primitive World,* 106). The nonhuman universe was, therefore, not at all indifferent to how it was treated by these early hunters but had instead a life of its own as the enveloping "system of moral consequence." Because our modern, Western society views nature in purely physical terms as simply the occasion and opportunity for expedience and practical exploitation, this primitive view seems to us not only backward but superstitious and ignorant as well. Despite our misgivings and downright prejudice against this reverential, intensely religious view of nature, the fact remains that in pre-civilized societies where man acted practically toward nature in order to get his living, his actions were limited by moral considerations toward a natural universe that was "part of the same moral system in which men, and the affairs of men, also found themselves" (106).

Because of his feelings of oneness with the universe, primitive man's actions with regard to nature were governed by his sense of an inherent, circumspectively immanent moral order, a view quite unlike our accustomed separation of purely physical nature into an unfeeling entity upon which we act as expedience suggests. To the pre-civilized and nomadic hunters and foragers, the taboos, religious ceremonies, and practical restrictions that formed a part of their everyday lives were actually the manifestations of this belief. It even spilled over into Christianity, and in Deut. 22:6 we find what is perhaps the first recorded regulation protecting the nests of game birds. The point is that everything prehistoric man did that involved his interaction with the natural world assumed out of hand an ethical relatedness to the encompassing moral order of the universe. It was not until he became able to produce his own food and so came out from his felt unity with the universe that he began to view nature as endowed with "physical qualities only, upon which he may work his will." As that happened, the universe lost its moral character and became to him indifferent (Redfield, 108).

In José Ortega y Gasset's *Meditations on Hunting,* he also refers to man's having fully achieved his humanity within the period of history when his chief vocation was the hunt. Of greater relevance to our present discussion are Ortega's comments on the special set of assumptions about the natural world that encompassed primitive man, assumptions that form a parallel and corollary to the practical side of hunting's indelible heritage. Ortega speaks often about hunting as a way for man to reenter the natural world, but once inside that primal unity the universe becomes more than simply a place to pursue and to kill game. It becomes instead an ethically sensitive cosmos where everything is infused with moral consequence as well as physical significance. In this uniquely primal world, Nature regains her omniscient moral identity and evaluates human actions on the basis of their effect on the enveloping circumambience of the universe.

It therefore appears quite natural that artistic portrayals of the self-reflective and morally responsible sportsman who reenters the natural world should depict from first to last a special kind of human experience, one wherein he reawakens his predatory instincts and rekindles something of the reverential attitudes of primitive man towards nature. Both Paul Shepard in *The Tender Carnivore* and Richard Nelson in *Make Prayers to the Raven* make this phenomenon abundantly clear in their studies of the Koyukon Indians, Alaskan aborigines who are so isolated from the mainstream of Western culture that they retain many of the customs, occupations, and ceremonies of their hunting and gathering forebears. While modern man can never hope to regain fully the view of nature that pervaded the Paleolithic world, he has clearly erected complex systems of institutionalized taboos that govern his conduct afield and demand respect through their enforceable systems of penalties and fines. Quite aside from the relatively recent environmental concerns fostered on us by rhetorically minded politicians and the circumspective media, one has only to refer to the burgeoning wealth of hunting regulations and sporting etiquette to realize that the environmental alertness demanded by the hunt also evokes an equally intense orientation to man's moral obligations to the ancient order of the universe. It is precisely this view of himself as an integral and properly reverential member of the natural world that Sam Fathers succeeds in instilling in the youthful Isaac McCaslin in *Go Down, Moses*. And forty-five years later, James Kilgo's narrator chronicles his journey backward into the mysteries of the Savannah River swamp in *Deep Enough for Ivorybills* with a voice deeply colored by many of the same themes and ideas, the most prominent of which are a brooding and profound lament for the destruction that man's loss of respect for the natural world has brought about and a celebration of the moral and environmental responsibility that its reemergence can foster.

As Ortega points out in his *Meditations,* "Man is at one and the same time a creature of today and of 10,000 years ago" (Ortega, *Meditations,* 136). On the one hand, the leading characters in the southern sporting narratives of the last 140 years are bound by the iron hand of the imperatives of their food-producing, civilized existence that views nature as an impersonal resource that should be exploited for profit and "progress." Even William Elliott's work assumes an unquestioning and uncritical acceptance of agriculture as the proper use of the land, and Elliott himself was a learned, remarkably progressive agriculturist who published extensively in the agricultural journals of his day. On the other, these same authors reveal that through their involvement with the chase, they have come to appreciate the value of a reverential view of nature that infuses each of its elements, and all of man's actions upon them, with a moral significance reminiscent of the primitive view of the universe as a nurturing, encompassing deity worthy of man's admiration and respect. From first to last, the authors addressed herein are, in fact, portraying the dynamics and meaning of this dilemma as their lament for the destruction of the wilderness intensifies with each passing generation. For these writers, the tenets of good sportsmanship are metaphors for the moral conduct and respect for nature that they revere. This is abundantly clear in *Go Down, Moses,* and Isaac McCaslin represents the ultimate flowering of their shared dream that the morally and environmentally responsible virtues they celebrate in their stories will help to reverse the moral decay, exploitation, and boorishness they abhor.

As our journey through the last 140 years of southern sporting narrative reveals, even the most highly self-conscious literary artists understand that the lament for the natural world and its wholesale, practically expedient exploitation parallels a civilized, moral decadence that is even more shocking to the sensitivities of the educated and morally responsible sportsman of the South. The southern sporting narrative therefore opens a window for its readers upon a view of the world that is deeply tinged with an often heart-rending sense of loss. As the wilderness disappears, as the South is defeated, and as nature becomes for its human occupants less of an omnipotent and nurturing deity and more of an indifferent resource to be exploited for what it can be made to yield, the integrity of the moral codes that govern responsible conduct in civilized life also decline in practical authority. Whether or not they fully realized the implication of it as they wrote, the sporting authors we turn to now are all concerned with castigating the immorality they found present in their cultures by defining it through the lens of man's primordial interaction with nature through the hunt. In its rituals, its etiquette, and its ability to restore temporarily the lost unity of man and nature, these writers found a wealth of symbolic and philosophical material out of which to fashion their communal lament. Well aware of the great law that change is the nature of the universe, they are unanimous in believing that in the world they knew, those changes brought about by irresponsible exploitation at all levels of society are unmistakably and irrevocably for the worse. That they are backward-looking instead of progressively optimistic there is little doubt, and that is one reason why they chose to celebrate the morally responsible sportsman as their ideal. It was he, they concluded, who alone of their fellows knew what it was like to reenter the primitive unity of nature and man and who could therefore comprehend something of man's felt responsibility to his surroundings—to the elements of the natural world as well as to his human peers and subordinates. Man's conduct toward all of these is therefore of major concern to these writers, and it is not surprising that they felt it proper to integrate the ideals of aristocratic conduct with respect for nature, for consideration has always been both the hallmark and the bedrock of gentility. Though their work covers only a chronological fragment of the total sum of human history, it provides a rich and sharply focused critique of a small part of that evolution by evaluating the world in which its authors lived through the themes and imagery of the hunt.

Chapter 1 begins with the erudite and principled optimism of William Elliott's stories about the outdoor pastimes of the South Carolina planter aristocracy. In his *Carolina Sports by Land and Water* (1846), the patrician norms of his elite class and their view of field sports as integral parts of their day-to-day lives clearly suggest their function in reaffirming a close kinship with the land. Elliott describes an approach to nature that is soundly and solidly based on the idea of a mutual dependency, and the pageantry and excitement of the chase are portrayed in terms that accentuate his feelings of affinity with the struggles of the natural world. This emphasis on man as an extension of nature and involved with her in a reciprocal relationship is continued in chapter 2, but by the time that William Gilmore Simms wrote his Reconstruction-era stories of southern sportsmen, the economic and cultural decadence following southern military defeat had darkened his tone considerably. In the late short story "How Sharp Snaffles Got His Capital and Wife" (1869) and in his final published novel, *The Cub of the Panther* (1869), the sense of a mutual dependence on nature has changed from a largely philosophical to a decidedly pragmatic reality. To clarify further these kinds of changes, I contrast the bleak materialism of his late portrayals of southern field sports with the antebellum optimism found in *The Golden Christmas* (1852). In this early novel of plantation manners, the sportsmen do not hunt out of any need or necessity but instead share with Elliott's aristocrats a view of the chase as an opportunity to practice the values of their class in a communal celebration of their lives as further extensions of nature.

Chapter 3 moves beyond the worst privations of Reconstruction and addresses the work of three authors that reflects the southern transition from an impoverished, isolated, and regionally defensive existence into a period where her writers were at pains to move beyond and to heal sectional differences.

Alexander Hunter's *The Huntsman in the South* (1908) once again portrays southern sportsmen as those who pursue hunting and fishing for pleasure, and his narratives are marked by a penchant for preserving the code of sportsmanship and fair play introduced in Elliott's book. Archibald Rutledge, too, is deeply concerned with portraying the southern sporting ethos as an integral part of proper aristocratic conduct, and in *Plantation Game Trails* (1921), *Children of Swamp and Wood* (1927), and *An American Hunter* (1937), he emphasizes and articulates the connection between his code of sporting etiquette and a proper regard for nature. Like his literary predecessors, Rutledge continues to emphasize the southerner's reverence for and dependence on the natural environment, and his work reveals how the tenets of Theodore Roosevelt's ideal of the hunter-naturalist are simply northern varieties of the southern sporting code. (Even Roosevelt got a good dose of the southerner's involvement with the natural world from his mother, Martha Bulloch [1835–84], who was born and raised on Bulloch Hall plantation in Roswell, Georgia). Taken together, their work forms a sharp contrast to the often bleak isolationism of Caroline Gordon's equivocal hero, Aleck Maury. For Gordon's errant professor of the classics in *Aleck Maury, Sportsman* (1934), the traditions of southern field sports are all he has left of his genteel cultural inheritance. They sustain him in his efforts to avoid the crass materialism he sees taking root in the modern, industrial South, but Maury is a man who must travel his chosen path alone. He can draw on the intricate complexities of nature for spiritual regeneration, just as he can find solace in the disciplines and rituals of sport, but the communal faith in nature as the source of beauty and truth has by now retreated far into the past.

Chapter 4 continues to examine this sense of cultural breakdown and vanishing traditions in William Faulkner's *Go Down, Moses* (1942). Like Aleck Maury, Isaac McCaslin is heir to a culture in the process of profound social and economic changes that spell the end of a way of life. And like Gordon's hero, Isaac finds in the code of southern sportsmanship a way to reaffirm the moral imperatives of the past. Although his impractical idealism leads him to pursue the impossible goal of regaining a prelapsarian moral innocence, his otherwise admirable moral conduct is informed and defined by his commitment to a sporting ethos that ensures his sense of noblesse oblige.

As we come to the end of our journey through the last century and a half of southern sporting writers in chapter 5, "Whither the Tradition," Samuel Derieux, Havilah Babcock, and James Kilgo provide ample evidence that the aristocratic code of southern conduct as it is manifest in the etiquette of the hunt continues to fascinate and to inspire those able to regain man's primitive unity and respect for the natural environment. Unlike Isaac's self-defeating quest for an existence that is separated totally from his civilized world, these later authors reveal that both the honor and respect that form the hallmarks of a properly enlightened code of moral conduct continue to constitute an important part of the civilized life of the South.

In dealing with the moral continuities of sportsmanship as portrayed in the southern sporting narrative, this study attempts to bring together a more practical cultural perspective than separate, exclusively literary analyses often provide. In an effort to avoid repetition and to allow an examination of cultural underpinnings that could otherwise escape notice, there has been no attempt to employ the contemporary theoretical discourse involving issues of political correctness. I have tried, moreover, to avoid placing a template of contemporary values upon novels and stories that grew out of the traditions of an earlier, quite different period of American history or upon authors who were deeply involved in the life and culture of a now vanished past. The aim overall has been to offer a fresh look at the southern sporting narrative as a unique and viable form of cultural expression and perhaps to open new avenues of inquiry into a large but often undervalued body of southern writing.

Throughout the course of this project, many kind people have given me encouragement and support, and I wish to thank especially the following individuals without whose help I could never have written this book. First of all, I would like to thank Professor Keen Butterworth of the University of South Carolina for his learned guidance and criticism and for his patient willingness to review my work and suggest revisions. In addition to allowing me to draw freely on his broad knowledge of American literature and the scholarship that surrounds it, Professor Butterworth also introduced me to the work of the Spanish philosopher José Ortega y Gasset, especially his *Meditations on Hunting* (1942). This introduction proved to be another of his major contributions to my study, for while many have tried, no other writer has been able so powerfully to articulate the meaning and essence of the hunt. It is likewise a pleasure to thank Professor Patrick Scott, also from the University of South Carolina, who first encouraged me to pursue my topic and who has helped me to look beyond the purely literary dimensions of my work. Special thanks are also in order for Professor James Kibler of the University of Georgia, who has been willing to take time from his busy schedule to read my work and to contribute countless ideas that have broadened the depth and perspective of my research. I should also like to express my gratitude to Alexander Moore of the University of South Carolina Press for his patience, support, and unfailing good manners and to the librarians and staff of the Thomas Cooper and South Caroliniana Libraries at the University of South Carolina for their imaginative persistence in helping me to locate research materials. To these and to many others I am indebted and obliged, but above all I would like to thank my parents, Mr. and Mrs. J. Franklin Rivers Jr., who often made great sacrifices in order for me to bring this work to fruition.

CHAPTER ONE

Hunting, Fishing, and the Planter Aristocracy

William Elliott's *Carolina Sports by Land and Water*

William Elliott III (1788–1863) represents the aristocratic elite of the nineteenth-century southern scholar-sportsman. This Harvard-educated planter, statesman, and eventual owner of nine separate plantations was admirably suited to reveal in his writing the complex relationships between field sports and the cultural milieu in which they were practiced. Born in Beaufort, South Carolina, into a wealthy and distinguished family of soldiers, statesmen, scientists, and planters, Elliott would live to become the acknowledged patriarch of his family and to continue its proud traditions of leadership and public service. Elliott's father, also named William (1761–1808), was a prominent and civic-minded Beaufort planter who served in the South Carolina House of Representatives and was chosen as the delegate from St. Helena Parish to the state convention that ratified the Constitution of the United States (Skardon, "William Elliott," 3). Elliott followed the family tradition of becoming active in politics, and in 1814 he was elected to his father's old seat in the lower house of the South Carolina legislature. He served either there or in the state senate until 1832.

Politically, Elliott was something of a maverick. Although he served his constituents faithfully as a competent representative of the planter interest, he would not support the hotheads who wanted him to vote for nullification of the federal tariff law in South Carolina. When Elliott felt that he could no longer represent the interests of those who had elected him, he resigned from the senate in 1832 and returned to his home and plantations. As South Carolina drifted slowly toward what he viewed as the insanity of secession, Elliott joined his friends Joel R. Poinsett and James Louis Petigru in publicly denouncing secessionist fire-eaters such as Robert Barnwell Rhett. His published admonitions to his "Fellow Citizens" are on record in the fifteen-page *Address to the People of St. Helena Parish,* which he delivered in Beaufort on August 22, 1832. Elliott cautioned his constituents against blaming the state's economic woes on a single federal tariff and with characteristic foresight cautioned them against breaking so violently with the Union:

> You will remember my friendly caution, and look back with regret, but will you look back from the same point? Will you then, as now, be free to choose your course? When you have struck forward the ball of revolution, can you prescribe its path and regulate its motion? When your voice has shaken and loosened the impending avalanche, can your voice arrest it? (Elliott, *Address to the People,* 6)

As the wording of this passage suggests, William Elliott does not fit into the stock role of the wealthy southern planter who took every opportunity to encourage his fellows to break with the Union simply because of a fashionable political agenda. While he considered South Carolina's rejection of the federal tariff to be unconstitutional, his primary reason for not supporting nullification was that he believed it would tragically compromise the health, safety, and prosperity of the society to which he was selflessly devoted.

In view of the interests, abilities, and achievements of his father, his grandfather, and his famous uncle, Stephen Elliott (1771–1830), and considering their proud traditions of public service, leadership, and civic responsibility, it is not surprising that William Elliott felt naturally inclined to express his political beliefs, agricultural expertise, and sporting adventures in terms that emphasized the aristocrat's duty to his society. While his literary reputation may rest on his single volume of sporting anecdotes, *Carolina Sports by Land and Water* (1846), Elliott also wrote and published during his lifetime a series of widely circulated and influential pamphlets and magazine articles, in addition to numerous book reviews and a five-act Elizabethan closet drama, *Fiesco; A Tragedy* (1850). A prolific writer for most of his adult life, Elliott's final publication was a six-part series of articles in 1857 for the Charleston-based *Russell's Magazine* describing agricultural and economic conditions in Cuba.

What makes Elliott's *Carolina Sports* an important introduction to the sporting narratives that followed are his insights into how the field arts of hunting and fishing were actually overt manifestations of deeply rooted cultural values, especially for the educated elite in the rural, antebellum South of his lifetime. Moreover, his collection reveals at length and in considerable detail many of the major themes of the southern sporting narrative that reemerge consistently in the work of his literary descendants. As Bruce Dickson has suggested, to the planters of Elliott's time and place hunting was "one feature in an image of plantation life they hoped to project to themselves and to the outside world"

(260–64). For Elliott and those like him, the hunt was an innocent and a manly amusement that grew naturally out of the southerner's beliefs about his relationship to nature, his proper role in society, and his view of life as a constant struggle for survival. Though perhaps difficult for some scholars of the modern, urban South to comprehend, hunting and fishing, at least for the men of Elliott's time and class, were integral parts of their education. They provided an important preparation for the struggle for survival, an education into the mysteries and beauty of nature, and an opportunity to practice and develop the sustaining virtues of their class: bravery, loyalty, generosity, consideration for others, and a deep and abiding love for the land and its game.

Strategically poised at the broad intersection of leisurely plantation elegance and the vigorous arts of the chase, William Elliott was admirably suited by both temperament and experience to portray in his writing the complex relationship between southern field sports and the cultural milieu in which they evolved. Though unmistakably tempered by the courtly manners and classical erudition of an accomplished tidewater cavalier, the true inspiration of his unique authorial perspective grew directly out of his deep and genuine involvement with the land and the game that he loved. The imaginative interplay of these complementary facets of his particular cast of mind are reflected clearly in his work, stories and tales that afford the modern reader valuable insights into the aristocratic southern sportsman's views of himself and his proper place in the garden of the southern universe. His work is therefore invaluable as an introduction to the study of the southern sporting narrative, for it shows how the field arts of hunting and fishing were integral parts and natural outgrowths of the society in which he lived. As practiced by Elliott and his peers, the rituals of the hunt were both extensions of their values and expressions of their beliefs. In the pages of Elliott's stories and sketches, we find that the gentleman planter who was also a sportsman carried with him into the field the same set of principles that he felt should govern his behavior toward the larger society of which he was a part. As he encountered and engaged the natural world through the rituals of the hunt, his allegiance to the land and his sense of moral accountability were not at all diminished by his rustic surroundings, nor did they render him any less insensible to the potential censure of public dishonor. Ever mindful of his responsibility and influence, he was compelled by his position of leadership to observe the proprieties and set the good example in every facet of his sport. As Dickson has rightly pointed out, the etiquette and equipage of the hunt were high priorities on the list of things that identified one as a gentleman in antebellum society. As such, the manner in which one hunted functioned as a badge of propriety and wealth, as well as a mark of refinement.

In addition to these matters of status and rank, the sports of the field also operated as integral parts of the antebellum southerner's education into many of the most cherished beliefs and assumptions of his society's conceptual universe. In his frequent trips afield, the young sportsman was acculturated into communal beliefs regarding man's relationship to the natural world and his proper role in society. By reentering and interacting with nature through the formalized rituals of sport, the southerner prepared himself for the rigors of life and leadership through an immersion in the mysteries, the beauties, and the struggles he found in the natural world that enveloped him. In Elliott's charming vignettes of sporting life in the South, we find that while hunting may very well have taken place away from the civilized life of the plantation, it was nevertheless grounded in and governed by the sustaining virtues of the antebellum planter class who practiced it. Long before the first appearance of *Carolina Sports* in 1846, Elliott and those like him had elevated the chase into a ritualistic celebration of the bravery, loyalty, compassion, and sense of fair play that they revered.

On a somewhat different level, Elliott's work also looks forward to José Ortega y Gasset's famous essay, *Meditations on Hunting* (1942). Elliott realized, nearly a century before the Spanish philosopher, that hunting was more than simply an indigenous pastime and that the seemingly mystical, restorative powers of the chase were brought about by man's temporary return to his natural role as predator. Most striking, however, is not the similarity between Elliott's and Ortega's views of hunting as an authentic and restorative immersion in nature but rather their shared belief that the craft of hunting, when properly pursued, can enable and allow its practitioners to achieve their maximum potential as civilized and rational men. In view of this common conviction, it comes as no surprise that both thinkers conclude their respective volumes with celebrations of the hunt as the great promoter of intellectual acuity—Elliott celebrating the increased capacity for "forecast," "observation," and "sagacity," and Ortega praising the hunter's learned habit of "perpetual alertness." As the latter observes, "Only the hunter . . . sees everything and sees each thing functioning as facility or difficulty, as risk or protection" (Ortega,

Meditations, 151). For both the twentieth-century Spanish philosopher and the nineteenth-century southern aristocrat, hunting involved much more than the pursuit and killing of game. Their education and temperament enabled them to see past these surface realities into the true nature of the chase: the basic activity of all reasoned endeavor.

For Elliott and many of his antebellum contemporaries, man did not exist as a sovereign entity separate from nature but rather as an integral part of a vast and interrelated web of existence. That he occupied a position above the lower animals in this stable and prearranged hierarchy was preordained in what Ortega would later call the "inexorable hierarchy among living beings" (112). Elliott would have moreover agreed with Ortega that "Every animal [including man] is in a relationship of superiority or inferiority with regard to every other" (112). Since the accepted law of nature in the antebellum mind was that life and rebirth are dependent upon death and decay, and because an integral part of man's natural identity as predator was his ability to kill, the venatic act was considered by Elliott and his like as a reaffirmation of man's position within the natural order through a disciplined and highly structured ritual. The killing of animals did not therefore concern them as a moral issue, because they viewed themselves in their roles as hunters as ritualistically reenacting a part of their proper and natural identities. But even for those who did not themselves engage in the sports of the field, the killing of animals would not have presented a moral dilemma. The South of Elliott's place and time was largely rural, and its inhabitants, at all levels of society, were well acquainted with the slaughtering of domestic animals for food, a common household practice whose frequency was necessitated in large part by the absence of refrigeration. Unlike the present case in the modern, urbanized South, where animals grown for food are located miles away from the people who ultimately eat them, most citizens of antebellum South Carolina accepted without qualm that the cattle, swine, and poultry that formed a natural part of the visual landscape were raised exclusively to be killed and eaten. Whether he actually hunted or not, the antebellum southerner would hardly have considered the killing of animals for either recreation or food a legitimate cause for serious moral concern.

Elliott's famous book was assembled from sporting narratives he had published previously, under the pseudonyms of "Piscator" and "Venator," in Charleston newspapers such as the *Charleston Mercury* and the *Charleston Courier*, in the *American Turf Register*, and in the *Southern Literary Journal* (Scafidel, "Planter and Politician" 109–10). The resulting volume was well received by its contemporary reviewers for the most part, but in spite of the strong emphasis on the importance of fair play that recurs frequently throughout its pages, the mildly negative, really conjectural commentary of one review temporarily misinterprets *Carolina Sports* by calling its author's moral propriety into question. The reviewer says that he has little experience in either hunting or fishing, and he later admits that "After all, our objections to the 'Carolina Sports,' are not very important. . . . We make them not because they are entitled to much weight, but that we might not seem to review only to commend" ([Simms?], Review of *Carolina Sports,* 79–80). The criticisms are directed at the chapter on devilfishing, and the anonymous writer (probably William Gilmore Simms) for the *Southern Quarterly Review* charges Elliott with wantonness and lack of courage:

> We are *half disposed* [Italics mine] after reading it, to entertain but scant sympathy with the amusement of killing a creature so harmless and so useless. It savors of a destruction of life that seems wanton, unattended, as it is, by circumstances that justify the taking it. The victim is useless . . . They are not eatable by men or dogs . . . They afford no exercise to the sportsman's courage like the lion, tiger, or elephant, for they appear to be a timid animal and seek only, like Mexican generals, to run away (79–80).

Why Simms would choose to ignore the ever present dangers of the sport and Elliott's deep concern with the moral elements of the chase are unclear, but Elliott himself harbored no such misgivings about either his sport or his book. He had no qualms whatever about placing his name proudly on the title page of *Carolina Sports*, nor was he apprehensive about leaving it as the mark of his literary accomplishment. In 1859, he wrote to his wife that "if anything I have written will live after me it will be these 'Sports.' . . . At the worst they can only drop into oblivion, but should they acquire notoriety, it will be a sort of legacy of honor to my posterity who need not then be ashamed of claiming descent from old 'Venator'" (Scafidel, "*Letters,*" 977). Elliott's appraisal proved to be correct, and the volume has been reprinted seven times since its 1846 debut, including an 1867 London edition by the house of Richard Bentley. Among the landowning southern gentry, stories of hunting and fishing were in great demand, and Elliott's collection ranks among the very finest. Like the sports it chronicled, its stories of devilfishing and deer hunting did more than provide amusement; they also spoke reassuringly to a largely homogeneous audience about the virtues and way of life they admired. The fortitude of the hunters, the courage of their dogs, and the struggle for survival spoke time out of mind to the deepest values of the southern aristocrat. Appropriately, the book concludes with a thirteen-page philosophical chapter titled "Random Thoughts on Hunting," in which Elliott most explicitly articulates the sporting ethos he both believed in and practiced during his life.

While Elliott is perhaps best known as a writer of hunting stories, over half of his *Carolina Sports* is concerned chiefly with fishing. The chapters on bass, drum, and sheepshead provide entertaining yet practical introductions to conventional forms of angling for these popular species, and the descriptions of the scenery, tactics, and equipment reveal their author's meticulous eye for detail. Even the unique events he chronicles in "Devil Fishing," the first and longest section, are thoroughly believable and probably accurate in regard to material fact, but the reader soon learns that this particular kind of fishing has little in common with other, more traditional methods of catching fish. In a very real sense, devilfishing is not fishing at all. There is no attempt to lure the devilfish to strike a natural or an artificial bait, and the enterprise has about it more the quality of a military campaign than a restful, contemplative sport. It is instead a maritime form of hunting, most closely akin to the whaling we get in Melville's great classic, and like Melville, Elliott was well aware of the imaginative and rhetorical possibilities of this material. The long leading episode both introduces and establishes the narrative and sporting ethos realized throughout his book, and through an artistic shaping of his experiences Elliott transforms the facts of his actual adventures into a sporting dialectic that celebrates the virtues of his class. The series of reprinted magazine sketches, original narratives, journal entries, and biological debates are not designed simply to amuse or inform. Instead, they are presented and arranged in such a way that a particular type of world view or philosophy is advanced. Through the medium of Elliott's principled, deliberate, and rhetorically self-conscious narrator, the piece as a whole is designed to identify and revere the sustaining virtues of the cultured southern aristocrat.

That "Devil Fishing" could more accurately be titled "Devil Fish Hunting" is suggested in the opening sketch, "Fishing Extraordinary," in which Elliott provides an account of his grandfather's founding of the sport. Aiming his authorial barb not at a devilfish but rather at "contributors [who] talk of their capture of perch and trout of two pounds weight, and other fish of that calibre," Elliott says that devilfishing "bears the same relation to your lauded trout-fishing as a Bengal tiger hunt to a match at snipes" (16). While this claim might be interpreted as tall-tale bragging, it also reflects Elliott's sense of the danger involved. Like so many others whose ancestral roots reached deeply into traditional societies, Elliott and his fellow aristocrats considered courage to be chief and first among the virtues. Without it, they believed, no society could long endure. For those who pursued the lordly devilfish, courage was an absolute requirement.

Well aware that many of his readers would require an orientation to the physical size and power of his prey in order to understand the nature of the risks involved, Elliott provided a brief description of the devilfish:

> Imagine, then, a monster measuring from sixteen to twenty feet across the back, full three feet in depth, having powerful yet flexible flaps or wings, with which he drives himself furiously through the water, or vaults high into the air: his feelers (commonly called horns) projecting several feet beyond his mouth, and paddling all the small fry, that constitute his food, into that enormous receiver—and you have an idea, an imperfect one, of this curious fish (14).

Near the end of the opening sketches, Elliott follows up with a "scientific description" of the devilfish, primarily from James E. De Kay's *Zoology of New York* (1842), and takes occasion to correct several of De Kay's observations regarding color and length (Elliott, *Carolina Sports,* 88–93). From Elliott's descriptions, it appears that the fish that he and his friends pursued was actually the Atlantic manta (*Manta birostris*), the largest of the family Mobulidae, whose range includes the South Carolina coast.

Perhaps the first real hint we have that Elliott will be concerned with representing himself and his fellow sportsmen as latter-day knights-errant, complete with a code of honor and dragons to test their manhood, is the early account of his grandfather's initial encounter with the devilfish. According to Elliott, there exists a type of "vague tradition" that his grandfather had engaged his maritime opponent only because the fish had offered him a personal indignity. In the following passage, Elliott adopts a tone of mock heroism to describe the insult but in so doing initiates a view of the devilfish as opponent rather than mere game:

> It is the habit of this fish to ply these arms [feelers] rapidly before its mouth while it swims, and to clasp with the utmost closeness and obstinacy whatever body it has once enclosed. . . . It was in obeying this peculiarity of their nature, that a shoal of these fish, as they swept by in front of my grandfather's residence, would sometimes, at flood tide, approach so near to the shore as to come in contact with the water fence, the firm posts of which they would clasp, and struggle to uptear, till they lashed the water into a foam with their powerful wings. This bold invasion of his landmarks my grandfather determined to resent (17).

The elder Elliott, however, appears not to have taken any active part in the initial encounter but rather only to have ordered the attack. What is more to the point is that his grandson, composing his first devilfish story from what he calls "these hints" of the encounter, takes occasion to dwell on the courage of the African harpooner named May. May is said to have been Grandfather Elliott's favorite slave, and throughout this part of the narrative May's courage alone endears him to his master. Eager to please and apparently fearless, May acts with decision when once the shoal of devilfish has been reached: ". . . grasping his staff [harpoon] in both hands, he sprang into the air, and descended directly on the back of the largest devil-fish, giving the whole weight of his body to the force of the stroke!" (18). Elliott is not content to let May's temerity pass as merely the apparent foolhardiness of an overzealous slave. Instead, he observes admiringly that "we have few sportsmen who would venture on the daring feat of the African 'May.'" If May, as Elliott suggests, had belonged "to the Saxon or Norman race, he had probably been knighted, and allowed to quarter on his shield the horns of the devil fish, in token of his exploit" (19).

Although Elliott resumes the narrative proper, after giving us "Piscator's" initial entry, by saying that "a few leading incidents only of this story are founded in truth" (22), he promises in what follows to confine himself "strictly to the facts" (23). Nevertheless, his intention to present a tailored version of the character of the devilfish and the adventures of hunting him is now well established. From what Elliott has already let slip, those who go out after devilfish have the bravery of a knight, whether they be master or slave, and that worthiness is won through the rash physical courage that enables them to overcome not only their opponent but also their fears of death at his hands. That Elliott would place himself in this category is unmistakable, especially in view of his earlier comment that he has "been brought more in contact with the devil-fish than any man living" (15).

Having firmly identified himself and his fellow sportsmen as possessed of knightly courage, Elliott proceeds to narrate those incidents in which their courage is put to the test. Not that overt, premeditated valor is often discussed, but scene after scene depicts the "fishermen" risking annihilation at every encounter. In dealing with Elliott's work, it is always important to remember that man in the antebellum South viewed himself as a further extension of the natural world. His courage, then, was not just an abstract quality but a necessary part of his equipment for survival. Elliott, meditating on the absence of devilfish from their accustomed territory on a recent but fruitless hunt, concludes that the fish have merely followed their food supply wherever it led them. Linking himself and his friends to their game and to the larger world of nature, he observes that finding "*subsistence easily and abundantly, is an impulse that pervades all animal life.* It is the great law which governs the inferior animals, as well as man" (61). His awareness of this "great law" and its all-encompassing authority was an integral and characteristic element of the southerner's view of life as a struggle for survival; in the staged encounters with their prey, Elliott and his companions sensed they were reenacting in their sport the inescapable laws that governed their non-sporting lives as well.

In reading the devilfishing section of *Carolina Sports*, one is tempted by the nature of the subject matter to approach the narrative as written by a sportsman who is not also a sophisticated author. Nothing could be farther from the truth, for those who accept Elliott as a kind of authorial "straight man" are missing entirely the tinge of self-deprecating irony with which the section is colored. Elliott's education and cultural and scientific knowledge allow him, or enable him, or perhaps just incline him to give us the devilfishing section with a slight irony. He could see, that is, that his portrayal of the "fishermen" as knights with lances and codes of honor is slightly humorous—that *Don Quixote* was a very present reality for his educated readers and that not a few of them would sense that his narrative has an edge of irony to it. With sublime narrative artistry, Elliott deliberately casts the hunters and fishermen in a mock-heroic light in order to express his own realization that, yes, it is somewhat ridiculous so to represent them. Elliott knew that a devilfish was not a dragon and that his fishermen were not Arthurian knights, but he also knew that courage was required for such pursuits and that the qualities developed through hunting on land or sea were valuable to society nonetheless. He deliberately included this slight tone of self-mockery to make a subtle statement to cultured men like himself who happened to read the book. Instead of producing a straightforward and unwitting melodrama, Elliott intentionally poked fun at himself and his friends in an effort to encourage his educated readers to look beneath the humor of his tale and to think seriously about the deeper meanings and values in the sporting adventures he relates. These kinds of activities formed an actual and important part of his culture, though he would hardly have argued that they were its most serious or most valuable outgrowth. What Elliott had done was to use them as a vehicle for imaginatively portraying his view of life as a difficult and dangerous game, one requiring in equal degrees the courage and audacity that he celebrates in these early opening narratives.

Despite his sense of the ridiculous, Elliott could not bear to represent himself and his fellows as unaware of the value of the natural bounty of which they availed themselves. While reemphasizing that "the sport is not without its perils" and that "There is danger enough in the pastime to give it the highest relish" (61), he continues by identifying his amusement as far removed from the wasteful slaughter attributed to the sport by his critics. He is also at pains to define himself and his fellow sportsmen as respectable and responsible members of the natural world in which they hunt. In one example, he notes that killing devilfish has its practical advantages as well: "the liver yields an oil useful for many agricultural purposes, and the body cut into portions convenient for transportation, and carted out upon the fields, proves an excellent fertilizer of the soil" (61). Because man existed as an integral but superior part of his natural environment, he thereby exercised a type of dominion over the lower animals of the world. To recreate the struggle for survival by hunting and killing them with the proper ceremony was really to offer a kind of homage to "what is divine [and] transcendent in the laws of Nature" (Ortega, 112). The sportsman was nevertheless human and as such required amusement to relieve the tedium of his civilized life, but that amusement must not lead to wanton slaughter or needlessly waste its prey. Instead, as Dickson observes, the hunter's aim was "to enter nature as an active participant rather than an intruder" (Dickson, "Hunting," 279) and to match his courage and intelligence fairly against that of the game. To do so, however, was often to place oneself in extreme physical danger.

Elliott incorporates the risks quite naturally into the devilfishing episodes. From threats of "extensively and exceedingly violent [storms capable of] destroying fences, uprooting trees, and falling on some devoted spots with the force of a tornado," to risking being "beaten to pieces" against the breakers in the shoal water while subduing the prey (48), Elliott makes it clear that the sportsman must accept risking his life if he is to comport himself properly. The most colorful risks, however, and those most effectively conveying the dangers of the chase, come from the devilfish themselves. As Elliott again reminds us, "The reader must not suppose that there is no risk in the pursuit and capture of such formidable game" (70). A harpooned devilfish can not only tow his pursuers twenty-five miles out to sea or catch the arm of his assailant with one of his tremendous feelers but can also perform aerial acrobatics that, considering his two-plus tons of weight, can easily destroy both his pursuers and their craft. Perhaps the most dramatic of many examples Elliott provides for his claim that "no precautions can absolutely secure the sportsman against danger" (70) is his account of his son's close brush with death. Assuming the post of harpooner, the younger Elliott took aim at a particularly large devilfish from the bow of his boat. In the following passage, we are afforded an insight into how suddenly dangerous and unpredictable the quarry can be:

> It was my son's fortune to reach him first. His harpoon had scarcely pierced him, when the fish made a demi-vault in the air, and, in his descent, struck the boat violently with one of his wings. Had he fallen perpendicularly on the boat, it must have been crushed, to the imminent peril of all on board (77).

Fortunately—one could almost say miraculously—Elliott's son was thrown forward and onto the back of the harpooned fish but managed to make his escape "without being entangled in the cordage, or receiving a parting salute from his formidable wings" (71). In either case the younger Elliott would likely have been killed. As the author and his contemporaries would view the incident, however, the young harpooner had not merely had an adventure but had rather passed through a major stage in his education into life as a struggle for survival. What we actually have in this scene is an example of how hunting provided not only an education but also a preparation for the future. That Elliott believed such violent indoctrinations invaluable is certain, especially in view of his eldest son's death in 1830. By taking his next oldest son devilfishing, Elliott shows that he was willing to risk the life of the heir apparent to his fortune and family name in order to afford him this dangerous but necessary introduction into the hunt and the rigors of the struggle for survival.

Between the long chapter on "Devil Fishing" and the second section of the 1859 edition titled "Sports of the Field," Elliott includes four brief chapters: "The Sea Serpent," "Drum Fishing," "Bass Fishing," and "Sheepshead Fishing." Of these, only the last three are found in the original 1846 printing by Burges and James in Charleston. "The Sea Serpent," a not-very-successful sequel to the devilfishing episodes it follows, was written by Elliott in New York while he was negotiating the details of the 1859 printing. The editors at Derby and Jackson may have felt that readers would like to have one further installment of maritime hunting before moving into the accounts of more traditional forms of angling, but their more practical concerns were to "broaden the book's appeal by recounting incidents that reportedly took place in New England waters" (Rosengarten, introduction to *Carolina Sports,* xxvi). In addition, the political climate of 1859 may also have had some influence on the New York editors' decision to include a story that shows Elliott and his comrades at their worst, as Theodore Rosengarten plausibly argues:

> The sea-serpent story, added to the New York edition of 1859, reads more like a tall tale than a true adventure; furthermore, the mock heroism and frivolity which precede the unmasking of the Monster undermines the artistic humbling of the hunters in the second part of the book. Probably the Yankee publishers hoped the comedy would boost sales. Perhaps, at a time when anti-southern feeling was running high, they were covertly editorializing by projecting an image of superstitious aristocrats who spent their time chasing chimeras and practiced planting on the side (xxvii–xxix).

Whether for political or for economic reasons, adding "The Sea-Serpent" to an otherwise serious volume of sporting adventures in the antebellum South did little to enhance or to improve the book as a whole. The chapters on drum, bass, and sheepshead fishing, though far less valuable in suggesting the values of Elliott's class of sportsmen, are at least serious attempts to depict the excitement and surroundings of actual sport. Of these, only "Bass Fishing" and "Drum Fishing" describe incidents and practices that indicate the courage and noblesse oblige required of the conscientious sportsman.

The black drum (*Pogonias chromis*) takes his name from the peculiar noise made by the males of the species during their courtship rituals in the spring. Elliott tells us that on a quiet afternoon the "drumming" can be heard at a distance of several hundred yards from the water (110). Not as formidable as the devilfish, the drum of Elliott's day averaged about thirty pounds in weight and four feet in length, and its value as a food source was considerable. The planters dined on only the delicacies of the smaller fish and their roe, but their servants received the windfall of the larger fish, "salted and cured like cod-fish, from which when dressed they are scarcely distinguishable in flavor" (112). In the following excerpt, Elliott provides his readers some idea of how the planter-sportsmen of his day combined their love for sport with the obligations of their class:

> The planters of this vicinity are skillful fishermen and much devoted to the sport. They succeeded in taking, during the last season, at least twelve thousand of these fish; and when I add, that except the small number consumed in their families, the remainder were salted and distributed among their slaves, not in lieu of, but in addition to their ordinary subsistence, you will perceive that this is a case wherein the love of sport, and the practice of charity, are singularly coincident (112).

This added bounty, however, was not obtained without considerable effort and risk. Elliott tells us that "the patience of the fisherman may be severely tested; sometimes you have the mortification to hear them drumming beneath your boat, while they stubbornly refuse to be taken" (14). Should the fisherman be successful, he faces the rigors of pulling the fish in—not with modern reels and fiberglass rods but with stout lines that are pulled in by hand: "In the sport of this day [Elliott tells us], my gloves were torn into shreds by the friction of the line, and my fingers so blistered by the severity of the play that I was incapable of renewing my sport for several days" (115). As uncomfortable as such abuse may seem to modern anglers equipped with the latest in angling technology, the element of real danger only appears when the fishing has been especially good. Opportunists as they are, the sharks of Port Royal Sound took a decided interest in the successful drum fisherman's good fortune. On one occasion in particular, Elliott's fully loaded boat was nearly capsized:

> *Thirty* fish were all that the boat could conveniently contain; her gunwale was but a few inches above the water, and we slung the *ten* (which were *de trop*) alongside, by a rope. In this situation we were attacked by sharks. These "grim companions" would range up alongside, and make a rush at them to cut them

> off; and we were compelled to beat them off with boat-hooks. A little more boldness in their attack, and we must have fallen victims, for a single blow from their tails would have filled our overloaded boat. As it happened we were unattended by any other boat which could have rendered assistance, and were full three miles from shore (114–15).

The sharks of Beaufort Harbor continue to play a major role in providing the spice of danger in Elliott's next chapter on "Bass Fishing." The bass, as Elliott calls them (*Corunia oscellata*), are currently classified as red drum (*Sciaenops ocellatus*) in *The Audubon Society Field Guide to North American Fishes, Whales, and Dolphins* (Boschung, *American Fishes,* 117, 623). More elongated and "elegantly shaped" than their black cousins, they are still referred to as spot-tail bass by the anglers of Beaufort County. In the July 1847 number of the *Southern Quarterly Review*, the reviewer correctly observes that "the bass fishing of Broad River resembles very much the drum fishing just described" ([Simms?], 80). However, when the angler leaves his boat and wades into the surf to try his luck, he abandons not only his comfort but also his margin of safety. F. G. Carey notes in the October 1846 number of the *North American Review* that "'Bass Fishing' is particularly agreeable for the graceful touches, which disclose a nice perception of the dispositions of both fish and men" (Carey, review of *Carolina Sports,* 329). These "dispositions" are nowhere more powerfully portrayed than in Elliott's account of surf fishing for bass where he is cut off from land by sharks.

Following a set of detailed directions with what Carey calls "a precision worthy of the chief topographical engineer among fishermen" (329), Elliott tells of a trip that was very nearly his last. Having waded out onto a sandbar that is covered at high tide, Elliott and his servant, Cain, are enjoying their sport and the "clear transparent wave[s]" that push "pearly fragments of sea-shell by you with the flux and reflux of the tide" (126). Nevertheless, the seemingly tranquil sport is not without its dangers, and we learn that the sportsman must take care not to step on the "jagged spines of immense sting-rays . . . one incautious step, and your leg may be transfixed by the venomed weapon!" (126). So absorbed were Elliott and his servant in their sport and in avoiding the barbs of the rays they didn't realize their danger until nearly too late. Waist deep in the surf and 150 yards from shore, the fishermen suddenly realize that the scent from their bait basket has attracted three large sharks, "paused to reconnoiter before they rushed on their prey" (127). Anyone familiar with the power and disposition of our coastal sharks would be quick to agree with Elliott that "If they attacked *us*, we were gone!" (127).

Fortunately for himself and his servant, whose eyes were "almost starting from their sockets," Elliott has the presence of mind and the nerve to realize "one of those frequent cases, in which we find safety in audacity" (129). Calling for his spear and telling his servant to keep close and to shout when he does, Elliott mounts his attack:

> Repeating my order to Cain, and grasping my spear in both hands, I rushed upon the leading shark, and struck it down violently across his nose—shouting, at the same time, at the top of my voice—while Cain, in a perfect agony of fear, gave a loud yell, and fell at full length in the water! The manoeuvre succeeded; the sharks ran off for deep water, and we took the crown of the ridge, nor looked back, until we had accomplished the one hundred and fifty yards over which we had to wade before we regained the bank! (127–28).

The escape profoundly affected the author, convincing him to abandon forever the pleasures of "*bass fishing in the surf*" and causing him to reflect on the fragility of life itself. Moreover, the scene brings together and underscores the themes of natural mortality, courage, and noblesse oblige that recur both in the chapter on "Bass Fishing" and in the first half of the book as a whole. Like the natural destruction of the small island at Bay Point, formerly a great nesting ground and egg bank for "curlews, seagulls, and other aquatic birds" (125), but now obliterated by hurricanes, and like the fate of the person and residence of Gen. Charles Cotesworth Pinckney, both "swept away in one of the fearful hurricanes that vex our coast" (119), Elliott's experience has caused him to understand better and on a more profound level that his days, too, are numbered by the laws of the natural world. His encounter with the sharks has caused him to realize that, like "the storms of the equinox," nature's power operates "with a force that nothing can resist" (120). He will return to this theme in "A Business Day at Chee-Ha" (181–82), as James Kibler's review of the 1994 edition makes clear, and it is here in this later story that Elliott's subtle artistry reveals how the natural world abounds with imagery that affirms the transience of all living things.

But even in the face of nature's invincible power and its unmistakable allusions to man's mortality, the sportsman and the gentleman must not allow himself to abandon his courage, honor, and consideration for others. Earlier in the chapter on "Bass Fishing," Elliott tells us that "I like my full share, I confess, but not the monopoly of the sport" (121). Having properly positioned his boat and taken as many bass as he wants, he invites a neighboring boat to anchor to his drop. Looking back, he comments on "the satisfaction, while I sailed away from the ground, to see him merrily engaged in the sport" (122). Moreover, the sportsman cannot allow himself to be cowed by the power of the natural world. May, Grandfather Elliott's slave, was not contemptuous of the devilfish or its power but with knightly zeal jumped astride the wide back of his opponent in a gesture that clearly earned Elliott's respect. In a more deliberate rendering, Elliott charged the sharks that had cut off Cain and him from the shore, saving both their lives by the attempt. The values and virtues that Elliott imaginatively articulates in the first half of *Carolina Sports* are those of the traditional English aristocracy, qualities that are revered highly by the planter class he represented. Whether harpooning devilfish or angling for drum or bass, the ideal of the sportsman we find in the first half of *Carolina Sports* is a brave and generous man, intensely aware of his close ties with the natural world that surrounds him and duty-bound to fulfill his obligations both to that world and to his fellow human beings.

In the second half of *Carolina Sports*, titled "Sports of the Field," Elliott moves from the fishing he obviously enjoyed to accounts of hunting that are so vividly portrayed that no one can doubt his enthusiasm for the sport. The continuing themes of courage, fair play, and noblesse oblige remain prominent, and the opening section, "A Wild-Cat Hunt in Carolina," reveals an author absorbed in his true element. In later episodes such as the "Chee-Ha" series and in "Random Thoughts on Hunting," Elliott displays a fine perception of his place in the universe through meditations delivered when the hounds are at fault or his sport lags. In "A Wild-Cat Hunt," however, he is at pains to communicate the matchless thrills of the chase. As the *Southern Quarterly Review* writer pointed out in an 1847 review, Elliott is at his best when he writes about "the excitement of action . . . passages of spirited narrative . . . lively and vigorous and strongly indicative of the ardor with which the writer seems to throw his whole soul into the sport" ([Simms?], 69).

As Dickson suggests, hunting allowed the southerner to enter into the natural world in a way that reaffirmed his kinship with nature: "the total involvement of the experience as much as the actual kill . . . provided the sense of being a natural man" (Dickson, 276). In "A Wild-Cat Hunt," this total involvement is unmistakable, and it provides occasion for us to observe Elliott at his fast-paced best. In the following excerpt, the author is not simply reporting his experience but is also recapturing for his readers the consuming intensity of the chase:

> There they go!—look at them!—listen to them! Does it make your pulse quicken? Is there not a thrill of pleasure shooting through your frame? Can you tell your name? Have you a wife? A child? *Have you a neck?* If you can, at such a moment, answer such questions; you do not feel your position, and are but half a sportsman! (147).

Elliott's choice of words and images in this passage tells us a great deal about how he and his friends felt about their sport. His comment that the man able to remember his own name is "but half a sportsman" clearly attests to the total involvement in the natural world that many southerners experienced through the pageant of the hunt. Even the strong sense of a hierarchical society with which the story opens is forgotten. There are no lines of caste or class in this scene—no judges or doctors; no neophytes or veterans; no blacks or whites; no masters or slaves. Instead, through their total involvement in the magic of the chase, the men have transcended their societal positions and temporarily exchanged them for their primordial identity as predator. Much later, William Faulkner would voice the same sense of transcendence in *Go Down, Moses* (1942):

> It was of the men, not white nor black nor red but men, hunters, with the will and hardihood to endure and the humility and skill to survive, and the dogs and the bear and deer juxtaposed and reliefed against it, ordered and compelled by and within the wilderness in the ancient and unremitting contest according to the ancient and immitigable rules which voided all regrets and brooked no quarter . . . (184).

Elliott was astute enough as an author and devoted enough as a sportsman to identify and to capture the same phenomenon that Faulkner would later write about. Hunting was not only the way that southerners of Elliott's time and class reaffirmed their kinship with nature but also a means of transcendence wherein the accretions of political society could be temporarily ignored and forgotten.

Following this introduction to field sports in the second section of his book, Elliott moves into four loosely connected stories about hunting at Chee-Ha plantation, located in an area called the Chee-Ha Neck—a fourteen-mile stretch of land between the Ashepoo and Combahee Rivers in what is now Colleton County, South Carolina (Skardon, 114). In this area, still quite probably "the best hunting-ground in Carolina" (Elliott, *Carolina Sports,* 152), we continue to find "no fancy sketch" but rather the sporting adventures of a lowcountry planter less concerned with using his material to suggest themes outside of the sports themselves than with celebrating his own experience. Nevertheless, Elliott is self-consciously aware that he faces no simple task when "a word too little makes you vague, and a word too much makes you tedious" (141). Moreover, he is also aware that the sportsman who "gives you a true description of his sports, *must be an egotist*" (162), simply because "the things which *he* has seen or done are precisely those which make the liveliest impression" (162). To compensate for these inescapable hindrances, he promises to provide his readers with a deliberate "*celerity of movement*" (162) and consciously to include a "*want of repose*" in his narrative: "could I rouse for you an elephant, gentlemen critics, you should have repose with a vengeance. But, for your lighter game, dash splash on, with whip and spur!" (162). Although criticized for a certain rashness in his writing, what one reviewer called a want of "the grace of ease" ([Simms?], 69), it is through this very headlong intensity that Elliott best achieves his purpose of depicting for his readers and of communicating to them the exhilarating transformations he experienced while hunting.

The four Chee-Ha narratives are best approached in pairs, the first with the second and the third with the fourth. In the first pair, Elliott fulfills his avowed role as egotist, but the rapid pace and brilliant descriptions more than compensate for any slight smugness that readers may detect. In "A Day at Chee-Ha" (152–61) and "Another Day at Chee-Ha" (162–72), we not only can trace the transformation of the refined, educated hunter from a civilized intruder into the natural man at one with his element but also can find ample evidence to suggest that while transformed by the excitement of the chase, the sportsman was yet governed by respect for the values his class and society revered.

The planter-sportsman of Elliott's time was very much aware of his responsibilities to his fellow men—black and white, peer and servant—and the strong sense of noblesse oblige was an important part of his life and manners.

Elliott himself was a noble example of this sense of responsibility. He shared selflessly with his fellow planters his hard-won and extensive agricultural expertise through speeches, pamphlets, and articles and adhered to what James Kibler calls "a policy of strict planter responsibility" toward his slaves that prohibited "physical mistreatment or family splitting," and that included provisions for "careful medical attention and responsibility for the slaves's moral and religious betterment" (Kibler, "William Elliott III," 113). In fact, Elliott celebrated these kinds of civic and moral responsibilities as one of the hallmarks of his class under the heading of "liberality of character" (Elliott, "Cultivation of Male Cotton," 354). As he says in one of his numerous articles on southern agriculture, he prefers "the risk of tediousness, to the imputation of reserving for my private advantage, any hint, suggestion, or information whatever, calculated to advance that great interest, which is the basis of all Southern prosperity" (Elliott, "Cultivation and High Prices," 162). His writing reveals that he was, in both private and professional life, a man of compassion and conviction and possessed of an abiding sense of his responsibility to his fellows. Not surprisingly, many of these same qualities are manifest in his narratives of the chase.

In "A Day at Chee-Ha" we find these virtues in abundance. With Elliott on this day are two novice hunters who, in continuing the metaphor of hunting as a species of warfare, are described as not yet having "'fleshed their maiden swords'" (153). One of these, addressed by the black driver Robin as "Maussa Tickle," was fortunate enough to bring down his first deer and was duly "bloodied" by a veteran companion. His deer, however, had been fired at several times, and we learn that "Loveleap had given the mortal wound, and that Tickle had merely supplied the 'coup de grace' to a deer, that, if unfired on, would have fallen of itself, in a run of a hundred yards" (156). Nevertheless, Elliott tells us, "we were quite too generous to divulge this unpleasant discovery to our novice, in the first pride of his triumph!" (156). As if for emphasis, the following page begins a second chase in which a deer again is hit but continues to run, this time swimming a river and gaining the fastness of an impenetrable marsh that Elliott calls an "impracticable Serbonian bog" (157). While Elliott remains mounted, his Negro servant climbs a tree in an effort to spot the dogs and deer. He is unable to do either, but the cry from the pack tells Elliott that the chase has stopped and that the dogs have the deer at bay. In what Elliott calls "the excitement of the moment," he orders Robin to advance before the hounds tear the deer to shreds. Robin, however, is reluctant: "'Got maussa . . . if he be water, I swim 'em—if he be bog, I bog um—if he be brier, I kratch tru um—but who de debble, but otter, no so alligator, go tru all tree one time!" (158). The stalemate is broken when the deer rallies and, with what Elliott calls a "masterly manoeuvre," escapes again. Though he has accused his servant of cowardice, Elliott quickly realizes that he had momentarily forgotten his responsibility for Robin's safety: "The thought was just stealing its way into my mind, that under the excitement of my feelings, I was giving an order that I might have hesitated personally to execute" (158).

In "Another Day at Chee-Ha" the image of the hunt as a form of warfare is continued as Elliott and his friends prepare "to perpetrate a *raid* against the deer" in a type of "sylvan war" (163). The beauty of the "glorious winter's day—sharp but bracing" is not lost on the hunters, and, as if sensing the fleeting nature of such weather and scenery, they "felt that such a day was not to be trifled away in talk" (163). The account of the chase and the kill is no less well-rendered in this second section, but there is less emphasis on the noblesse oblige than in the first. The huntsman Geordy does adhere nobly to the highest standards of his sport by making sure of the deer he's hit instead of firing as others of the herd pass him, and Elliott's "Done like a sportsman . . . one dead deer is worth a dozen crippled ones" suggests his attitude toward irresponsibly wounding game. What strikes the reader most is the exhilaration evident in Elliott's tone after he has killed two running deer at point-blank range. Profoundly moved by the encounter, he berates northern sportsmen for their lack of adventure and wildness and celebrates his own quite different brand of hunting: "They were wild deer, of the wild-woods, that we slew, this day at Chee-Ha!" (172). For Elliott, the hunt not only brings him release from the tedium of work and allows him to "fling the cares of life far, far behind" (172), but it also allows him "to feel an otherwise inexpressible sense of what it meant to be a part of something as awesome as nature" (Dickson, 273).

Put another way, Elliott's experience in reaffirming his natural role as predator has enabled him to understand and to relish his close ties to nature. This is why he lashes out at the tame and artificial sport of his northern contemporaries. From the start, the Puritan experience was to live in stockades and villages and to fear the wilderness that surrounded them. Their goal was to conquer the wilderness to the point of terrific control thereof, creating an artificial and arrogantly man-willed world devoid of mystery and governed by his science and empiricism. While Elliott himself may not have been fully aware of this fundamental difference between the northern and the southern views of nature, he nevertheless understood that a mere simulation of the hunt was as self-defeating as it was unsporting. As Dickson says, "the necessary relationship with nature evoked by hunting would have been impossible on a preserve" (Dickson, 277). Shooting pen-raised birds in surroundings that only simulate nature could never evoke for the sportsman a sense of his proper place in the universe. Perhaps José Ortega y Gasset says it best:

> Man cannot re-enter Nature except by temporarily rehabilitating that part of himself which is still an animal. And this, in turn, can be achieved only by placing himself in relation to another animal. But there is no animal, pure animal, other than the wild one, and the relationship with him is the hunt (Ortega, 139–40).

Thus far into *Carolina Sports*, Elliott has been concerned primarily with describing scenes of hunting and fishing that celebrated the character of the sportsman as he practiced the virtues of his society and class. Brave, generous, responsible, and ever mindful of the beauty and power of nature, the hunters and fishermen conduct themselves admirably whether afloat or afield. Above all, Elliott presents the recurring image of a genuine southern nobility as the members of this elite class interact with nature in such a way that they are able to reaffirm their position in the natural world. We are not encumbered by much in the way of politics and domestic social life, nor does Elliott open to us the world filled with the tedious and unrelenting cares associated with managing the great plantations. Instead, the world thus far presented is, to a large degree, ideal, unmarred by the superficialities and petty intrigues of society. Beginning with "A Business Day at Chee-Ha" (173–91), however, the magic circle that Elliott has drawn around his group of sportsmen is broken, and excepting the brief sections on identifying the birds and animals of the chase and the philosophical "Random Thoughts on Hunting," the remainder of his book depicts the pitfalls of indolence and self-indulgence, both of which are portrayed as ruinous to the aristocratic ideal of noblesse oblige. While Elliott continues to celebrate the principles of the planter-sportsman as the touchstone for evaluating moral worth, he now reveals what can happen when greed, irresponsibility, and wantonness cause the gentleman to abandon his trust.

In "A Business Day at Chee-Ha," the "occasional failures" that Elliott promises are designed to foreground the pitfalls of shirking one's duties. Appropriately, the sporting and domestic scenes that follow are filled with incidents and imagery notably lacking in a sense of authenticity, undercut as they are by false appearances that only suggest the existence of reality. Preparing like other planters to revisit his plantations near the end of October, Elliott first draws our attention to the theme of duplicity and false appearances by placing the two words *business* (173) and *hunt* (174) in italics. We learn as well that this allegedly duty-bound planter has chosen Robin the hunter as his body servant and his "hunting pony" as his mount as he prepares to examine his property. His horn and shotgun are thrown into the gig, and he tells us further that if hunting "was not exactly the direct object of my visit, it might readily become a collateral one" (174). From this point on, Elliott portrays himself as falling victim to the "irresistible" appeal of hunting with Loveleap, and the *business* trip soon deteriorates into a farce.

At every turn in "A Business Day," Elliott is at pains to include textual hints that the planter who neglects his professional duties is only asking for trouble. Not that the narrator is unaware of his responsibilities: "business before pleasure; that's my motto" (174), he says, and after promising to conclude his inspections in three hours, he reflects self-consciously on his dilemma:

> Oh! It is wonderful how we stride over the field of business, when we have hitched to the fence beyond, some favorite hobby which we are impatient to mount and ride! (176).

Nevertheless, every scene is shot through with suggestions that, because he has been remiss in his duties to his proper work, he has subsequently forfeited the true pleasures and meaning of the chase. At the plantation, for one example, the rice ricks, apparently too capacious and promising of profit, are "plated" with only the most choice sheafs of grain, hiding the inferior rice beneath: "the light, and the mow-burnt, and the bird-pecked was safely bestowed, far from the reach of inquisitive eyes, in the very center of those proud looking ricks" (178). In addition, the conversation with his Negroes is little more than slapstick, cut mercifully short by a shrill whistle from Loveleap. Putting off the Negroes' requests for clothing until he can "find time to attend to them," Elliott gives the excuse of going "to visit the sick." In the space of one line—"The sick were visited, examined and prescribed for" (180)—he dispatches his duties there and to the seemingly endless requests for favors answers the aging Negro in charge: "Not a word more!" as he flings himself into the saddle. Realistically, no absentee plantation owner could possibly conduct the necessary inspection and maintenance of his plantation in three hours, but when Loveleap advances we learn that Elliott has spent only two. His inspection has been no more thorough than glimpsing his corn, pea, and cotton fields that he galloped over on the way out, and one senses that the awareness of his irresponsible conduct has served to make him uncomfortable. And well it might, for though Elliott was wealthy, he was constantly tasked and intimately involved with the details of managing nine separate plantations that stretched across a hundred miles. While Rosengarten would reduce the entire episode to supposed guilt over the question of slavery, such a convenient interpretation totally ignores the practical side of the issue. The opening pages of "A Business Day" do not portray a man beset with thoughts of racial injustice. The slaves are to him simply one more of the troublesome aspects of owning and of operating a plantation. There are instead two more universal and straightforward issues that disturb Elliott's narrator and put him ill at ease. The first is that instead of looking after his family's financial interests with proper and deliberate diligence, he has shirked his duty to go off on a hunt for deer. And the second, as James Kibler points out in his review of the 1994 edition, is suggested by Elliott's refusal to be called "Old Master" by his slaves and the "unpleasant memories that flashed across [his] mind" (181). Taken together, they suggest that Elliott wants his audience to identify with a very human character whose uncharacteristic lack of diligence stems directly from his feelings of being overwhelmed by the pressures of his existence. In one sense Elliott does wish to escape, not from any sense of racial guilt but from the grueling responsibilities of plantation management and "the recognition by a forty-five year old narrator of his own mortality, a narrator created by an author whose father had died at age forty-seven" (Kibler, "Imperialism," 338).

The remainder of the narrative is filled with scenes and incidents that serve to underscore both the penalties for this type of negligence and the contrast between appearance and reality. For example, the "coverts; so solitary, so undisturbed" (182) yield only deer that are so wild that they outstrip even the best efforts of Elliott and Loveleap to cut them off—hardly the kind of reaction expected from game unused to being hunted. Finally, Elliott does get a shot, but his previously infallible aim is at fault. The deer at first goes down, but it quickly recovers and escapes. Nimrod, the magnificent hunting dog who was "a cross with the West India bloodhound," catches the deer, but he can only hold him for a moment. Elliott's final shot is good, but the deer falls into the river. When Robin refuses to swim out to retrieve him, Elliott undresses to swim out himself. He decides not to after all, because Loveleap offers to go instead. Nevertheless, Loveleap ultimately decides against the attempt as well. What had begun as a story about discharging the duties of an absentee planter has by this point deteriorated into a mockery of both the business of planting and the craft of hunting. Neither, it would seem, can be properly executed by men who abandon their diligence and their proper attention to duty.

The themes of artificiality and of misleading appearances are carried over into "The Last Day at Chee-Ha" (192–217). Although "the day was fine, and many a familiar face was noted at the gathering place" (192), this final hunt at Chee-Ha is a far remove from the simple, good-natured, and sustaining amusements offered in the first half of the book. Excepting Elliott's amazing shot on two bears, killing them both with a single barrel of his shotgun, there is very little of actual hunting in this section at all; almost immediately, we are returned to the theme of misleading appearances. The first of the two bears, though "*stone dead*" (195), is killed with a brain shot that effects a type of instant rigor mortis that, with the help of a convenient sapling, maintains the animal in an upright position. The famous pack of Port Royal hounds, supposedly fearless, are so cowed by the upright bear that their conduct "amounts almost to terror" and can never be induced to follow the scent of the other two bears that escaped. In addition, a hunter called "The Laird" claims to have wounded a buck at point-blank range but can only offer what he says is bone marrow in proof. And after the hunt, Venator reads for his friends a piece titled "Phantasmagoria" (210–12), which begins by describing his vision of demons but ends by revealing their origin in a malarial fever and an overdose of quinine. It seems that nothing on this "Last Day" is authentic or genuine.

With "The Fire Hunter," Elliott moves from reporting his own adventures to an admittedly fictionalized account of actual events connected with the death of a Negro slave. His aim, he says in the brief afterword, is "to expose the dangers to property and to life" of this highly illegal practice, and, "unlike the sketches which precede it," this story is "illustrative of life—rather than . . . a sketch from life" (231). Fire hunting today is simply called night hunting or jacklighting, a practice in which deer are blinded with powerful spotlights long enough for them to be shot. In Elliott's day, the practice was no less illegal, but a large frying pan filled with fat-lightered splinters was used instead of today's electronically powered lights. No matter the equipment or the century, night hunting for deer has never been considered proper sporting form, and those who practice it have always been subject to the true sportsman's disdain. In fact, South Carolina passed the first law prohibiting night hunting in 1780, eight years before the author of *Carolina Sports* was born (Halls, *White-tailed Deer,* 71).

Elliott's strongest message in "The Night Hunter" has to do with what can happen when the sportsman completely abandons his proper sense of noblesse oblige, thereby cutting himself off from his fellows in the kind of modernist introversion we saw earlier in The Laird's insistent arrogance that, despite the well-deserved ridicule of the other hunters, he preferred to cling to his own self-aggrandizing fantasies. While one may quite reasonably not expect the same high level of honorable conduct from a slave and an underbred overseer as he might from the landed aristocracy, Slouch and Pompey's behavior constitutes a complete disregard for their duties and societal obligations. They not only steal the plantation's game and sell part of it for profit but also succeed in killing a fine colt whose mother they plan to plant in a neighboring field as a ruse. Unconcerned with this further duplicity, Slouch drives the point of a sharp stake through the dead colt's body to make it look like an accident, and as for the mother, he calmly replies, "If they knock her brains out, I don't care; she'll be out of sight for one day, anyhow" (266). To register his disdain for such conduct, Elliott concludes the section with the following lines: "We shall now leave the faithful Slouch, after having acquitted himself thus honorably of his trusts, to retire to his rest; which, we may assure the reader, was disturbed by no qualms of conscience" (226–27).

On a somewhat different level, the absentee planter, the would-be hunter of his plantation's deer that have already been killed by Slouch, has done nothing more than to plan a hunt for himself and his friends on land that he legally owns. Nothing in the wording of the following excerpt suggests that Slouch is intended as anything but what he appears to be—an ungrateful and faithless employee determined to steal what he cannot legally own:

> Here he's been writing to me, as if I were a nigger; telling me to keep them bucks till he comes over with his friends to hunt them. Dang me, if I do. Who

> gave them to him? Were they born in his cattle-pen? Have they got his mark and brand upon them? All that have white tails are in my mark, and I'll shoot them as I please, and ask no odds (219–20).

Perhaps it is Elliott's unconscious design to berate the absentee planter for his irresponsible proprietary control, but if Louis D. Rubin is correct that the "imaginative sympathy works directly against what as landowner Elliott wishes to demonstrate" (Rubin, *William Elliott Shoots,* 27), then why should he so forcefully emphasize Slouch's insubordination and portray its outcome in such unmistakably offensive terms? The safer course is to accept Elliott's denunciation of Slouch and Pompey at its face value and to move on to the tragic circumstances of Toney's death as an episode more clearly related to the absentee planter's true negligence.

When Pompey discovers his brother, Toney, shot by another fire hunter and bleeding slowly to death, the incredulous slave is not unsympathetically rendered. Pompey's concern for his brother is depicted as genuine and moving, as are his indignation at the act and his angry promises for revenge. Elliott clearly feels a sense of moral outrage and a fine disdain for the absentee planter who refuses to live on and take care of his property. As the dying slave says, "Maussa musn't say I die like a tief!—tell 'um all 'bout it! *If he bin here, de fire hunter neber bin shoot me*!" (230, emphasis mine). Rubin correctly identifies this passage and properly suggests its true significance:

> Because the land-owner will not guard his own property, the helpless slave must die. And the slave dies when on an errand of mercy: getting sugar for his sick wife. If the master had been there where he should have been, the slave would not have needed to borrow the mule and ride to the distant store for sugar (Rubin, 25).

In brief, the indictment of the nameless absentee plantation owner in "The Fire Hunter" is the same as it was for the hasty plantation examiner in "A Business Day at Chee-Ha." Neither character has properly discharged his duty to his family's pecuniary interests or to the necessities of his labor force. Both characters ignore their responsibilities to their proper code of honorable behavior and to those who depend on them for protection. While it is true that Elliott's indignation is aroused and severe, his disdain is directed toward supposed "sportsmen" who, whether from intentional disregard or simply from convenience, indulge themselves at the expense of other human beings. That he may have unconsciously revealed, as Rubin suggests, an unease over matters of racial injustice may or may not be the case. What is clear is the intensity of Elliott's concern over matters of honesty, proper conduct, and moral responsibility.

The opening of this chapter suggested that Elliott's concluding section, "Random Thoughts on Hunting," provides a type of summary and encapsulation of the cultural ideals that inform his work in general and his philosophy of sport in particular. Here we find Elliott the sportsman once again celebrating the innocent, manly, and ennobling virtues of the chase, and again his social position and education are clearly revealed. Elliott is convinced that, despite its sober-minded detractors, recreation of one type or another is "indispensable" and that in the realm of rural amusement, "They who denounce them should withhold their censures, until they can substitute a recreation more commendable than hunting" (250). Not only does he argue that hunting can teach and develop the virtues of "*forecast, punctuality, observation, and sagacity*," he also promises that "the man who habitually applies himself to this sport will become more *considerate*" (251). Having earlier taken to task the Puritan-minded "ascetic innovators, who would make life as unjoyous as their own natures" by denouncing amusement as sin, he is at some pains to delineate the cause of their narrowness. It springs, he says, "from this intense self-esteem—and their utter inability to get beyond themselves, so as to understand the relations and wants of others" (248). By denying the value of wildness and nature to the point of assuming absolute control of an artificially man-willed world, the men to whom Elliott refers are the victims of a life-denying and myopic agenda. As Elliott says, they look at life and the universe through the medium of a prejudice "so inveterate, as to discolor or distort whatever is graceful or beautiful in nature or art" (248).

Although he draws a broad and clear line between landed aristocrats, men who are nevertheless "proprietors *and* tax-payers" (emphasis mine), and the poor who poach with relative impunity upon rich men's properties, his arguments are not couched in terms that suggest his aim is to enact laws that forbid poor men to hunt. Instead, he simply argues for the common law maxim "that everything upon a man's land is his own . . . and he can thus shut it out from his neighbor without wrong to him" (255). As Elliott points out, he is speaking about "land which [the owner] has purchased with the proceeds of his industry—and for which he pays tax to the state" (255). His purpose is not to encourage the passing of laws designed to restrict the practice of hunting but only to outlaw the practice of "unrestricted hunting" that, in his era, allowed professional fire hunters to slaughter game for commercial purposes and to destroy fences, crops, and livestock in the course of their sport.

Like other southerners, Elliott viewed himself as an integral part of the natural world, nor would he deny his less fortunate fellow hunters the opportunity to recreate themselves in the beauty of nature. "I like my full share, I confess," he says in the chapter on bass fishing, "but not the monopoly of the sport" (121). Instead, though his imagination could accept and make use of the plight of the poor and the slave, he wrote primarily for others like himself and for true sportsmen everywhere, urging them tacitly to practice the virtues of courage, fair play, and noblesse oblige in their domestic, professional, and sporting lives. Meditating on the authors of southern sporting narratives at large, Dickson aptly concludes that "their narratives of their exploits were constructed in a way that was consistent with their assumptions about human nature, society, and the world" and that, in describing the rigors and rituals of the hunt, "the Southern writer made his society's theory of the universe personal and concrete" (Dickson, 281). This is a large part of the message of Elliott's book, from the devilfishing episodes on through its final pages. For this reason, if for no other, attempts to define *Carolina Sports* as a political treatise or to identify its author as a frustrated social reformer can only rest precariously on the uncertain ground formed by tentative assessments of Elliott's unconscious intentions, a dubious business at best.

CHAPTER TWO

Field Sports in the Reconstruction South

William Gilmore Simms's *The Cub of the Panther* and "How Sharp Snaffles Got His Capital and Wife"

After the Civil War and the subsequent extinction of circumstances that allowed Elliott and scholar-sportsmen like him to flourish, the southern sporting narrative and its aristocratic orientation virtually vanished until well after the turn of the century. What stories of hunting have survived from the Reconstruction period do not suggest the restorative powers of an immersion in the natural world but rather reflect the bleak, impoverished struggle of men trying to wrestle a living from the ruins of a ravaged landscape. In two of the few surviving narratives by a major southern author in which hunting plays a leading role, "How Sharp Snaffles Got His Capital and Wife" (1870) and *The Cub of the Panther* (1869), William Gilmore Simms suggests how the changed cultural atmosphere after the war is reflected in the ways men approached the sports of the field. Not surprisingly, the enforced cultural decadence and Simms's personal and professional losses are clearly reflected in the ways in which he portrayed the southern sportsmen. Struggling against grinding poverty and the oppression of northern occupation, Simms and the postbellum sportsmen he presents in his later works have altered their perceptions of hunting from a sport to a necessary means of pragmatic exploitation. What follows examines these narrative themes and contrasts them with the optimism that informs the hunting scenes in Simms's earlier novel of plantation manners, *The Golden Christmas* (1852).

In the early spring of 1852, Simms published a light novel of plantation manners that playfully parodies the foibles of antebellum planter society in the South Carolina lowcountry. Very much a part of this elite and aristocratic group, Simms was able to draw on firsthand experience for his portrayals of its culture, and he included descriptions of the hunting scenes that formed an integral part of a plantation Christmas. Though tinged with a light irony, Simms's renderings of the hunts for deer and boar in *The Golden Christmas* are even more emphatic than *Carolina Sports* in depicting the sportsmen as knightly adventurers. Evident, too, is a playful optimism that clearly reflects its author's sense of confidence in both the strength and the stability of his society. Not until well after the turn of the century, in collections like Archibald Rutledge's *Plantation Game Trails* (1921) and *My Colonel and His Lady* (1937), would southern planters who were also hunters again be portrayed as secure in their privileges and wealth.

As David Aiken remarks in his introduction to the 1994 reprinting of *The Golden Christmas*, the 1850s were a time of prosperity when the wealth and abundance of the South were "well known and widely envied" (Aiken, i). In 1852, Simms and his family were living comfortably at Woodlands, his wife's three-thousand-acre plantation home in the Barnwell District of lowcountry South Carolina. Even as late as 1857, the extent of their hospitality would prompt Simms to complain in a letter to young Mary Lawson about the inconveniences of entertaining a continual stream of guests: "We have had besides a world of Aunts and Cousins (my wife's) spending (self-invited) some five weeks with us, so that we have not had quiet for a moment in all that time. Think of dining 20 or more persons daily, for six weeks!" (Simms, *Letters*, 3:498). Although Simms may have considered himself "very poor" by the comparative standards of the tidewater aristocracy, the plantation's profits and the sales of his books were quite enough for him and his family to live elegantly and well and to entertain their relations on a gracious scale. Moreover, if he occasionally despaired of the freedom to write the "Great Work" his friend James Henry Hammond desired, his creative energies and output remained exceptionally high and would continue to do so. During the period from 1850 to 1859, Simms published no less than six major works of fiction, including the four novels that rounded out what John Guilds identifies as the "lofty theme [of] America's struggle for freedom and independence": *Katherine Walton* (1851), *The Sword and the Distaff* (1852), *The Forayers* (1855), and *Eutaw* (1856) (Guilds, *Life,* 195).

Even a casual review of the circumstances surrounding Simms's life during the different times he wrote *The Golden Christmas*, on the one hand, and "Sharp Snaffles" and *The Cub of the Panther*, on the other, reveal important differences that undoubtedly influenced his work. Having published extensively in the genres of poetry (seven volumes), biography (two volumes), and short fiction (two volumes) during the years from 1845 to 1849, in addition to various satirical essays and the book-length *Views and Reviews in American*

Literature, History and Fiction (1845), and at the beginning of one of his recurring "sustained waves of creative energy," Simms returned "vigorously and imaginatively" to the prose fiction that had first earned for him a secure place in American letters (Guilds, 191). Not only was his reputation as author and poet secure, but his worldly affairs were as well. Though his letters from the early 1850s often contain allusions to the expenses of maintaining a family and upholding "the aristocratic family tradition of genteel hospitality," Simms could nevertheless afford to decline James Henry Hammond's offer to fund him in the "Great Work" for the five years Hammond envisioned it would consume (Simms, *Letters,* 3:168 n). And while Simms complains that he could "make & put up money, were I not compelled to live in Carolina" and that "in N.Y. or Phila. my income would be trebled by the very same amount of toil," he also reveals confidence in his ability to earn enough by writing to continue his gracious lifestyle:

> Look where I will, I see nothing at present before me, but the necessity of toiling on, as I do now, assured that my drudgeries will, at least, provide me with the means of staving off necessities and enabling me to maintain myself & family in the degree of comfort which they at present enjoy & to which they are accustomed (3:194).

Simms could not have known what the war and its aftermath held in store for himself and his family. Relative to the inconveniences of 1852, the hardships he faced later were severe indeed. By the time he came to write "Sharp Snaffles" and *The Cub of the Panther*, his society and most of his plantation home at Woodlands were in ashes. In an excerpt from his letter to Joseph Henry in December 1868, Simms succinctly reveals his losses: "My property, save my lands, is all destroyed. One day, I was the owner of some $150,000 in slaves, land & c. I have nothing now, but what I can extort, from what Ben Jonson styles 'Brain Sweat.' My house destroyed, my Library, which cannot be replaced even by money, more than 10,000 volumes" (5:180). That the loss of his library, the death of his wife, and the defeat of the South affected Simms's outlook is hardly surprising. Writing to Paul Hamilton Hayne from the partially rebuilt Woodlands in 1869, the declining author suggests the pragmatic view he then took of his work: "I do not write now for fame or notoriety or the love of it, but simply to procure the where-withal of life for my children; and this is a toil requiring constant labor" (5:213). No doubt Mary Ann Wimsatt is correct in arguing that Simms "retained to the last his conception of literature as an art requiring serious imaginative commitment" (Wimsatt, *Major Fiction,* 253), but this excerpt from an 1868 letter to his protégé, John Esten Cook, suggests how little Simms relished his incessant labors:

> For my part, I can boast of nothing that I have done, though I have been doing not a little. Still, it irks me that I am forced to tone my mind down to the miserable requisitions of stupid [serial] publishers, and low-toned readers. I cannot labor gracefully or gratefully simply for popularity, though this becomes the essential necessity of those who lack money (Simms, *Letters*, 5:190).

Simply put, the contrast between Simms's emotional, financial, and political circumstances before and after the Civil War was considerable, and his changed situation, reflecting the widespread effects of the military and cultural defeat of his society, figures prominently in his work. However, unlike the portrayals of professional hunters in his postbellum fiction, men for whom the chase represents the means of surviving and achieving material wealth, his fictional sportsmen of 1852 could still engage cheerfully in a type of indigenous recreation that was free from the goad of necessity.

The Golden Christmas is properly classified as a comedy of manners, and Simms uses his short novel to provide what Wimsatt calls "satiric descriptions of errant city socialites," a theme he expanded later in *Katherine Walton* (1854) and *The Cassique of Kiawah* (1859), in which certain leaders of the planter class are presented in a "mildly unflattering light" (Wimsatt, 159). The volume was first published serially under the title *The Golden Christmas: A Chronicle of St. John's, Berkeley* in three weekly supplements to the *Southern Literary Gazette* in 1852 (Simms, *Letters*, 3:39 n). The firm of Walker, Richards and Company, which also published the *Gazette*, issued the short novel in a single volume later in the same year. Although it produced little in the way of remunerative or contemporary critical rewards, Guilds is correct in calling it "perhaps [Simms's] best [effort] at social satire in a comedy of manners." Guilds continues: "*The Golden Christmas* captures—with wit and good humor, yet with an admirable objectivity—the nuances, the distinguishing characteristics, the strengths and weaknesses, of southern society at its most sophisticated and gracious level" (Guilds, 203–4). In both the urban and pastoral settings, we are amply provided with detailed descriptions of how important caste, class, and bloodlines were to antebellum planters, and quite often, Simms's wit seems to sharpen upon itself.

As a part of his efforts to present the southern agricultural system at its finest and to provide a faithful portrayal of its customs, Simms includes lengthy descriptions of two hunts, both of which reveal a celebration of the courage, noblesse oblige, and generosity that are strikingly similar to those found in the earlier *Carolina Sports*. And like William Elliott, Simms incorporates a wry, sidelong glance of self-deprecatory irony into the hunting sections of *The Golden Christmas* to insure a comic tone. The first hunt at the Bulmer Barony is for deer, but the narrator of Simms's tale is not at all the practicing *aficionado* of *Carolina Sports*. Dick Cooper is unprovided with either fortune, lands, or leisure, and the hard-working young attorney can only look back to better times for memories of his sporting prime:

> Though a bookworm of late, and a city lawyer, I had been once a famous fellow for the chase, was a free rider, a good shot, and altogether a good deal of a hunter. It had been a passion with me once, but—what has poverty to do with passion! (Simms, *Christmas,* 54).

Nevertheless, the virtues of the sportsman are celebrated and revered in Dick's adventures much as they are in Elliott's earlier work. And there are other similarities too, such as the narrator's comments on the growing scarcity of game and the use of the Manton shotgun (54), a high-quality English import manufactured by the London gun maker Joseph Manton. Simms's narrator tells us that the once impenetrable swamps are now largely accessible, and the human population, now "greatly increased, give the deer no respite" (54). As a result, the deer are "terribly thinned off," and the presence of a nice buck, or even of his tracks in the pea field, has become an event of special note. On the four thousand acres of the Bulmer Barony, however, game still exists in huntable numbers, and the opportunity to prove oneself in its pursuit remains an important mark of manhood.

Though "fresh from the dingy chambers of the law and the ponderous volumes of the frosty wigs" (57), Dick proves that city life has not greatly diminished his prowess afield. As Major Bulmer says after the deer he and Dick fire at are found, "The law has not spoiled you for a gentleman and a hunter yet"

(57). But while the visitor's performance has earned him "quite a feather in [his] cap," he is not so overwhelmed by his marksmanship that he forgets his sense of the obligation of those born nobly to conduct themselves honorably. It seems that Major Bulmer shot at the buck Dick has killed only moments before, and though he confides to the reader that "the shot that killed him was mine," he notes, too, that "the exulting Major discovered other button holes in the jacket of the beast, to which he laid confident claim" (57). In this same spirit of generosity that prompted Elliott and his friends not to undermine Mr. Tickle's killing his first deer, one that had already been mortally wounded, and to avoid divulging "this unpleasant discovery . . . in the first pride of his triumph!" (Elliott, *Carolina Sports,* 156), Dick and the hunters "readily recognized the claim of the old man to have certainly made his mark" (Simms, *Christmas,* 57). By so doing, both the major's self-esteem and the camaraderie of the hunt are preserved.

In his introduction to the 1994 reprinting of *The Golden Christmas*, David Aiken emphasizes Simms's reliance on actual people and events for the scenes of sport and culture: "The lasting impression of the novel is realistic. Simms wants to document life on a Low country plantation, not only at Christmas time but throughout the year" (Aiken, v–vi). As he says, the book is drawn from Simms's "personal experience, filled with characters based on people known to the author, and with places familiar to him. . . . it is authentic" (i). The Christmas hunts form an important part of this authenticity, as do the games, dances, and social pretensions of the aristocrats like Paula Bonneau's grandmother, Madame Girardin, and the posturings of Major Bulmer himself. But there is another, quite different strain of realistic depiction in the short novel that is valuable in contributing to the verisimilitude of the narrative, and in chapter 14 of *The Golden Christmas*, Simms interrupts the lighthearted tone of his story and draws the reader quietly aside for a no-nonsense orientation to the habits of the game:

> You are aware that, in the larger swamp and forest ranges of our Low Country, whose population is sparse, the hogs run absolutely wild . . . They turn readily upon the dogs, and it requires a very vigorous cur, indeed, and a very bold one, to take them by the throat. They will sometimes give fierce battle to the hunter even, on horseback, and have been known to inflict serious if not fatal wounds upon the horse; while the rider, himself, must be wary enough in the

> encounter if he would escape from hurt. The long white tusks of an angry boar, which has never been honored by the annual tribute of the barn, or mollified by the pickings of the farm-yard, are no trifling implements of battle, rashing short and sudden, against the thigh or ribs of the heedless hunters (115).

Unlike pursuing the devilfish, hunting wild boar occupies a long-standing tradition among both European and American sportsmen. Indeed, it is Major Bulmer's desire in *The Golden Christmas* to perpetuate the old English tradition of having a boar's head at the center of the Christmas table that prompts him to initiate the hunt (115). While the excerpt below from the *New Hunter's Encyclopedia* describes Americanized Russian boars introduced into North Carolina in 1910, along with their crossbred descendants on wild razorbacks, animals that more closely resemble those discussed in *The Golden Christmas*, the warnings are surprisingly similar:

> Big game hunters claim that in the heat of battle these boars are the most vicious of all animals that roam the American forest. They reign supreme in their territory and even the black bear is no match for this powerful, belligerent brute. Mother bears selecting one of these pigs to feast their cubs have been found with bellies ripped inside out and littered on the battle ground in the boar's own inimitable manner of destruction . . . (Camp et al., *Encyclopedia,* 40).

With an eye toward incorporating the details of the hunt with "the Social and Domestic Life of the Parishes," as he had earlier advised William Elliott to do (Simms, *Letters*, 2:493), Simms tells us before the boar hunt that "the jousts and tilting of the knights of the middle ages" have recently been introduced into the parish of St. John's and that these "served, perhaps, to suggest the present enterprise to his mind" (Simms, *Christmas,* 115). Accordingly, Major Bulmer selects his huntsmen from "six or eight young knights who had distinguished themselves at the last tournament . . . each armed with boar spear and *couteau de chasse*" (115). All have assumed titles, including Dick Cooper as the Knight of Kiawah and a particularly unfortunate though nameless young man who calls himself the Knight of the Bleeding Heart. Even the dogs are afforded chivalric roles, especially "a gaunt, gray beagle" who had not "waited for enlistment, received no bounty, and, seeking only the honor of the thing, went as an obscure volunteer" (116).

The hogs are brought to bay and the huntsmen arrive, finding "three hogs of immense size . . . long bodied animals, with long legs, grisly and angular in aspect and outline, and all with ominous tusks" (117). The dogs rush in as the hunters appear, but "the sharp bark was followed by a sharper cry, and we could see the blood-stains instantly upon the shoulders of one limping beast, and the gash along the ribs of another, who howled himself out of the fight, only to sink down, seemingly fainting in the water." As Major Bulmer observes, "Bull has got his quietus, I'm afraid" (118). The danger to the dogs is real, but so is the danger to the hunters. Though well-mounted, Major Bulmer and his knights do not carry firearms. Instead, Simms reminds us that, on this hunt, "It was not allowed, be remembered, to use any other weapons than spear and knife. There had been little sport . . . but for this restriction" (120). This self-imposed handicap is in keeping with what Ortega would observe almost a hundred years later in his chapter titled "The Essence of Hunting." While he acknowledges the great truth that hunting occurs throughout the animal kingdom in relationships of natural inequality—that is, "between two animals, one of which is the agent and the other the subject"—he also points out that man cannot employ his reason and technology without some restraint if the "precise boundary beyond which hunting ceases to be hunting" is to remain intact (Ortega, *Meditations,* 53–54). Without articulating this concept or giving it more than a passing mention, Simms seems to have divined this truth instinctively. No doubt plantation gun rooms of the 1850s were well-stocked with rifles capable of effectively dispatching wild boar from a safe and comfortable distance, but Major Bulmer disdains their use, choosing instead to restrict himself and his friends to the spear. It is this gesture, this deliberate and voluntary relinquishing of technical superiority, that reveals more than anything else Simms's instinctive rapport with the essence of hunting. As Ortega would later observe, "progress in weapons is foreign to the essence of hunting . . . *since hunting cannot substantially progress*" (53). His point is that hunting is actually a game played between two competing sets of instincts, and these must be allowed to function freely without superimposing a great handicap on the one by affording the other an overwhelming and artificial technical advantage. To the master of this antebellum boar hunt, this nice point of sporting etiquette is important, not only as a practical means of preserving the sports of his ancestors but also as a necessary element of the fair play required for a real hunt to take place. Even though the actual encounter with the game is depicted with a tinge of mock heroism reminiscent of Elliott's devilfishing scenes, the major's sense of fair play very nearly costs a man his life.

The boar's primary defenses are his tusks, and as Dick, considering it "a point of honor to give the Knight of St. John a chance" and abstaining from further combat, watches his friend make a charge on one of the boars, the Knight of the Bleeding Heart follows suit and is nearly killed: "He was taken completely by surprise, and, before he could anticipate the danger, or wheel out of the way, the sharp, white, felonious tusks of the boar rashed against the fore-shoulder of his beast, swift and deep, so that you could hear the grinding of the keen instrument against the bone" (Simms, *Christmas,* 121). Thrown from his horse into the confusion of boars, dogs, and fellow hunters, the knight's escape with no more serious injuries than a bruised head and a bloody nose seems no less miraculous than young Elliott's escape from the devilfish in *Carolina Sports* (Elliott, 71). But while Simms does provide an exciting and detailed depiction of a hunt for wild boar in the classic style, complete with descriptions of the very real dangers that such an undertaking involves, he does not forget that he is involved in writing a comedy of manners, not a tragedy of sylvan warfare. As he says, "Had leg, or arm, or neck, been broken, the mishap would have risen into tragic dignity. As it resulted, it was simply ludicrous, and the Knight of the Bleeding Heart was everywhere laughed at as the Knight of the Bloody Nose!" (Simms, *Christmas,* 123).

As the author of an authentically representative, though mildly satiric, comedy of plantation manners in the lowcountry of antebellum South Carolina, Simms felt compelled to include in *The Golden Christmas* incidents of hunting as an important part of the cultural expression of the planter class. Courage, fair play, and noblesse oblige are the hallmarks of his sportsmen, just as they were for William Elliott's in 1846. And like Elliott, Simms presents the most dramatic encounters with a self-deprecating irony that couches otherwise serious but potentially melodramatic dangers in a mock-heroic rendering. The sportsmen are of the elite, and apart from Major Bulmer's need to preserve the sports of his ancestors, the hunters in *The Golden Christmas* resemble, on one level at least, the volunteer beagle that joined the boar hunt in "seeking only the honor of the thing" (116). But these chivalric episodes were written well before the ravages of Sherman's army. After the war, with his home, his library, and his literary career in ruins, Simms would return to accounts of hunting for the final phase of his career, although his fictional sportsmen would bear little resemblance to the "knights" of the Bulmer Barony. In his last published novel, *The Cub of the Panther: A Hunter Legend of the "Old North State"* (1869), and one of his final published efforts in short fiction, "How Sharp Snaffles Got His Capital and Wife" (1870), the aristocratic hunters of his and Elliott's earlier works are replaced by men whose very livelihoods depend upon their woodcraft, marksmanship, and courage. While there remains a striking continuity between the values revered by these lower-class, professional hunters and those of the elite in *The Golden Christmas*, the only aristocratic "sportsman" who appears in Simms's late work is sadly lacking in any moral values at all. Strangely like Elliott's decision to place as the final narrative in *Carolina Sports* his tale of Slouch and Pompey in "The Fire Hunter," Simms, though working on a much broader spread of fictional canvas, saves for his last novel the depiction of Edward Fairleigh, the most corrupt and vulgar element in the hunting fraternity.

"How Sharp Snaffles Got His Capital and Wife" originally appeared in *Harper's New Monthly Magazine* (41 [October 1870]: 667–87). Its companion piece, written during the same period, is "'Bald-Head Bill Bauldy'; and How He Went through the Flurriday Campaign!—A Legend of the Hunter's Camp." Both stories are from Simms's final period, 1865–70, and are based on notebooks he kept during several visits to western North and South Carolina in the 1840s. Simms turned to the Appalachian material he had gathered twenty years earlier at a time when his fortunes, reputation, and his narrative perspective were markedly altered from the optimism of the 1850s, a time when he could still envision latter-day knights-errant hunting deer and boar on a thriving lowcountry plantation. As a result of this shift, we find distinct differences in the portrayals of the hunters in "Sharp Snaffles" and in the physical setting itself. The most obvious change is that the aristocratic hunters on the fringes of a settled, thriving community are replaced by rough mountaineers, professional hunters in a wilderness environment who "traded in the meat that yet ran in the woods" (Shillingsburg, "Edition," 114). This alteration in the caste and profession of his characters meant that the studied impracticality of the earlier sportsmen is abandoned and that, instead of seeking honor and spiritual fulfillment, the mountaineers return to their natural roles as predators as a means of survival. They form an important part of Simms's larger design to portray the economic and cultural ruin that engulfed the South after formal military defeat, but their environmentally insensitive pragmatism is also a realistic if imaginative parallel to the great increase in unrestricted market hunting that peaked after the Civil War. As Richard Nelson points out in *Heart and Blood* (1997), the "binge of exploitation" that marked the latter half of the nineteenth century greatly escalated the extensive damage already done to American wildlife over the past three hundred years (Nelson, 101). In the South, the dire necessities of Reconstruction did little to encourage either its professional hunters or their hungry patrons to reflect on the negative effects their wholesale slaughter would ultimately have on the environment.

In contrast to the leisure that would allow him to take a month's hunting trip on which he took the notes for his 1847 journal, the strained circumstances of 1869 left Simms with little time for hunting and fishing. Writing to Charleston merchant James Nicholas Robson from Woodlands in 1869, Simms admits that "my own personal exercises in field sports are now pretty well ended" (Simms, *Letters*, 5:200) but continues by saying that he has nevertheless "devolved upon my boys mostly the use of rifle and shotgun. In these they are pretty expert." (5:206). His further comments praising the virtues of the DuPont gunpowder that Robson had sent him, "that it gives out but little smoke upon discharge; that it fouls the piece less than any powder they have known, and that its force is evidently much greater," bears testimony to his thorough familiarity with the muzzle-loading arms of his time. However, these "great and goodly qualities" are not applauded for their value in improving the quality of the sport but rather for the practical value of putting food on the table. As he goes on to say, "we have need to rest our hopes, of fresh meat, upon what trespassers we may arrest with our guns in the shape of duck, partridge, rabbit and squirrel" (5:200). A quick glance back at the preparations for the great dinner party in *The Golden Christmas*, where thirty slaughtered hogs and a freshly shot beef are complemented by "a wilderness of mince-pies," "seas of jelly," and "mountains of blanc mange," suggests something of the contrast between plantation life before and after the war (Simms, *Christmas,* 138). If Simms did look back to the bounty of an antebellum plantation Christmas, the memory could only have served to intensify his present predicament.

Working doggedly to meet his literary engagements in the bleak days of 1869, Simms was faced with any number of obligations, disappointments, and physical complications that undoubtedly contributed to the perspective with which he chronicles the sports of the field. His published letters from this later period in his life provide ample evidence that the years of poverty and drudgery after the war taxed the aging author to the maximum extent. Despite his precarious health, each summer from 1865 until 1870 Simms returned to New York to seek new writing contracts and to attempt, often without success, to collect payments for his previous publications. Left nearly destitute by the war, Simms had no recourse but to use his talents as author for the survival of his family, and to that end he directed the whole of his being. Though markedly disinclined to accept contracts for serial writing, he wrote to Paul Hamilton Hayne in December 1869 in an effort to explain his current production:

> For my part, and for the last six months, I have been literally *hors de combat*, from overwork of the brain—brain sweat—as Ben Jonson called it—and no body sweat—no physical exercise. In the extremity of my need, I took contracts in N.Y. in the autumn of 1868 for no less than three romances, all to be worked, at the same time. I got advances of money on each of these books, and the sense of obligation pressing upon me, I went rigidly to work, concentrating myself at the desk from 20th Oct. 1868 to the 1st. July 1869—nearly 9 months, without walking a mile in a week, riding but twice and absent from work but half a day on each of these occasions. The consequence was that I finished two of the books [*Voltmeier or the Mountain Men* (*Illuminated Western World*, 6 March–28 August 1869) and *The Cub of the Panther* (*Old Guard*, January–December 1869)] and broke down on the third [see Simms, *Letters*, 5:194 n], having written during that period some 3000 pages of the measure of these which I now write to you. Dyspepsia, in its most aggravated forms,—Indigestion, Constipation, Nausea, frequent vomitings, occasional vertigo, and, as the safety valve to this, hemorrhoids (5:282).

During the "final harrowing months of his terminal illness," Simms also managed to write two "backwoods dialect tales of exceptional merit": "How Sharp Snaffles Got His Capital and Wife" and "'Bald-Head Bill Bauldy;' and How He Went through the Flurriday Campaign!—A Legend of the Hunter's Camp" (Guilds, 315–16). A common source that links these late tales together is Simms's use of "notes and memories of his several visits to western North and South Carolina in the 1840's . . . but the trip that mattered most for his imaginative writing was his tour of Western North Carolina in the early fall of 1847 with his friends and professional hunters" (Wimsatt, 220). These notes, now in the Charles Carroll Simms Collection in the South Caroliniana Library, "comprise 43 leaves in a manuscript volume titled 'Personal and Literary Memorials'" (Shillingsburg, 2). Transcribed as appendix A in Shillingsburg's unpublished dissertation and referred to in her table of contents as the "1847 Journal," these extensive but hastily taken notes provide a picture of a younger, still optimistic Simms gathering material for his later work.

Of the two serially published novels, *Voltmeier* (1869) and *The Cub of the Panther* (1869), the latter draws most heavily on the 1847 journal and is especially revealing of the lives and legends of the professional hunters with whom Simms traveled in 1847. There we find the clash of rich and poor, common in Simms's later romances, in the leading portrayals of the debauched but aristocratic Edward Fairleigh and the formally uneducated but naturally gifted professional hunter, Mike Baynam. Fairleigh, the villain of the tale, who seduces then abandons the socially pretentious mountain girl, Rose Carter, and turns her out carrying his unborn son after a fraudulent marriage, is a gentleman and a sportsman in name only. Cast unsparingly as a "thoroughly depraved character," Fairleigh represents a new tone of cynicism that Shillingsburg identifies as a "strain of bitterness in the novel that is not typical of Simms" (Shillingsburg, 19). Significantly for the present study, Shillingsburg also considers whether the tragedies of the war and Simms's incessant labors had begun to affect his characterizations: "It is almost as if Simms has allowed some kind of personal antagonism to slip into his writing—not generally characteristic of his other works" (20). This tone of bitterness is not confined to Edward Fairleigh alone; even the more virtuous mountain folk are occasionally portrayed as unfeeling and cruel, but by far the most striking example is the character of the "Cub" himself, Fairleigh's bastard son by Rose Carter. Charles Watson singles out the Cub as the "most original character in the novel" (Watson, "Simms," 36), but his true originality has little to do with the strange circumstances surrounding his illegitimate birth or even with the panther-shaped birthmark that appears on his forehead: "an ineffaceable mark which, in his excited moods, seemed to glow and burn, as if with a life of its own" (Simms, *Cub of the Panther,* 193). What most effectively identifies this boy as a new and frightening fictional species is his unexpected and unnatural indifference to violence and bloodshed. The Cub is portrayed at the age of twelve as vicious, almost savage in his temperament: "quick in quarrel; irritable and resentful, if not absolutely revengeful" (193). Watson believes that the Cub can profitably be considered as "a brother to the boy heroes of Thomas Bailey Aldrich and Mark Twain"

(Watson, 36), but there is about this particular youth a passionless competence and a self-contained aloofness that is part of Simms's plan to create a character whose basic humanity is severely compromised by the animalistic indifference in his nature. Simms can, of course, be excused a good deal of fantasy in his "Hunter Legend," and in the opening lines of "Book Third" he feels it necessary to appeal to "the higher susceptibilities of the reader's imagination, or what is spiritual in his nature, to prompt sufficient credence in our legend" (Simms, *Cub of the Panther,* 157). All this is in good romantic order, but the attributes Simms affords this particular young hunter do not serve simply to mark him as an exceptional prodigy whose character borders on the supernatural but rather as a youthful scourge whose dispassionate rapport with violence and death suggests the presence of an amorality only intensified by the character's youth.

Aware of the need to prepare his readers emotionally for the patricide with which the novel concludes, Simms provides us with two episodes that present the Cub's indifference and unshakable self-possession. In the first of these, the Cub rescues his uncle from the close hug of a wounded bear. The initial rendering of this repeated and violent motif is successful in presenting the Cub as not only surprisingly cool under fire for his fifteen years but also a bit more sanguinary than readers either then or now would prefer. Approaching a downed bear whose strength seems exhausted, Sam Fuller is attacked and held in an upright embrace. His arms pinned to his side and his knife fallen to the ground, Sam calls out and the Cub responds at once. Thrusting the muzzle of his rifle up to the bear's eyes, but "not giving heed to the near neighborhood of the bear's nozzle to that of his uncle, and steady as if all his nerves were made of steel, he blew the bullet through the head of the beast" (201). Leaving nothing to chance, the Cub drops to his knees, recovers Sam's knife, and "drove it himself into the belly of the bear . . . slashing into the body of the beast, so deeply, so thoroughly, that his bowels rolled out upon him" (201).

Perhaps Sam's mortal danger could account for the Cub's dramatic performance, but in his next encounter with a bear, the savage efficiency with which he saved his uncle is intensified, though unmitigated by any actual necessity. In this second scene, the Cub has trailed a female bear to her den high in the mountains. Separated from the entrance by only twenty steps, he hides behind a large boulder to plan his attack when unexpectedly, the old bear emerges and starts out toward him. Waiting until the last possible moment, he stands erect and screams "such a shriek and a howl" that the bear recoils, loses its footing, and plunges to its death below. In the following passage, we get the first real insight into the Cub's total lack of compassion:

> He penetrated the cavern, and found a jolly pair of fat cubs awaiting him. They pawed him pleasantly; fawned upon him, and got between and hugged his legs. . . . In five minutes, he had drawn the edge of his *couteau de chasse* over both their throats; had born them out of the cavern, to the edge of the precipice, and tumbled them over into the near neighborhood with their dam! (208).

This particular variety of pragmatic ruthlessness forms a striking contrast with the tone of the hunts in either *Carolina Sports* or *The Golden Christmas*. On the Bulmer Barony only the boars are killed by the hunters, and the sow and pigs are captured and taken back alive. That their ultimate destination is the plantation dinner table is not important insofar as the boar hunt itself is concerned, for the sportsmen show no interest in harming either the young pigs or their dam. Much later, perhaps, that duty would fall upon the slaves responsible for processing the plantation livestock, a purely domestic enterprise entirely different from hunting game in the wild. But by the time Simms wrote *The Cub of the Panther,* there were no longer any herds of plantation livestock and few plantation mansions left standing at all. Re-envisioning his lost society from the ravaged wasteland of the Reconstruction South, Simms created images for expressing his painful sense of how profoundly his culture and its way of life had been damaged. We find one of his most successful efforts in the Cub, a hunter whose youthful immorality constitutes a powerful antithesis to the traditions of generosity, compassion, and fair play that informed the code of southern sportsmanship.

In *The Cub of the Panther*, the bulk of the action is set in the antebellum South when owners of mountain plantations like the Fairleighs were still in possession of their affluence and wealth. But things have changed dramatically. In contrast to the high-minded aristocrats like Major Bulmer of *The Golden Christmas*, the master of Fairleigh Lodge is governed neither by the ethics of the sportsman nor the obligations of the gentleman. While the bitterness of his characterization may indeed stem from the long list of tragedies his creator was forced to endure, Edward Fairleigh himself is deliberately portrayed as the very antithesis of the principled and aristocratic outdoorsmen who precede him. Described as slender and graceful in his youth, the picture we get of Fairleigh at thirty-six complements the progress of his moral dissipation: "He had grown obese; his face had become beefy and rubicund, and attested the frequency and potency of his draughts, at all hours, of peach and honey, applejack and usquebaugh!" (212). Living only to "hunt by day, feed heavily at evening, [and] drink deeply by night," Fairleigh exhibits none of the redeeming qualities that distinguish the sporting gentleman. Moreover, instead of attending properly to the affairs of his mountain estate, we learn that he has "grown neglectful of those large interests which his mother had so long and so ably economized" (212).

As a major part of his negative characterization, totally unmitigated by the courage, consideration, and refinement that should be his heritage as a member of the southern sporting gentry, Fairleigh's social and moral deficiencies are further delineated through a series of detailed descriptions of his unethical conduct afield. In two separate but thematically related episodes, Simms deliberately depicts Fairleigh's contempt for proper sporting etiquette and for the cultural values of which they are an extension. In both portrayals, he is at pains to punctuate the action with earthy, realistic details that suggest his desire to emphasize the concrete and wholesome concerns of the lower-class hunters and also to castigate the vulgar element of debauched aristocracy represented by Edward Fairleigh. The outcome of the first of these scenes is foreshadowed by the plain-spoken warning of the professional hunter called Wood, who, encountering the Fairleigh party as they ride out that morning after bear, notices that the wealthy sportsmen are armed only with shotguns. Realizing instantly the danger of attempting to take black bear with weapons whose projectiles lack sufficient penetration for the thick, tough layers of hide and bone protecting the bear's vital organs, Wood offers the following caveat:

> Well, I'd jist idvise you, ef you happens to hit a full grown b'ar with one of them we'pons, you won't do more than graze his hide, and melt a leetle of his fat! That'll jist put him in a mighty bad humor for the rest of the day, and you must be mighty quick to git out of his way when he comes tearing down upon you! (213).

With a fine disdain for Wood and his homely speech, Fairleigh rudely expresses his vanity in his fine Manton shotguns, proclaiming proudly that they are fully up to the task at hand, having been "made in England . . . by the finest gun-maker in the world" (213). While the Manton doubles of this period were considered elegant and exceptionally well-made, the "fifteen pellets in each barrel" that Fairleigh boasts of are only buckshot, fully capable of shooting through the thin skin and light skeleton of a deer but not at all designed to penetrate the "thickness of a b'ar's jacket" referred to by Wood in his warning. As Wood concludes, however, "It's no use idvising these fine gentlemen" (214).

Later that morning, Fairleigh gets his chance to prove his claims, but though he hits the bear that is driven to him with right and left, the second shot delivered when the bear was "not ten paces off," the charge has no apparent effect, and Fairleigh is thrown to the ground and mauled savagely. Simms describes the scene with feeling:

> He struck at the beast with the butt of the gun, but was hurled to the ground at the same instant, and the bear swept over him, then wheeled about and threw himself headlong upon the prostrate man, whom he grappled with his forepaws, while ripping and tearing him with his claws behind, just as one uses his rowels upon the steed (216).

If not for the timely intervention of the Cub, who puts a bullet through the bear's head before finishing him with his knife, Fairleigh would have been disemboweled and killed. In the struggle, however, the Cub inadvertently nicks Fairleigh with his knife, and it is this, and not the boy's courage or assistance, that Fairleigh seizes upon as the rest of the hunting party arrive. Instead of thanking the boy for saving his life, or even acknowledging that his assistance was needed, Fairleigh stoutly defends his towering vanity: "Saved h—l, man; what are you talking about? I had the bear in my power, and in another moment my own knife would have cut him down from throat to navel" (217). Finally caused to admit that the Cub had at least fired at the bear, Fairleigh tells his companions to search the carcass "and you'll be sure to find my pellets" (218). The pellets are found, but as Wood had warned, they barely penetrated the skin. Nevertheless, Fairleigh argues that the presence of his shot in the bear entitles him to the meat. Even his friend Bulkley, "taken by surprise at this exhibition of his meanness," rebukes Fairleigh's conceit: "Don't make yourself ridiculous, Fairleigh. . . . The bear belongs to the boy, if ever boy had a right at all" (218).

With pleasing consistency, Simms's portrayal of Edward Fairleigh in the second of these two major scenes continues to develop the vanity, greed, and ruthlessness that mark his behavior. With little regard for his fellows and especial contempt for the local, professional hunters, Fairleigh begins his leisurely, belated hunt with the call to "liquor all round, before we begin business" (245). As Simms tells us the "good deer hunter will take the field . . . while the morning dew still glistens upon grass" (244), as Mike Baynam and his party have done earlier that morning. Fairleigh and his group have other priorities, including the "phlegm-cutter" taken before breakfast, as well as the "*air-expeller*" following the morning meal (245). Not surprisingly, Fairleigh shows no appreciation for the beauty of the natural world around him, regarding it as simply a convenient place to drink. As Simms tells us, Fairleigh is rather bored on the hunt and has "made provision against any undue tax upon his patience . . . [with] a pocket flask containing '*the ardent*,' and has scarcely taken his stand ere he has taken another swallow" (246). Thus fortified, Fairleigh's shooting is "somewhat disordered by his potations," and when the buck comes bouncing by he fails even to slow it down with his fine Manton gun. Really drunk by this time, Fairleigh "staggers to his horse" to ride to the sound of the shot he heard in the direction the buck has taken. Arriving to find the Cub astride the same deer at which he had fired, Fairleigh strikes the young hunter with his whip for his impudence as a commoner in interfering with "the sports of the country gentry" (248). Fairleigh's revenge is short-lived, however, for the Cub, "lithe as the panther . . . sprung upon the haunches of Fairleigh's horse, and in an instant . . . had driven his knife deep into the body of his assailant" (248). Fairleigh falls from his horse, but the boy has no time to spare looking after his victim. Instead he "sprang off " but reappeared quickly, "rifle in hand, and mounted, with the slain deer fastened behind him; as cool and quiet of demeanor as if nothing unusual had occurred" (248). Even when Sam Fuller identifies Fairleigh as the Cub's own father, there is no apparent effect. As Wimsatt says in her concluding analysis, "The final picture of the Cub is of an amoral child of nature, a 'wild-eyed and strangely-branded boy' who stands before his dying father and gazes upon him indifferently" (241).

From the portrayals of Edward Fairleigh in the scenes noted above, the picture emerges of a thoroughly corrupt man whose many vices are only intensified by his wealth and social rank. As a sportsman he fares no better, and his outrageous conduct afield intensifies his grievous moral deficiencies. To complete his negative characterization, his seduction and abandonment of Rose Carter are thematically linked to his disavowal of the Cub's assistance in the fight with the bear; in neither case does Fairleigh show the least sign of the noblesse oblige that should govern his behavior. Remorseless, irresponsible, and habitually drunk, Fairleigh is totally lacking in any of the virtues that either level of society portrayed in the novel admires. However, more frightening by far is the picture of his illegitimate son, the Cub, whose cold indifference makes even Fairleigh's dissolutions seem human.

More sympathetically rendered are the poor mountain hunters Mike Baynam and his brother-in-law, Sam Fuller, but they are to be distinguished from Simms's earlier, lower-class heroes by the leading roles they are afforded in the narrative. As Wimsatt argues in her *Major Fiction*, "For the first time in his long fiction, he makes plain people rather than aristocrats the principal actors in the plot and uses them to convey his standards of value" (238). The homespun mountaineers not only have "sounder values and better judgement" than their patrician counterparts, their characterizations are more complex and afforded more extensive development. While William Trent attempted to account for this dramatic shift in creative focus by arguing that Simms realized the day of the romancer who extolled the virtues of the ruling class was over, Trent seems to have forgotten the impact of the drastic changes brought about by southern military defeat. A more convincing approach is Miriam J. Shillingsburg's in her afterword to the University of Arkansas Press edition of *The Cub*: "Simms had to portray Southern life before the Civil War in a way that would be acceptable to Northern audiences and still be truthful . . ." (259). In a very real sense, he was forced, primarily by the antipathy of northern readers to celebrations of the antebellum southern aristocracy, to choose what Shillingsburg calls a "politically neutral setting" where "conduct that may have been condoned in the old order could no longer be assumed to be appropriate" (262).

As the leading foil and antagonist to the aristocratic but morally corrupt Fairleighs, Mike Baynam's melancholy but upright virtues lend a quiet, authentic dignity to his portrayal. It is Mike, for example, who rises in the night after his vision to search for Rose in the mountains after she escapes from Fairleigh Lodge and Mike again who raises Rose's and Fairleigh's illegitimate son (the Cub) after Rose's death. Even his language is different. As Miriam Shillingsburg observes in "Simms's Last Novel, *The Cub of the Panther,*" "[Simms] is consistent in his distinction between the rustics and the other characters in the book. Mike Baynam is never pompous in his language, but he is correct, characterized by neither the country idiom, mispronunciation, nor incorrect grammar" (117). Though unmarried and a professional hunter, Mike is aware of his duties to his family and his society as a whole. Realizing that his nephew, Sam's son, Bayn, has little aptitude for hunting but a genuine interest in reading, Mike convinces his father to "let *me* have the managing of the boy" (Simms, *Cub of the Panther,* 210). He gives Bayn books to read and funds his education in the nearby town of Spartanburg. As Mike points out, "God does not make everybody to be a hunter" (210). Conscious of the eventual arrival of civilization in the now remote mountain country, Mike's wisdom and foresight are directed toward preparing his nephew to play a major role in accomplishing that goal. As he says of Bayn's future contributions to his homeland as an educated professional, "It is on these mountains that he'll find his best uses," and by the novel's end we learn that he was "admitted to orders in the Episcopal Church, and became a famous pulpit orator" (251).

As for Mike Baynam, though afforded qualities most often associated with the landed gentry, he is hardly portrayed as an aristocratic sportsman pleasuring himself in the beauty of nature. Instead we see a professional hunter who "sells his five hundred deer hams every year to Walker in Spartanburg, and other deer and bear meat, hams and shoulders, to other people in Asheville and Greenville" (22). Mike's is a wild region and largely undeveloped, with hunting instead of farming the principal occupation of the residents. Because of this frontier setting, it would be wrong to place Mike and his friends in the same category with the fire-hunting professionals that Elliott attacks in the closing pages of *Carolina Sports*. Mike and his rustic companions are linked instead to the aristocrats of Elliott's collection and to the elite sportsmen of *The Golden Christmas* by their industry, courage, sense of duty, and their genuine regard for their fellow men. When these qualities are abandoned, we find the hunter no different from any other romantic villain, here represented by Edward Fairleigh: cowardly, cruel, irresponsible, vicious, and the very antithesis of the traditional southern hero.

In *Figures of the Hero in Southern Narrative* (1987), Michael Kreyling presents a history of the development of Simms's concept of the hero, and Kreyling's insights have special relevance to the unique position of the hunter in the southern sporting narrative as a genre. Citing Simms's comments in the 1842 review "The Writings of James Fenimore Cooper" (see Simms, *Views and Reviews,* 269–70), Kreyling notes that for Simms, Cooper's heroes lacked the all-important interest in "the long-range project of establishing a civilization" (Kreyling, *Figures,* 35); more significantly, he points out that Simms objected to

Cooper's heroes primarily because of their "model of moral individuality in solitude" (34). For whatever reason—cowardice, dissipation, or simply bad luck—the title character in Simms's "Bald-Head Bill Bauldy" rejects his proper roles as soldier, husband, and father, rejoicing at the end of his story that "the Lawd be praised, I'm a free white man to this very day!" (Simms, "Bauldy," 521). Unlike Mike Baynam, Bill Bauldy has no interest in the future development of his region.

In contrast to the retreat from women and his proper role in society, Sam ("Sharp") Snaffles has been married thirteen years by the time he tells the tale of his courtship at the Saturday night story-telling called the "Liar's Camp," and he takes considerable pride in having become the father of nine healthy children. The fanciful tale of his rise to material success and romantic fulfillment is presented within the familiar framework of the dramatic convention that posits a wealthy and overweening father adamantly opposed to his daughter's marriage with her otherwise admirable but habitually impecunious suitor. Squire Jeff Hopson, Merry Ann's father, is presented as a bitter caricature of the self-made man, a physically powerful and domineering patriarch whose heavy-handed authority terrorizes both his wife and his only child. Well aware of Sam's poverty and determined that Merry Ann will never wed a pauper, the Squire encourages the aging but prosperous John Grimstead to court his unwilling daughter. At the next of Sam's and Merry Ann's frequent but clandestine meetings, she tells him her father has given the "open mouth incouragement" to Grimstead, a dryly malodorous old bachelor more than twice her age. Resolving instantly to confront the squire and to ask for his daughter's hand, Sam is nevertheless beset by a flurry of thoroughly believable fears. Recalling the events for his listeners, Sam describes the plight of a man whose courage is put to the test. His fears no doubt were real, but the imaginative requirements of the Liar's Camp allow him to phrase them in language that humorously underplays their intensity:

> I was jubous; I was mighty oncertain, and a leetle bit scary myself; for, you see, old Jeff was a fellow of tough grit, and with big grinders; but I was so oneasy, and so tired out waiting, and so desperate, and so fearsome. . . .
>
> Well, Jedge, as I tell you, I put a bold face on the business, though my hairt was gitting up into my throat, and I was almost a-gasping for my breath, when I was fairly in the big room, and standing up before the old Square (Simms, "Snaffles," 428–29).

Though Sam does manage to state his intentions manfully, Squire Hopson convinces him that because he lacks "capital," Sam is not a complete man and so unworthy to wed Merry Ann. With a telling and withering scorn, Hopson states his case succinctly: "You may think, in your vanity, that you air a man; but you ain't, and never will be, onless you can find a way to get capital; and I loves my gal child too much to let her marry any pusson whom I don't altogether consider a man" (433). Hard hit and profoundly moved by what he has heard, Sam returns to Merry Ann, acknowledges her father's accusations, and promises to find the needed capital to make a "good, comfortable home" for his future bride. Returning to his cabin later that evening, Sam continues to reflect on the truth of the squire's words: "It's all true! How kin I bring that beautiful yaller flower of the forest to live in sich poor accomydations? She that always had everything comforting and nice about her" (435).

Luckily for Sam, his marginal skills as a hunter are augmented by a sustained run of unbelievably good luck. Having hunted hard from dawn to dusk on the day after his interview with the squire but with nothing to show for his toil, Sam comes at length upon the shore of a small mountain lake where he decides to rest until moonrise. The day has been long and grueling, and soon he falls into a deep and exhausted slumber. What wakes him are the cries of thousands of Canada geese for whom the lake provides a secluded retreat. The sight and sound of flocks of the great birds pouring into the safety of their evening roost is a welcome vision to the cold and hungry hunter, and Sam immediately begins to plan how he will turn them into "capital."

The scene is the beginning of a series of fanciful venatic triumphs in which Sam captures, by his own calculations, 3,150 geese in a net of his own manufacture. Though the flock flies off with Sam in tow, they soon become entangled in the trees and drop him into a hollow tree where he lands neck deep in honey. Unable to extricate himself, he is miraculously saved when a bear backs down inside the hollow. When Sam grabs hold of his tail, the bear panics and drags the honey-soaked hunter to safety. As they reach the top of the hollow, Sam gets his arm over the outside rim and pushes the bear with his free hand. Exhausted and off balance, the bear slips off the edge and falls to his death below. Though he has had a "mighty bad skeer for life," Sam now has the means to get the all-important capital, for to the income from the geese, he will be able to add the sale of a five-hundred-pound bear, as well as two thousand gallons of wild honey. To say the least, Sam's fortunes have changed indeed, but they have not changed his love for Merry Ann nor his sense of responsibility for her happiness and comfort. Instead of squandering his newly found wealth on narcissistic pleasures, Sam buys a farm with a suitable home, a wagon load of fine furniture, and a "fine milch cow that giv eleven quarts a day" (450). As soon as the house is ready, Sam rides boldly up to the Hopson homestead and marries Merry Ann that very night. With their wealth and their happiness now intact, Sam and his bride can begin their life in comfort and security.

As Meriwether points out in his analysis of the story, Sam, though enjoying the entertainment during the "annual masculine ceremonial of the hunt," has become "a respectable middle-class farmer, a husband and father who has made his way up in the world through determination, and who obviously is content with society and his place in it" (Meriwether, "Simms's 'Sharp Snaffles,'" 69). His success as hunter and his standing in society are complementary aspects of his character as it is presented to the reader, and even the acquisitive, pragmatic nature of his younger days is largely mitigated by his motivations and his current value to society. It is well to remember that Mike Baynam, the "melancholy hunter" of *The Cub of the Panther,* is portrayed as a productive member of his sister's extended family, and it is an important part of Mike's characterization that he raises Rose Carter's illegitimate son and provides for the education and training of young Bayn. Unlike Bill Bauldy, Mike is both responsible and brave; unfortunately Mike cannot, as Watson observes, "transfer the hunter's qualities into courtship" (Watson, 33). While the hunters in Simms's Appalachian fiction are a far remove, both in their social class and venatic aspirations, from the gifted aristocrats of *The Golden Christmas* and *Carolina Sports*, they share with their more polished brethren a reverence for moral and physical courage, an awareness of civic responsibility, and an abiding respect for the power and the beauty of nature. Even in the story of Sam Snaffles's rise to affluence and wealth, there remains about him and his fictionalized history an aura of moral respectability.

As part of his greater design, what Guilds calls Simms's attempt to "envision, design, initiate, and consummate an epic portrayal of the development of our nation" (Guilds, 333), "Sharp Snaffles" has consistently earned the highest praise from those who have read it with an informed and objective eye. One of the reasons for this continuity of positive, critical response is suggested by Donald Davidson in his introduction to volume 1 of Simms's *Letters*. Acknowledging the unevenness in Simms's total literary output, Davidson points toward what he believes lies at the heart of Simms's narrative power:

> . . . the real strength of Simms is in his unself-conscious nearness to what might be called, for want of a better term, folk tradition. . . . The best of Simms's fiction is not a long step away from saga and folk tale. And in the stories it often is actual folk tale, surrounded perhaps by a literary framework. . . . On the other hand the remarkable and wholly delightful "How Sharp Snaffles Won His Wife" is almost pure folk tale, but lightly worked over. It stands almost without a peer, surely, among the "tall tales" recorded or written in the United States (Simms, *Letters*, 1:li–lii).

Much later, William Faulkner, another southern author concerned with the evolution of his region and with the importance of the oral hunting narratives it produced, would look back with genuine regret and matchless artistry to the great society of hunters that thrived in the last days of the Mississippi Delta wilderness. For Faulkner, too, the tradition of orally transmitted hunting tales was an important source of strength, and in "The Bear" he comments on the importance of the spoken narrative:

> . . . the best game of all, the best of all breathing and forever the best of all listening, the voices quiet and weighty and deliberate for retrospection and recollection and exactitude among the concrete trophies—the racked guns and the heads and skins—in the libraries of town houses or the offices of plantation houses or (and best of all) in the camps themselves where the intact and still-warm meat yet hung, the men who had slain it sitting before the burning logs on hearths when there were houses and hearths or about the smoky blazing of piled wood in front of stretched tarpaulins when there were not (Faulkner, *Go Down, Moses,* 184).

At the very heart of this early oral tradition and occupying the innermost nucleus of its focus is the hunt: not simply because of its freedom and pageantry, but because, as Ortega would argue, "it is essentially the same thing that Paleolithic man did" (Ortega, 136). Ortega continues:

> By hunting a man succeeds, in effect, in annihilating all historical evolution, in separating himself from the present, and in renewing the primitive situation. . . . The only difference—doubtless decisive—is that for the latter hunting was the center of gravity for his whole life, while for the sportsman it is only a

> transitory suspension, almost parenthetical, of his authentic life. But that other creature which is going to occupy the parenthesis is also authentic. The duality which makes the situation so difficult is based on this. The hunter is, at one and the same time, a man of today and one of ten thousand years ago (136).

It is quite natural that this prehistoric identity, muted by modern life but lying just beneath the surface in what Ortega calls the "permanent availabilities in man" (134), should not only require but demand a voice of its own to talk about hunting, for 99 percent of human time the "essential fact of his condition" (135). The "capital" that Sam must amass in order to pave the way for his marriage to Merry Ann is initially in the form of honey, geese, and bear fat, and the imaginative requirements of the camp demand that he cast his achievements in acquiring these items in the guise of a very tall tale. As the narrator explains before Sam begins, the raconteur is encouraged to deal "in all the extravagances of invention" and to "confine himself to the bald and naked truth, is not only discreditable, but a *finable* offense!" (Simms, "Snaffles," 423). In "The American Dreams of Sam Snaffles" (1986), Ian Marshall explains Sam's inventions as a deliberate if rustic parody of "the story of how a man makes his way in the world," a familiar motif found earlier in Benjamin Franklin's *Autobiography* (1791) and Horatio Alger's *Ragged Dick; or, Street Life in New York* (1867). It seems more likely that in his eagerness to identify correlations between Simms's alleged disillusionment during this period and the deliberate fictions of the Liar's Camp, Marshall has overlooked an important function and practical dimension of the fictional setting. The narrative artistry on which the "Big Lie" (The Big Lie is the master of ceremonies at the Liar's Camp in "Sharp Snaffles" and "Bill Bauldy.") insists allows the natural pride and self-esteem of the successful hunter to find expression in terms that no one would find objectionable. In the tale that Sam tells, his identity and professional life begin as a hunter, and it is through his efforts (and luck) as a hunter that he succeeds in making his way. When, years later, he recounts the tale of his capital and courtship to the Liar's Camp, his fictions are not designed to undercut the American dream of success but rather to describe a time in his life when he was forced to rely on the Paleolithic heritage common to us all. By having Sam speak for himself in the dialect of the isolated mountain hunters, Simms allows the natural pride, excitement, and spontaneity of man's original profession to shine through without the slightest hint of insolence or ostentation.

As Gerald Donovan argues in his study of the similarities between late-nineteenth-century Irish and American writers who sought to transform their countries' oral heritage into written fictions, Simms's "great achievement in 'Sharp Snaffles' is that he reproduced accurately the oral style of American frontiersmen in the postbellum South . . . [and] preserves the particular dynamics of the tall tale that might have been lost in formal reworking" (Donovan, "Irish Folklore," 194–95). And as Davidson says of Simms's best narratives, "They might have been in being, one feels, as stories told or waiting to be told before they found in Simms the medium through which they burst into utterance" (Simms, *Letters*, 1:li). For the prehistoric man whose life revolved around the hunt, the dream of success already existed. Surely he must have dreamed of more plentiful game, of exceptional prowess afield, and of the security and comfort these things would bring to him and his band. And from the dawn of language itself, he must have shared these dreams with his comrades, willing listeners to whom the dream of success began to assume the importance of whatever religious doctrines they had by that time developed. The result of Simms's deft handling of these ancient dreams and the oral traditions in which they survived is an authentic and imaginatively successful rendering where the inextinguishable dreams of the prehistoric hunter reemerge intact.

Had Simms been able to continue to enjoy the good health and relative prosperity of the 1840s and 1850s, perhaps the authorial voice that narrates the story of Sam Snaffles's rise in the world would have been more nearly like those early dreams of success, fancifully optimistic and free from the surprisingly cynical undertones that Ian Marshall identifies in this final example of Simms's published short fiction. As Marshall observes, "cynicism is not a characteristic usually associated with Simms" (Marshall, "American Dreams," 105), and Shillingsburg had marveled earlier at the "unexpected touch" of bitterness in *The Cub of the Panther*, an unusual quality to find in Simms's work and one "not altogether congruous with the humor so manifest in this book" (Shillingsburg, 19). Certainly Marshall is correct in arguing that "if ever a man had reason to turn cynical, such a man was Simms in the last years of his life" (Marshall, 105), but whatever fault finding Simms displays in "Sharp Snaffles" and whatever misgivings the story suggests about the motives of human nature, they are not directed toward the hero of the tale, nor toward his rustic version of how a man achieves the American dream. Sam is both happy and successful, in the frame as well as in the story he relates. His rise to success may be presented through the established conventions of the tall tale and within the context of a Liar's Camp, but that does not mean, as Marshall would have it, that Simms intended to depict the American dream as "a fiction not to be believed, a whopping lie to outdo any stretcher that the group of hunters has ever heard" (97). As Meriwether points out, Sam is "content with society and his place in it" (Meriwether, 69). While the "underlying indictment" that Marshall identifies is real, it is not an indictment of the American dream of upward mobility, nor does the unlooked-for strain of bitterness identify Simms as a "full-fledged pessimist" (Marshall, 106). The real target of Simms's authorial disdain is the myopic materialism of Merry Ann's "close, money-loving father," Squire Jeff Hopson, a man perfectly willing to sacrifice his daughter's happiness by giving her in marriage to an aging "skunk of a bachelor" more than twice her age simply because he has the proper kind of "capital." As a negative corollary on the demoralizing necessities of the ruined society in which he found himself after the war, Simms makes it clear that Sharp has found it necessary to take on some of the squire's traits. He has become a wealthy man, a man of "capital," and he is rather too much proud of his wealth and the power it exerts over people like the squire. His capital is gained only through an exploitation of nature in a way that Elliott's hunters would never have dreamed. That Sharp *must* do so is part of Simms's negative commentary of the postbellum South. We don't so much blame Sharp or the tenets of the American dream as we do the dictates of the Reconstruction economy in which Sharp must act.

Despite the dramatic shift in narrative perspective between his hunting scenes of 1852 and those of the late 1860s, there remains a striking continuity in the values these narratives endorse. On the one hand, Major Bulmer in *The Golden Christmas* is willing to risk his own life and those of his dogs, horses, and human guests in an effort to ensure the fair play his sportsmanship requires. In this mock-heroic rendering, he proudly congratulates Dick Cooper on his sportsmanship by saying that the law "has not spoiled you for a gentleman and a hunter yet" (Simms, *Christmas,* 57). Much later, the rough-hewn hunters of the Appalachian Mountains neither entertain nor express any such ideas, but even the rustics of Mike Baynam's mountains place a high premium on courage, compassion, and generosity, and they intuitively recognize the value of these qualities to society. Not surprisingly, their wilderness lifestyle naturally caused them to express these values in terms of the hunt. It is a tribute to Simms's artistic integrity that his final, fictional sportsmen are morally defined in terms suited to their counterparts in real life, and in "Sharp Snaffles," it is the backwoods industry, persistence, and courage of Sam's struggles to win his bride that are celebrated at the expense of Hopson's and Grimstead's bleak and sterile materialism. In every case, Simms's approbation is awarded to men whose conduct both in and out of the woods is governed by a code of honor that manifests itself in their courage, compassion, and noblesse oblige. In examining the pattern that begins to emerge in sporting narratives by nineteenth-century southern authors such as Simms and Elliott, we see that, while there may very well be a change in the ways that their cultural and moral values are portrayed, there nevertheless exists a striking continuity in the essence of those values themselves.

In the next chapter, we move beyond the hardships of Reconstruction to the early 1900s, a period that witnessed the end of the South's intellectual isolation and an effort on the part of her sporting writers to chronicle their society's values in narratives carefully designed to minimize the sectional differences between North and South. Following close on the heels of the plantation fiction epitomized by Thomas Nelson Page's *In Ole Virginia* (1887), Alexander Hunter, Archibald Rutledge, and Caroline Gordon were careful to couch their cultural arguments in more universal terms that would boost their region's credibility instead of engulfing readers in an improbable flood of romanticized southern ideals.

CHAPTER THREE

Preserving the Cultural Heritage

Alexander Hunter's *The Huntsman in the South,* Archibald Rutledge's *Plantation Game Trails, Children of Swamp and Wood,* and *An American Hunter,* and Caroline Gordon's *Aleck Maury, Sportsman*

While the sporting writers whose work began to appear after 1900 still looked back with longing and regret to the days when the plantation community formed the social and moral center of the southern universe, the fictional worlds they created suggest a resigned yet optimistic perspective rarely marked by bitter references to the war or the indignities of Reconstruction. Largely unburdened by the massive tragedies that plagued Simms in his final years, their reemerging optimism allowed them once again to employ the imagery of southern sporting life to celebrate the courage, compassion, and noblesse oblige that formed the hallmarks of aristocratic conduct. In their abiding concern for the environment and the ennobling virtues their lost society revered, the writers we turn to now present a moving cultural commentary that reveals both the changes and the continuities in the evolution of the southern sporting narrative.

Although their literary ambitions, narrative perspectives, and material circumstances varied widely, Alexander Hunter, Archibald Rutledge, and Caroline Gordon were involved in dealing with two common dilemmas. First of all, they were intensely regional writers with distinguished southern pedigrees who were forced to curb their sectional loyalties because of the prevailing political environment. And second, they faced the difficult task of promoting the real values of sport hunting in a way that defined it for an increasingly urban audience as a responsible form of wholesome recreation and a valuable tool in enlightened conservation practices. On a tactical level, their positions resembled those facing attorneys-at-law, themselves the authors of controversial texts, who must maintain the difficult equilibrium of aggressively promoting their clients' best interests while at the same time remaining equally enthusiastic in supporting the authority and countenance of the court. For these writers, the court was represented not only by the northern audiences they hoped to reach but also by public opinion informed by the conservation movement that had begun to take hold on the American environmental consciousness. Granted that Hunter's authorial aspirations were a far remove from the more intensely literary ambitions of Gordon or Rutledge, even Hunter faced the unavoidable necessity of keeping his narratives as free as possible from residual sectional bitterness and any trace of profligate indifference to the wildlife he pursued. Taken together, their work deals with this common set of problems in three major ways: by foregrounding the virtues of those who pursue field sports with the proper regard for aristocratic southern values, by drawing attention to the excitement of the hunt and the beauty of its natural surroundings, and by maintaining an intense awareness that their work would be viewed as a type of southern apologia regardless of their intended goals. The artistic techniques and narrative strategies these authors adopted to deal with the political and cultural environments within which they had to maneuver argue convincingly that while the old South lay in defeat, many of its most fundamental values remained pervasive, viable, and admirable realities that informed the thoughts and actions of its descendants, both in their larger sense of societal responsibilities and in their use and management of the nation's natural resources.

Despite their need to avoid regional defensiveness and to demonstrate the moral and environmental responsibility of their leading characters, this small but aristocratic grouping of non-canonical southern writers succeeded splendidly in creating a solid body of sporting literature that celebrates the cultural values of their society in innocuous and inoffensive terms: Hunter, through a stylized book of sporting etiquette that also includes renderings of local color from the tradition of the educated observer; Rutledge, through a naturalist's interpretation of hunting and fishing; and Gordon, through a portrayal of southern field sports as a fitting vehicle for transporting antebellum values into the spiritual wasteland of the modern world. Like other literary modernists of the time, these writers reached back into the past for models of order, harmony, and virtue with which to confront their sense of widespread moral chaos and environmental destruction. Moreover, the sporting symbols they revived and the imaginative renderings they employed form an important part of the background against which the more formal codifications of southern values in *I'll Take My Stand* (1930) took shape. In much the same way that Ransom and the Twelve Southerners employed agrarian imagery for expressing what they saw as the dominant cultural values of the old South, the writers examined here used the southern sporting code as a symbol for the values they revered. In *The Huntsman in the South* (1908), Alexander Hunter masks his purpose by appearing preoccupied with simply reporting the selective preferences of a privileged and wealthy sportsman. In reality, his sporting proclivities are metaphorical encryptions of the larger code of moral conduct to which he and his fellow sportsmen subscribed. While his sketches may lack the broad scope of societal concern often found in Simms's best work because of the more narrow focus on the insular world of aristocratic field sports, there remains in Hunter's collection a strong element of concern for ethical conduct and a deeply rooted commitment to the future of the land, its game, and the society of which he was a part.

Alexander Hunter (1843–1914) was born and raised on his father's antebellum Virginia plantation and grew to manhood surrounded by thousands of acres of prime wildlife habitat. When the war came he served with distinction in the Confederate army, was wounded and captured several times, but survived the conflict intact and wrote *Johnny Reb and Billy Yank* (1905), a 720-page account of his adventures, and *Women of the Debatable Land* (1912), a book-length tribute to the courage and sacrifice of Confederate women in wartime Virginia. In addition to his published books, Hunter also contributed frequently to contemporary magazines with articles such as "The Club Houses of Currituck Sound" (1892). His most famous and controversial work was "Booth and Bessie Hale" (1878), in which he attributed the motive for John Wilkes Booth's assassination of President Lincoln to a rivalry between Booth and Lincoln's son, Robert, over the daughter of former United States senator John P. Hale. Hunter is valuable as a transitional figure whose career spans the Civil War, but unlike Simms, he survived the war and Reconstruction without having to face the grinding poverty and physical afflictions that plagued his famous predecessor. More importantly, Hunter was no professional man of letters dependent on his writing for his livelihood and responsible for supporting a good-sized family; rather, he was a privileged aristocrat whose authorial output was more on the order of an ornamental flourish for his civilian career in the General Land Office in Washington and briefly as a member of the Virginia General Assembly in the House of Delegates from 1877 to 1879 (Alford, "Alexander Hunter," 6). In *The Huntsman in the South*, we find the genial reportage of a well-heeled gentleman who has left behind the dire necessities and harsh realities of the war and who is free to devote his remaining leisure time to depicting the finer points of the chase. In fact, he dispenses with the war very early, suggesting that instead of an embittered conflict, it was merely an inconvenient interruption in the lives of the planter-sportsmen:

> The winter of '60 and '61 ended my shooting days for a long time. The boys on the Southern plantations dropped their fowling-pieces and seized the musket, the saber, and the lanyard; the setters and pointers became house-dogs, the pack of hounds ate their heads off, and the game had a rest from their natural enemy, man; for the sportsmen, North and South, instead of killing game, were busy shooting one another (Hunter, *Huntsman,* 30).

If not for this kind of understated and infrequent reference to the great and recent conflict, one might suppose the author knew little of the war itself instead of having served gallantly through four years in some of the bloodiest fighting. Hunter clearly suppresses his involvement, and as Stuart Marks points out in *Southern Hunting in Black and White* (1991), southern veterans of Hunter's class "often tried to disguise, if not to deny, the . . . major discontinuities in political and economic life" caused by the war, perhaps in an effort to downplay the extent of their actual losses (Marks, 293). Marks's observation seems appropriate in the present case, for Hunter is scrupulous in avoiding pointed references to the war and its attendant tragedies. While there is an occasional, offhand reference to a character like "Captain Blow, my uncle, [who] had followed the hounds for nearly half a century . . . save when the bugle displaced the hunting horn" (Hunter, *Huntsman,* 87), or an incidental reference to the falling off in the numbers of a plantation's hunting stable, for the most part any mention of the war or its costs are studiously avoided. Perhaps the strongest suggestion that Hunter writes from the perspective of a hardened survivor is what Marks calls his Darwinian "conception of nature and society." Noting that Hunter pauses to reflect on the resilient adaptability of bobwhite quail despite their being "snared, gunned, baited, trapped, hunted, shot at and worried" (Hunter, *Huntsman,* 114), Marks reveals one of Hunter's few, subtle references to the actualities of the postbellum South: "In quail, Hunter had found a metaphor for enduring on a capricious landscape, and he hoped that similar survival skills were present in his class of leisured gentlemen" (Marks, 42).

Had Hunter chosen, he could have punctuated his narrative with similar kinds of figurative references to the plight of the postwar South, but had he done so his book would have become more of an inspirational survivalist's manual than the cultural form book it remains. As we have it, *The Huntsman in the South* is more concerned with tacitly arguing that, as practiced by the southern gentry, field sports, and especially hunting, embody the most cherished ideals of the planter class and that loyalty to these ideals forms the primary reason that "throughout these mutations the love of sport has survived all changes, all vicissitudes" (84). For Hunter and his friends, participating in the rituals and abiding by the rules of the chase were important ways of rekindling and reaffirming the values of their lost society.

The 318 pages of Hunter's memoirs are divided into fifteen separate chapters that provide artistically rendered and detailed descriptions of his pursuit of fish and game along the Virginia and North Carolina coasts. Included are separate sections on such varied topics as "An Old Virginia Fox Hunt" (chapter 4, 82–102), "Among the Quail in Virginia" (chapter 6, 113–38), "Among the Currituck Bay Birds" (chapter 10, 213–33), and a concluding, largely technical section on "Guns and Dogs" (chapter 16, 315–18). Although the title page includes the announcement "Volume 1—More Volumes to Follow," the State Library of Virginia in Richmond indicates in its OCLC (Online Computer Library Center) records that no other volumes were ever published.

Beginning with chapter 1, "Sporting in the Olden Time" (11–31), Hunter reveals something of the freedom, abundance, and hereditary prerogatives of his early life as the heir to a great plantation dynasty. Looking back on his youth from the perspective of sixty-five years, his opening lines suggest his solid grasp of the stern realities of survival in the natural world and his awareness that life in the wild is a far remove from the pastoral utopia envisioned by those who denounce sport hunting:

> It is the inexorable law of Nature that all living creatures prey upon one another. By beak, talons and claw the fight was commenced, and it will only end when this world is no more. To say that sporting is a cruel pastime is to ignore the fact that all fin, fur, and feathers batten upon one another, and if the rifle or gun did not end their days, they would be killed anyway (11).

Like William Elliott before him, Hunter viewed human life as a further extension of this elemental, animalistic kind of struggle, and he felt strongly that early training in the sports of the field provided an excellent way to educate children into the rigors of this inescapable reality. He believed as well that "the greatest gift Nature can bestow upon a child is to endow him with a love of the forest, the field, and the stream" and that intensive training in the sports of the field "will make the boy and the man stronger, healthier, and happier" (11).

In view of Hunter's aristocratic background and his emphasis on the ennobling virtues of field sports, it is not surprising to find a striking similarity between his narrative perspective and that of William Elliott. Nevertheless, the physical and political landscape of Hunter's South is markedly different from the region as portrayed in *Carolina Sports,* and his writing reflects the changes that had taken place in the partly reconstituted South of the early twentieth century. In particular, Hunter reveals to us a South now crisscrossed by interstate railroads and fully accessible to northern sportsmen. As he says, "It is but a question of time, and a very short one at that, when the eastern North Carolina coast will be as well-known to the Northern sportsman as the Adirondacks" (103).

Seizing opportunely on the potential for profit afforded by sportsmen traveling to the South, both northern and southern railroad companies aggressively promoted the region as the mecca for fish and game. Hunter himself describes train rides from Richmond to the base camps of favorite clubs, but it was northern enthusiasts who were most often rich enough to travel long distances for sport and who were subsequently the primary targets for the railroads' advertising campaigns. As part of their promotional designs, railroad publishing offices often printed exhaustive pamphlets outlining the quality of southern field sports. One such booklet published by the Southern Railway Company is *Hunting and Fishing in the South* (1904). This sixty-four-page advertisement shows considerable attention to detail and includes a surprising number of reproductions of black-and-white photographs of hunting and fishing scenes. Dedicated to "the army of sportsmen who have found an ideal field in the South for sport and recreation," it promises to provide "the best locations in the South for various kinds of Game and Fish," as well as "the Game Laws of Virginia, North Carolina, Kentucky, Georgia, Florida, Alabama, Tennessee, and Mississippi." Maps and railway schedules are provided, but to these are added glowing descriptions of southern game fields and individual profiles of each state. Designed as free brochures to promote the railways' profits, booklets like those provided by the Southern Railway show a high degree of advertising ingenuity. In page after page of unreserved praise, excerpts like the following promise the South-bound sportsman unexcelled opportunities:

> Its forests and mountains abound in four-footed game, its wooded uplands are the favorite resort of quail, partridge, woodcock, and the lordly wild turkey, its marshes and bayous are frequented by myriads of migratory wildfowl, and its crystal streams are the haunts of thousands of trout.

A similar, fifty-nine-page brochure was also provided by the Seaboard Air Line of Richmond, and its *Guide to the Famous Hunting and Fishing Grounds of Virginia, North Carolina, South Carolina, and Georgia* (1898) follows a format similar to the Southern Railway pamphlet mentioned above. What again strikes the modern reader in the format of this early advertisement is the extensive detail of the booklet's offerings. Not only are there individual narratives promoting the particular attractions of specific areas, which are profusely illustrated with excellent sporting photography, but the South as a region is portrayed as an earthly paradise where the "extremely cordial and hospitable nature of the people" is guaranteed to welcome the visitor with unparalleled hospitality.

As never before, the advance of technology was beginning to open up southern game fields to anyone who could afford it. Together with the perfection and mass production of the breech-loading shotgun in the United States and England around 1870, the advent of the railways and their promotional campaigns enabled and encouraged great numbers of northern sportsmen to invade what had formerly been the exclusive territory of the region's inhabitants. While narratives like Hunter's acknowledge the presence of these outsiders, his primary emphasis remained on the southern sportsman engaged in the recreational customs of his region. Even in the midst of this influx of northern hunters and the affluence of their wealth and prestige, the southern sportsman, at least as we find him depicted in Hunter's work, must continue to uphold the larger values of his society. In the type of point and counterpoint portrayals of characters and events that inform his basic narrative strategy, Hunter's depictions of a variety of sporting scenes argues for a code of behavior not far removed from that found in *Carolina Sports* (1846), though the antebellum optimism of Elliott's perspective affords him a more frank, bold, and forthright narrative stance. Nevertheless, it seems most profitable to consider the code that Hunter advocates as one that reflects the moral beliefs of the planter aristocracy in the mirror of southern sport and one that could easily accommodate the "ethics and responsibilities of sportsmanship" that were being codified by northern periodicals like *American Sportsman* (1871–77), *Forest and Stream* (1873–1911), and *American Angler* (1881–1900). As examples of the similarity between the kinds of values these early periodicals promoted and Hunter's own code of sporting ethics, these excerpts from the November 1872 issue of *American Sportsman,* reprinted in John F. Reiger's *American Sportsmen and the Origins of Conservation* (1975), reveal that their authors are concerned with moral qualities whose importance to society transcends the pleasures of the field:

> It is not the mere killing of numbers, much less the mere killing at all. . . . it is in the vigor, science [correct technique], and manhood displayed—in the difficulties to be overcome, in the pleasurable anxiety for success . . . and above all, in the unalterable *love of fair play*, that first thought of the genuine sportsman, that true sportsmanship consists (Reiger, 28).

Attributed to editor Wilbur F. Parker, the statement above is followed by the comments of an anonymous contributor who identifies more specifically the qualities involved in true sportsmanship:

> The pastimes of stream and woodland, champaign and valley, are the characteristic exercises of many of the noblest properties of man's nature. They call into exertion courage, perseverance, sagacity, strength, activity, [and] caution; they are the wholesome machinery of excitement. . . . *Instead of being antagonistic meanings, the sportsman and the gentleman are [becoming] . . . synonymous terms* (29).

Though Hunter's book strongly endorses a great many of the same ideals celebrated in these 1872 excerpts from the *American Sportsman* magazine, it is not a part of his rhetorical strategy to include such overt and formalized statements of his beliefs. Unlike the narrator of Elliott's "Random Thoughts on Hunting," who waxes philosophical in his enumeration of the ennobling challenges of the field, Hunter provides only the briefest mention of the sporting principles he admires. His pastoral polemic is more reserved, more discreet, and more subtle, allowing instead the rendering of character and event to carry the rhetorical burden of his arguments. In contrast to Elliott's more straightforward delineations of aristocratic sporting ideals, Hunter couches his didacticism in extended sporting metaphors that alternate between foregrounding behavior that is either virtuous and responsible or morally reprehensible. At first, he suggests his contempt for poor sporting form through renderings of comic caricatures whose behavior is merely undesirable. Later his tone darkens, and the concurrent scenes of moral depravity become both shocking and profound. To relieve the somber tone of these powerful metaphorical censures, he balances his figurative admonitions with corresponding portrayals of ethical conduct that serve to maintain the narrative symmetry of the book. This type of recurring pattern of thematic development is clearly evident in the description of Hunter's visits to Goose Creek and Hog Island and in his hunt at the Ragged Island Club with President Benjamin Harrison. He begins, however, with a general and lighthearted review of the conduct all real sportsmen should avoid.

Concerned with selecting a "good quartet" with whom to enjoy a few weeks' shooting along Currituck Sound on the North Carolina coast, Hunter discusses personal shortcomings that are especially to be avoided in one's prospective companions. The first involves the man with no regard for the modesty, generosity, or consideration required of a gentleman. This particular type of undesirable citizen is called "'the good shot,' selfish and opinionated." Instead of appreciating the natural beauty of his surroundings or the companionship of his fellows, his "sole object is to make others feel small, and he never loses an opportunity to boast of his prowess." Patently indifferent to the best interests of anyone but himself, this stock variety of sporting egotist summarily appropriates the best blinds or stands, and "like a bantam rooster, he is continually on the crow" (213–14). A second breech of etiquette is attributed to what Hunter calls the "envious man." This malcontent is utterly consumed with the misconception that, because of his innate superiority to his comrades, only the best of everything is good enough for him. Suspicious that others do not recognize his value and are "leagured against him," he turns the slightest inconvenience into an excuse for abandoning his responsibilities to the joint enterprise entirely. Then we learn of the "penurious man," a miserly and miserably cost-conscious individual who wants to see a clear-cut and profitable relationship between dollars spent and game killed. What should be a trip for pleasure is for him only a "business transaction," and his constant haggling over every expense proves that the natural world and his human associates are to him nothing more than purchasable commodities. Finally, Hunter presents the image of the "constant grumbler," a man possessed of negative qualities that are "worse than all the others combined." This chronic killjoy is described as "a sawyer to your pleasure-boat floating down the stream" and as a "prophylactic snag" who, like the "good shot," places self-aggrandizement at the top of his list of priorities (214).

Initially presented as comedy, these intentional caricatures serve as the imagistic foundation for the further development of similar themes that follow. In his colorful depictions of the sloth and corruption of the residents of Goose Creek and Hog Island, Hunter moves from satiric playfulness to a bold and forthright indictment. Against this backdrop of unsparingly negative characterizations, the contrasting portrayals of his more ethical sportsmen stand out in sharp relief. In the following discussions of selected passages involving these widely divergent types, we can see that by vividly depicting the contrasts between the motivations and conduct of these sporting polarities, Hunter clearly reveals his penchant for adhering to the finest traditions of the southern sporting code.

Dramatically opposed to the sporting ideal that these traditions would help to promote, the Goose Creek Islanders who greet Hunter and his friends at the abandoned lighthouse installation from which they plan to hunt on Pamlico Point display an alarming lack of self-respect and enterprise. When Hunter arrives, he finds a group of uninvited and taciturn individuals "leaning, reclining and slouching around the house" (237). Though tall and powerfully built, the men in the party rarely stand up straight, "except when yawning . . . simply for the reason that it is too great an effort to hold the backbone erect" (237–38). To Hunter's consternation, the families remain on the premises several days, "eating, drinking, and lounging, until they cleaned out our whole large stock of wet and dry groceries" (239).

In the course of their stay, Hunter learns a great deal about the practices of the Goose Creek style of duck hunting, and we see that these lower class "pot-hunters" are anything but sportsmen. Hunting after dark and only on nights when the inlet is calm, the islanders silently approach ricks of bunched waterfowl in specially designed watercraft. Their equipment is simple: a large-bore fowling piece, a kerosene lamp, and a tin reflector. One can almost hear the fine disdain in Hunter's voice as he describes the Goose Creek stratagem:

> The gunner now opens the slide and a dazzling glare floats over the water. The ducks, bewildered by the light, mass together and swim slowly in a circle, blinking at the blinding gleam. The gunner fires at point blank range, and

> dozens are killed at the discharge, and as many more are crippled, and flutter away and die on the marshes (250).

Their sport ruined by illegal night hunters and inclement weather, Hunter and the one other sportsman who remains on the point fall victim to the objectionable habits of the abandoned lighthouse keeper with whom they are forced to live. He is given to the same indulgences and idleness as his nearby Goose Creek neighbors, and his indifferent housekeeping and nightly extravagances of shrill song and strong drink nearly drive Hunter and his companion mad before a ship can be hailed to take them back to the mainland. In the final scene, the lighthouse keeper refuses to use his boat at the critical point when they must row out to the waiting packet until Hunter pays him an additional fifteen dollars.

Faced with and surrounded by a like indifference to state statute, sporting etiquette, or even common decency during his forced seclusion at Pamlico Point, Hunter nevertheless manages to identify a single gleam of virtue in his otherwise depressing outing. This exception is found in the loyalty and persistence of his blue-blooded English setter, Jessie. Having seen her master wing a large Canada goose from his blind, Jessie dives into the frigid water to retrieve it. But the goose is barely hurt, and it leads the dog on a long and hazardous swim. For a Labrador, Chesapeake Bay, or Curly-Coated retriever to swim miles in icy waters to retrieve waterfowl is not uncommon, but for a setter, lacking the insulation of the retriever's dense, oily undercoat to protect it, a swim of fifty yards in freezing temperatures is often extremely dangerous. Losing sight of the dog from his blind as she swims after the goose, Hunter rushes to ascend the lighthouse where, with the aid of a telescope, he can barely make her out as she follows the goose out the mouth of the inlet. Silently upbraiding himself for sending his dog to make the retrieve, Hunter, much like William Elliott in *Carolina Sports*, regrets that the excitement of the moment has caused him to endanger his trusted servant (see *Carolina Sports*, 157–58). Fortunately, as Hunter and the lighthouse keeper prepare to launch a rescue boat, the setter reappears with the dead goose in her mouth. Promising the roasted goose as a reward for her fortitude, Hunter waxes eloquent in praise of Jessie's fidelity: "As for love, a dog's love is more honest and unsullied, more faithful and true, than any other in this weary old world. A man may sink into the gutter and kill the affections of all who are nearest to him, but his dog will cling to him through all" (245).

Perhaps included here to add a needed stroke of narrative humanity after the wholesale condemnation of the islanders, similar examples of this strong emotional bond between hunters and their dogs, and the strong sense of noblesse oblige these relationships engender, reappear regularly in Hunter's work, as well as in the writings of Rutledge and Gordon that followed.

Continuing this shift of narrative focus from the negative to the positive side of southern field sports, chapter 12 of *The Huntsman in the South* details the visit of President Benjamin Harrison (1833–1901) to Hunter's Ragged Island Club near Cape Henry, Virginia. Hunter tells us that Harrison had been in the White House over half his term (1889–93) when the officers of this elite club on Currituck Sound commissioned Hunter to invite the president "to make our club-house his headquarters during his stay in Virginia" (256). Since this would put the date of his hunt at Ragged Island in the winter of 1891–92, Harrison would already have been fifty-eight years old, but as Hunter explains, "the blood of sportsmen ran thick in the President's veins" (255). Indeed, Hunter is at some pains to describe the distinguished line of sportsmen from whom his guest is descended and to commend him for his fortitude, stamina, and unfailing good manners. The president is portrayed in glowing terms, and a review of *The Huntsman in the South* comments favorably on Hunter's depiction of Harrison as "a genial and thorough sportsman" portrayed in a "clever and graphic bit of writing" (Gladden, review, 609). Unwilling to take unfair advantage of the Republican surrounded by a party of staunch Democrats in this remote but elegant retreat, the members of the Ragged Island Club are all deference and tact. Equally unwilling to remind his hosts of his elevated position, Harrison abandons his presidential prerogatives handsomely. As Hunter tells it:

> He expressed a wish to be put into a blind as early as possible in the morning, and to be left there with a retriever, saying that he would hunt as the others hunted. He wanted no extra attention, and declared that he did not mind exposure, and could stand anything the rest could (257).

As the trip turned out, the president's hardihood would be sorely tested, but, warned that the weather would be cold and stormy, Harrison replies that, in his view, "The worse the weather, the better the luck" (258). Hunter neglects to give the particulars of the weather on the first day's shooting, saying only that "the rain froze as it fell." Nevertheless, Harrison was the last to return in the evening, with a nice bag of fourteen ducks, mostly canvasback. On the final day out, the president again is last to return from his blind, and Hunter's description of the nation's chief executive suggests his total immersion in the elements of his natural surroundings: "When we assembled in the club-house, the President was a sight. The lower half of his body was a mass of mud and the upper half was encased in ice" (263). As Ortega might explain the scene, President Harrison had succeeded in diverting himself from the ceaseless cares of his demanding office by returning to his primitive identity as a part of the natural world. In Hunter's view, Harrison had been able to rekindle "the touch of the savage in [his] composition" by "severing [himself] from all the luxuries and charms of civilized life" (235). Without intending it, Hunter's portrayal of the president's voluntary exposure to the worst possible elements argues much the same point that Ortega would later make in his essay on "The Essence of Hunting": "There is . . . in the hunt as a sport a supremely free renunciation by man of the supremacy of his humanity" (Ortega, *Meditations,* 59). Without this kind of deliberate and voluntary surrender, the sportsman can never hope to reap the full psychological benefits of his elemental encounter with the natural world.

Before Hunter closes his book with a lengthy description of the best guns and dogs to use for the great variety of southern game, he returns in his penultimate chapter to criticism of unethical sportsmen who refuse to abide by either the official game laws or proper sporting etiquette. The focus of his attack are the residents of Hog Island, Virginia, another lighthouse station where, in addition to the lighthouse itself, there are "forty-two dwellings . . . and every householder seems to be above want" (306). Once again, the islanders are criticized bitterly for their idleness and their illegal slaughter of waterfowl by blinding them as they gather on the water at night, but Hunter's strongest condemnation appears in his description of the hurricane that struck the island during his visit. Unable to remain bunched in offshore ricks, great flocks of American brant fly over the island seeking shelter from the approaching gale. This small member of the goose family, only slightly larger than the mallard, is known for its wariness, but confused by the hurricane they become strangely attracted by the lighthouse beacon. Circling around the tower in drove after drove, the birds are completely unaware of any human presence, and Hunter describes this rare opportunity to observe "every graceful curve of neck and head, and the set and balance of the body, and [the chance] to look into their brilliant eyes" (310–11). The excitement and imagery of this wild, rushing scene are among Hunter's finest, but soon the resident islanders have seen the brant and decide to turn their confusion to advantage:

> Some of the islanders asked the keeper on duty to allow them to ascend the tower and shoot the hovering birds. Certainly a man using a small gauge gun could have killed hundreds that night. I told the keeper that if such a murderous act was permitted the Government would dismiss everyone of the light-house employees (311).

On a first reading, Hunter's threats and the subsequent ousting of the islanders appear to be integral parts of a self-contained rendering intended to appeal to the reader's sense of justice and to validate the narrator's superior moral stance. And so it is, but simply to give a silent nod of tacit approval and move on would be to miss entirely the organic relevance of this highly figurative and subtly understated portrayal. In its paired contrasts, its emotional intensity, and its quiet celebration of the elevated principles that inform the code of genuine southern sportsmanship, the scene speaks volumes about Hunter's moral, thematic, and narrative rationale that resonates throughout the book. Like a camera lens coming sharply into focus, the native compassion, sense of fair play, and benevolent generosity of the southern sporting ethos are momentarily crystallized in this finely crafted though modest-seeming episode.

Hunter's position on the uppermost floor of the lighthouse is elevated indeed, morally no less than physically, and from his Olympian perch he is able to appreciate and to savor the beauty of the natural world in the brant's "graceful curve of neck and head" and "brilliant eyes." The islanders, however, are as blind to these higher levels of appreciation as they are to the pathos involved in the disoriented birds' confusion and fear. As the denizens of the metaphorical outer darkness below, the local residents are unable to see anything in the birds' plight except a golden opportunity to shoot them. More clearly than at any other time, Hunter defines for his readers the kinds of gaping, antithetical contrasts that separate those who are sportsmen, on the one hand, from those who are simply "murderous," on the other. Clearly emerging in a serious and distinctively chivalric iconography is the image of the sportsman as a responsible moral agent, a truly principled man whose appetite for good shooting and fine scenery is happily balanced by a code of ethics that prohibits wasteful slaughter and unfair indulgence. In a final and finishing stroke, Hunter reminds us at the end of the chapter that, as a member of the state legislature, it was he who "framed and formed the first game laws for the state" (314).

By the time that the little-known *Huntsman in the South* was published in 1908, the image of the sportsman as the protector and conservator of the very game he pursued had become solidified most prominently in the person of Theodore Roosevelt and in his pervasive ideal of the "hunter naturalist." Guided by Roosevelt's leadership and inspired by his example, men like William F. Parker, George Bird Grinnell, Gifford Pinchot, and Archibald Rutledge would continue to codify and bring to the public forefront a sporting ethos that helped to organize America's sportsmen into a powerful political force that fostered the great conservation movement of the late nineteenth and early twentieth centuries. For the first time in the nation's history and in the face of unparalleled exploitation of America's natural resources, the tenets of good sportsmanship were publicly endorsed as the soundest, safest, and most enlightened approach to ensuring the health and survival of the environment.

One of the most influential of the sportsman's organizations was the Boone and Crocket Club, formed in 1887 by *Forest and Stream*'s editor George Bird Grinnell and sport hunting's most powerful and prolific defender, Theodore Roosevelt. Like Grinnell, Roosevelt was an aristocrat from an old, well-educated, and wealthy family, and in their efforts to articulate the code of sportsmanship they may very well have been "subconsciously attempting to keep at least one representative element of the older elite's world free from the encroachment of the *nouveaux riches*" (Reiger, 33). On one level, their efforts to celebrate and to codify the proper methods for pursuing game and protecting habitat were ways not only of preserving the natural environment but also of perpetuating the moral values of a cast of mind and way of life they saw vanishing. In the face of an onslaught of economic development and environmental destruction that peaked in the Gilded Age, a "stylized, idealist type of hunter" that came to be known as the "hunter-naturalist" evolved (Alther, "The American Hunter-Naturalist," 9):

> Combining respect and aesthetic appreciation for nature and nostalgia for what they considered purer, wilder hunting in the past with the moral imperatives of gentle manliness, the hunter-naturalists championed the general code of sporting ethics called sportsmanship. Sportsmen from America's upper class sought to dignify hunting for sport and to check the savage hunting impulse (7).

Representing the culmination of the development of the hunter-naturalist ideal, the outspoken and determined Theodore Roosevelt brought the issues of conservation and the code of sportsmanship to the widest public attention. Roosevelt is best known for his considerable achievements in conservation during his term as president (1901–09), and in the following excerpt Reiger outlines a few of the most significant.

> . . . the addition of 100 million acres to the forest reserves, called "national forests" after 1907 . . . the establishment of five national parks and seventeen national monuments and the founding of an extensive system of wildlife refuges containing over fifty units (Reiger, 147).

Nevertheless, it was as sporting author and not as president that Roosevelt exerted the greatest influence on defining the code of sportsmanship that most clearly identified the hunter-naturalist. In early books like *Hunting Trips of a Ranchman* (1885), *Ranch Life and the Hunting Trail* (1888), and *The Wilderness Hunter* (1893), Roosevelt introduced a new element into the genre of the American sporting narrative. Not only were there carefully drawn and exciting portrayals of his encounters with game that invariably argued for observing the strictest codes of sportsmanship but also detailed descriptions of non-game animals, of flowers and scenery, and of the customs and traditions of the regions he explored. In his shorter works, reviews of books, and letters to associates, the ideal of the hunter-naturalist continued to receive its most eloquent and powerful support. Over and again, Roosevelt returned to his theme that hunters should also be "nature lovers. It is to be hoped that the days of mere wasteful, boastful slaughter are past and that from now on the hunter will stand foremost in working for the preservation and perpetuation of wildlife . . ." (Roosevelt, *Outdoor Pastimes,* 125). In addition, he joined the ranks of writers such as William Elliott and Alexander Hunter in condemning those whose only goal in hunting is to kill prodigious numbers of animals simply for the purpose of advertising their own prowess: "Laying stress upon the mere quantity of game killed, and the publication of the record of slaughter, are sure signs of unhealthy decadence in sportsmanship" (Roosevelt, "Master," 353).

Unfortunately, Roosevelt was correct in arguing that the average hunter writes a book "about as interesting as a Baedeker." Along with others of his gifts and experience, he wanted the nature writer to be able to express himself well: "I wish a good hunting book to be as interesting as a good novel!" (Roosevelt,

"Hunter Naturalist," 372). What Roosevelt had accomplished politically in establishing the national forests, national parks, and wildlife refuges, he aimed at doing on a philosophical level in his writings about hunting and the natural world. Like others who ascribed to the hunter-naturalist ideal, he felt that hunting was not only a sport but rather "the best mode of environmental perception, the truest appreciation of nature's ways and meanings" (Alther, 7). At a time when the concept of conservation was first taking hold on the American environmental consciousness, Roosevelt was able to define and to promote a sporting ethos that sought to incorporate into preexisting codes of sportsmanship a sympathy for the game and a keen interest in quasi-scientific observation. The influence of his thought and his writing were pervasive, and they would continue to affect the ways in which later sporting writers would envision and portray the hunters and fishermen they described. In the South, men like William Elliott and Alexander Hunter had already begun the task of formulating similar concepts in their region's sporting lore, but it would be left to Archibald Rutledge (1883–1973) to produce an extended body of work that fully articulates these principles. In collections like *Plantation Game Trails* (1921), *Children of Swamp and Wood* (1927), and *An American Hunter* (1937), we find the tenets of the hunter-naturalists and the aristocratic, southern code of conduct fully integrated into the character of the southern sportsman.

No other contributor to the genre of the southern sporting narrative brought to his work a stronger sense of cultural tradition or a more distinguished family pedigree than Archibald Rutledge of South Carolina. Descended from an aristocratic family who could claim among its many honored members a chief justice of the U.S. Supreme Court, a signer of the Declaration of Independence, and a governor of South Carolina, Rutledge would continue to bring honor to the family name through his prolific writing and his formal appointment in 1934 as the first poet laureate of South Carolina (Woodell, "Archibald Rutledge," 391). Born in 1883 at the family's summer retreat in McClellanville, South Carolina, to Henry Middleton and Margaret Hamilton Rutledge, the young heir to the proud family name proved to be exceptional in a number of different ways. Most importantly for his development as an author was an engrossing interest in the woods and game on the family's ancestral home of Hampton Plantation, a preoccupation of much intensity. Rutledge largely put aside the purely political identity that was his by the circumstances of his birth and created an imaginative universe that celebrated his culture's values through poems and stories about nature.

Though well aware that he was born into "a world that was ruined and a civilization that had passed," Rutledge was a literary man, an English teacher in the North who felt a natural disinclination for the commonly fascinating appeal that martial glory had for young southerners during Reconstruction (Owens, "Guide," 1). This is all the more surprising in light of the fact that the father with whom he shared a close and enduring relationship, Henry Middleton Rutledge II, had been the youngest colonel in the Confederate army, had commanded the Twenty-fifth North Carolina Calvary at Bull Run, and was shot from his horse into the Potomac River during the Confederate withdrawal at Sharpsburg (Wheeler and Neblett, *Hidden Glory,* 110–11), (I. Rutledge, *Flintlock,* 6). Even the efforts of his maternal grandmother, Caroline Pinckney, to inspire him with the "glittering sword and ornate uniform" worn by Gen. Charles Cotesworth Pinckney were to no avail. For him, military trappings seemed to become associated only with the ruin that the recent war had brought to his region. While he would later honor his father's achievements in *My Colonel and His Lady* (1937), even this book-length tribute downplays the colonel's distinguished military record in favor of his compassion, earthy wisdom, and pervasive sportsmanship.

In view of Rutledge's innate aversion to a martial career, and because of his deep involvement with the natural world of the plantation, it was undoubtedly difficult for him to adjust to the strictly regimented life at the military academy in Charleston where his parents enrolled him in 1896. Away from his family and the plantation's forests, Rutledge amused himself by sketching hunting scenes in his class notebooks and dreaming of the free, outdoor life he had enjoyed. Despite his loneliness, he distinguished himself as a scholar, winning gold medals for both French and English and graduating as class salutatorian in 1900. More important for his professional development was the award of a Lorillard scholarship to attend Union College in Schenectady, New York. At the age of sixteen, Rutledge found himself not only far removed from his family, friends, and the forests he had come to love but in the very heart of what was still considered "enemy territory" by most of his friends at home.

Through his diligence, good manners, and superior scholarship, the young southerner soon adjusted to the northern environment. His abilities as a writer also began to assert themselves. He edited the college newspaper, wrote and published a number of poems and stories, and graduated as class valedictorian in 1904. At Mercersburg Academy in Pennsylvania's Cumberland Valley, where he went for a temporary teaching position, Rutledge found his second home on the eve of his twenty-first birthday. Though known to his colleagues as "Johnny Reb," Rutledge found that the northerners were nevertheless eager to heal the wounds of sectional division. In "When the Yankee Band Played Dixie," the young Rutledge tells of finding the graves of Confederate soldiers decorated with flowers in the Mercersburg cemetery on Memorial Day in 1904 (I. Rutledge, 19–20). Of course, this particular section of rural Pennsylvania was a Copperhead region, whose inhabitants sympathized with the South during the war. These sympathies remained strong and may have helped Rutledge to establish himself there and to succeed in making it his second home. Except for the annual visits to South Carolina during winter and summer vacations, Rutledge remained in Mercersburg as a teacher and later chairman of the academy's English department until 1937, a tenure of some thirty-three years, when he retired and once again took up residence at Hampton Plantation as the state's first poet laureate.

A strong attachment to a particular region and homesite are characteristic of southern writers, whatever genre they may choose, and the strength of family ties, the sense of the weight of history, and the abiding sense of the presence of the past are hallmarks of the renascence in southern letters that began shortly after World War I. Archibald Rutledge shared these concerns with the more mainstream southern writers of the period, though his work is far removed from the intense emphasis on technical virtuosity and the dynamic intellectual environment of the Vanderbilt campus, where men such as John Crowe Ransom, Donald Davidson, and Allen Tate were plotting the new directions for southern literature. What has yet to be addressed is the difference between most of the Fugitive-Agrarians (writers who were indulging in a last look over their cultural shoulders at the old South prior to stepping fully into the modern world) and Rutledge, for whom antebellum cultural values informed a philosophy of life and a code of conduct that remained for him the perfect alternative to modern chaos. Most importantly, it is well to remember that Rutledge and the Vanderbilt Fugitives arrived at their disdain for romantically celebrating southern military honor by entirely different routes. For the men and women on the cutting edge of the renascence, characters like Page's Marse Chan and Ransom's Captain Carpenter represented a dysfunctional romanticism that in no way prepared southerners for dealing with the complexities of a modern world where the traditional icons had lost their cohesive and stabilizing power. On the other hand, though Rutledge revered his father's bravery during the war, he took a broader, more universal view of courage and sought to depict its exercise and value in a variety of different contexts. And unlike the southern writers after World War I who rejected the cavalier ideal of the Confederate hero because of his failure to provide an effective model for coping with the moral wasteland of modern existence, Rutledge objected to restricting the moral worth of the southern cavalier's code of bravery to the battlefield. He also believed that the romantic conventionalism of the past did not require a total restructuring to be relevant for the problems of modernity, only a shifting in focus to allow it to include a type of moral heroism not dependent on formal military engagements for its exercise. In the natural world of Hampton Plantation and Pennsylvania's Cumberland Mountains, Rutledge was able to find the perfect environment for his particular philosophy of life to enact itself. Through the lives of the wildlife he found there and the characters of the men who pursued it, Rutledge discovered a wealth of readily adaptable metaphors for expressing his traditional and distinctively southern views on honor and morality.

There is little doubt that Rutledge's extensive knowledge of natural history and his abiding code of sportsmanship combined to form a barrier against the deracination that would naturally have threatened him in the North. As a means of holding on to and preserving the values he admired, he used his writing as a means of solidifying and codifying the tenets of good sportsmanship he had learned as a youth. In his major works from his Pennsylvania years, we find that the values of the southern planter aristocracy inform his carefully worded though apparently straightforward nature stories, tales that parallel thematically the ideal of Roosevelt's hunter-naturalist and the great wave of environmental awareness that had begun to emerge around the turn of the century. When in *Plantation Game Trails* (1921) we find direct reference to these ideals, it becomes evident that Rutledge did not live his authorial life in a vacuum and that, in elucidating the values of the southern sporting code, he felt obliged to make reference to the concepts that are found in abundance in Roosevelt's earlier work.

Plantation Game Trails is dedicated to "My three sons, True Sportsmen of the Coming Generation," suggesting at the outset that Rutledge viewed his life, and his son's lives, not as discrete units of humanity but as part of the larger historical context. More important is his use of the term "True Sportsmen," for this seemingly insignificant accolade carries the burden of thematic continuity for the volume as a whole. For Rutledge and many of his well-bred, southern contemporaries, the terms "sportsman" and "gentleman" were largely interchangeable, for they alike implied a strict code of honorable conduct and a touchstone for evaluating experience. In the preface that follows the dedication, Rutledge enlarges upon his concept of sportsmanship. He promises a "faithful account of the observation . . . made as a hunter and lover of Nature," following, or at least paralleling Theodore Roosevelt's dictum that the hunter must also be a "nature lover" if he would be a sportsman and a credit to his society. But Rutledge goes even further in stressing this point, punctuating his message for clarity and force: "For the dual attitude of hunter and naturalist I offer no apology—save to confess that as the years advance the latter is acquiring a wholesome ascendancy" (viii). One might wonder why he felt it necessary to add this closing sentence to the preface of a volume clearly directed toward the active members of the hunting fraternity. It is possible he felt that the less discriminating of his readers would scoff at the idea of a naturalist writing a book for hunters or that his more refined audience thought hunting too savage a sport for a respected teacher and man of letters. More likely he sought to address the problem of stereotyping the two avocations as mutually exclusive. Like other hunter-naturalists of his day, Rutledge felt that hunting was the single most effective means of environmental perception, and he wished to cause his readers to abandon a narrow, unrealistic view of either the sport or the men who pursued it.

The world that Rutledge wrote about had changed markedly from the antebellum prosperity we find evident in Elliott and the early Simms. As Rutledge points out, he had seen his homeland "undergo great transformations. . . . the plantations have for the most part become waste tracts; many of the old families have died out" (vii). However, despite the passing of antebellum plantation society, its values and culture continued to provide for him a valuable source of strength and inspiration. The activities revolving around Hampton's land and game, rather than the formerly brisk social life at the plantation mansion, had now become for him the most vital source of cultural continuity. Though the old families of the many neighbors had died out (Rutledge's own father had died early in 1921) and the living descendants scattered, their memories of the culture of planter society continued to inspire the conduct of those who survived. For Rutledge, those memories remained alive in the natural world—not as a transcendentalist would have them but as a naturalist who could not ignore the similarities between the virtues of the people he had known and the characteristics of the game they pursued. This type of perspective and world view was not concerned with positing a natural fact for each corresponding spiritual idea but rather with expressing the values he had absorbed in terms of the forest and game that yet remained. The pageantry of the chase itself and his own keen powers of observation had provided him with a tremendous storehouse of information about the natural history of his region. Like many of our finest American writers, he was able to draw on this specialized body of knowledge to express his ideas, as Herman Melville had done with whaling and as Ernest Hemingway would do with bullfighting and war. For this reason, the most profitable approach to *Plantation Game Trails* is not as a simplistic and straightforward report of hunting adventure but rather as a form of highly figurative expression whose rewarding imagery subtly identifies a certain class of assumptions about the world.

For those unused to the narrative concerns of the hunter-naturalist, Rutledge no doubt confused many readers with the title of chapter 1, "My Friend the Deer." Instead of the lead-gray skies and piercing winds of winter, the opening suggests an Edenic, soothingly pastoral scene far removed from most descriptions of the chase. In the lines that open this first section, Rutledge sounds much more like a romantic lyricist than the author of a book on plantation hunting:

> It was the middle of May in the woods of South Carolina, and the time of the day was noon. I was riding along leisurely, trying to drink in a portion of the marvelous beauty of the scene which stretched away from me on all sides; a scene in which bright birds flashed, wild flowers gleamed and glowed, and great trees seemed to shiver and expand in the ecstasy of their springtime joy (1).

Although the scene that follows describes the "beautiful sight" of a doe that is "bouncing along gracefully" to her fawn nestled in the broomstraw, the descriptions suggest neither the excitement of the chase nor the romantic ideal of a purely benevolent natural world devoid of strife and complexity. The doe is described as a loving mother, but upon the narrator's approach she abandons her fawn and races with "reluctant speed" to a range of three hundred yards. Moreover, the narrator does not wax eloquent about the reunion effected on his retreat but launches instead into a twenty-page description of the deer and its habits. True to the hunter-naturalist penchant for accuracy, the details of the animal's behavior are faithfully and exactingly described—with admiration but without the starry-eyed romanticist's euphoria of having observed a scene of earthly perfection. Nor does Rutledge advocate using his remarkable skills as a woodsman simply as a tool for acquiring venison. Later in the chapter, he tells of a group of deer he observed by moonlight. Having located a herd who frequented an abandoned and sandy churchyard, he buries rock salt in the sand and builds an elevated blind some distance away. Though ascending his perch at sundown leaves him a three-hour wait before the game arrives, he goes often and is "richly rewarded" with the habits of the undisturbed deer. There is, of course, no attempt to kill any of the animals; instead, the chance to observe the game with "their air of superb readiness, of elfin caution, suppressed but instantly available," proves reward enough in itself (12).

The deer of the pine woods at Hampton are indeed beautiful to see, but in later descriptions we are told of a darker side of their lives that would hardly appeal to romanticists content "to stroll through a 'sylvan glade' and contemplate the 'beauty' around them" (Reiger, 35). Instead, the buck in mating season is described as aggressively combative and possessed of an "ugly and uncertain temper" (17). Though rarely attacking a man in the wild, they are "forever fighting their fellows" until ascendance is established. Even victory cannot satisfy the more sanguinary individuals, and Rutledge reports bodies of deer "which have literally been cut to pieces" by their rivals' repeatedly jumping on their fallen adversaries with their pointed hoofs. In addition, the ravages of anthrax are disastrous, and many infected deer are found still standing but "shaking and shivering as with the ague" (20). For those who survive these natural dangers, the many alligators of the lowcountry swamps pose a constant threat.

Though in later chapters, most notably "My Winter Woods" (178–93), Rutledge does leave off revealing the more somber side of the natural world he describes, the grim nature of survival in the wild has already been posited as a context and balance for these more nearly idyllic depictions. Even the cypress pond he finds so alluring has about it a sadness that cannot disregard Nature's indifferent cruelties. Says Rutledge, "A spirit broods here that is autumnal; it is rich and sad, full of haunting pathos and romantic charm" (190). It would seem that the report from Hampton Plantation is one that refuses to reduce the natural world into a simplicity it does not possess. There is beauty in abundance, and to observe it carefully brings pleasure, but really to appreciate the "magic vistas and mysterious swamps" and the animals who live there, one cannot concern oneself only with a stroll through the romantic's "sylvan glade." Instead, whether hunting or simply observing, the genuine lover of nature must seek to apprehend the awesome power and indifferent cruelty that informs the cycles of life and of death in the wild.

Writing during a period when American sportsmen everywhere were beginning to study the intricate dynamics of the natural world that formed the context for their sport, Rutledge had the great advantage of an extensive, first-hand knowledge of natural history, one gained against a cultural background that equipped him to excel in the very kind of outdoor writing then in vogue. His traditional southern upbringing and early training as a sportsman in the Reconstruction South had combined to instill in him a view of life as a struggle for survival and as a series of inescapable challenges that must be met by both man and beast with courage and even audacity. While the ideal of martial glory had little appeal for him as an individual, he was nevertheless steeped in the proud military traditions of his family and region. Because of these unique and complementary influences, he was able to adopt, perhaps more readily than his northern contemporaries, a comprehensive and sympathetic view of nature that avoided the factual absurdities and faulty sentimentalism of what Theodore Roosevelt labeled the "Nature-Faker" school of outdoor writing (Roosevelt, "Nature-Fakers," 267–83). Rutledge instead adhered closely to the responsibly accurate though artistically licensed guidelines set forth in John Burroughs's famous essay, "The Literary Treatment of Nature" (1905). Both Roosevelt and Burroughs agreed that literary renderings of natural phenomena faced a dual challenge. As Burroughs explains it, "the problem of the essay naturalist always is to make his subject interesting, and yet keep strictly within the bounds of truth" (207). Though Rutledge would often speak admiringly of the animals he described, he never forgot that his first duty was to portray accurately the history of their struggles and necessities and not to depict a romanticized and exaggerated interpretation of their habits and lives.

In *Children of Swamp and Wood* (1927), Rutledge reminds us that he is well aware that the fleeting encounters between hunters and game form only a small part of the dangers wild animals must face on a daily basis. In "The Courage of the Wild" (191–215), he takes as his thesis the idea that those who attribute little valor to the animals they pursue base their ideas on the necessarily unequal game played by hunters and their prey (see Ortega, 57–59). What Rutledge provides in "The Courage of the Wild" are descriptions of animals who exhibit intrepid behavior that is not only rarely seen by the rank and file of hunters but that also suggests something of the high regard that the narrator affords this virtue.

For Rutledge, there was "an element of divinity" in motherhood, human or otherwise, and he believed that without the "peculiarly superb quality of her devotion no species could survive" (202). Moreover, he argues that the female of all species is superior to the male in the "true moral intrepidity" that informs the most valuable types of courage. To illustrate his point, he describes his encounter with a ruffed grouse in the Tuscarora Mountains of Pennsylvania. Hearing muted calls of a brood of young grouse, Rutledge stepped forward into the bush for a closer look. The mother flushed but flew only a short distance and perched in a young hemlock. When the fledglings began to break cover, she attacked without hesitation, and Rutledge describes her circling and "buffeting my coat with pitiful strength—but with superb courage" (191). Admiringly, Rutledge notes that at any time he could have reached out and caught the bird in his hand, but the mother grouse, though well aware of her danger, was more than willing to sacrifice her life for her young.

In a second encounter, Rutledge describes the chance meeting of a whitetail buck and a wild bull on the marshes of Murphy's Island in South Carolina. The deer's valor in this episode is not prompted by the instinctual urges of parental protection, nor is there evident the natural rivalry among buck deer during the mating season. Instead, the scene is especially effective in supporting Rutledge's argument that, like their human counterparts, wild animals must quite often exhibit a great and sublime courage that can inspire in those fortunate enough to observe it a respect for this invaluable virtue. Watching from the cover of a red cedar grove, Rutledge observes a small herd of deer emerge to feed in the marsh late one afternoon. The buck leading them was in his prime but no more than 150 pounds in weight. From behind a sand dune that separated the jungle from the water, a wild bull appeared, apparently a descendant of cattle brought to the island a century earlier who had long since gone wild. When the bull, "merely from sheer truculence," advanced menacingly toward a crippled doe that was following the main herd, the buck turned and placed himself between them, lowering his head, apparently ready for a fight. The outcome of the proposed contest would have been certain, if for no other reason than that the bull outweighed the deer at least ten-to-one.

Nevertheless, faced with such determination and fortitude, the bull backed down and the crippled doe escaped unharmed. As Rutledge observes, the bull found resuming his grazing on the tender grasses more appealing than dealing with an adversary who was grossly inferior in strength but who nevertheless appeared "quite ready to take care of himself and of those under his protection" (125).

The decade between the publication of *Children of Swamp and Wood* (1927) and *An American Hunter* (1937) was for Rutledge a period checkered with both tragedy and reward. His prolific output of nature stories and inspirational poetry continued apace, and though continuing to teach and live in Mercersburg, he rarely missed a summer or Christmas visit to Hampton Plantation. During these years his writing continued to improve and to take on a philosophical complexity and imaginative fluency that in 1930 earned for him the coveted John Burroughs Medal, a national award for "the best nature writing of the year" (I. Rutledge, 40), and in 1934 a gubernatorial appointment as South Carolina's first poet laureate. While he failed to win the Pulitzer Prize in three separate nominations, he could at least console himself that he had come in second to some very stiff competition: Edna St. Vincent Millay, Robert Frost, and William Faulkner. To add to his disappointments, Prince Alston, his lifelong friend and hunting companion at Hampton, had died unexpectedly in 1928, and, in the depths of the Depression, his wife of twenty-seven years, Florence Hart Rutledge, died of a stroke while visiting friends in Charleston in 1934. In what would have been for a lesser man a deciding blow to his fortitude, the state of South Carolina announced its plans to dam and divert the Santee River that ran by Hampton Plantation to generate electrical power. Without the strong outward current of the Santee to force the nearby Atlantic's salty waters away from the land, much of the plant life for sixty miles inland would be killed. Unfortunately for Rutledge, his scathing public protests against this latest environmental outrage by the ideological descendants of the New South progressivists earned him the ire of the project's backers, and bills were introduced in the South Carolina Senate to abolish the post of poet laureate to which he had been recently named. He was saved from this indignity only through the efforts of loyal supporters who, in 1936, pushed a resolution through the state House of Representatives that vindicated Rutledge's right to free speech and verified his appointment (Bodie, *Hunt for Life's Extras,* 122–24). Despite these setbacks, Rutledge consistently avoided becoming embittered toward his homeland and remained convinced that obedience to the laws of patience, faithfulness, and courage remained the source of human happiness (163).

With the now-secure stipend from his post as poet laureate and the pension for thirty-three years service at Mercersburg Academy, Rutledge was able to return to Hampton Plantation late in 1937. Only months before his long-awaited move, he published his finest collection of hunting stories in a book appropriately titled *An American Hunter*. Dedicated to his three sons, the volume includes his classic essays "The Hunter and the Law" (112–21) and "Why I Taught My Boys to Be Hunters" (141–50). Taken together, these short sketches not only touch on many of Rutledge's most fundamental beliefs but provide as well a keen insight into the relationship between these values and the code of sporting etiquette he espoused.

By 1937, federal statutes and state laws regulating hunting seasons, licenses, and bag limits were well on their way to becoming the standardized and integrated regulations that we enjoy today. Enforcement remained a problem, but the history of game laws in America shows that funding for sufficient manpower to regulate hunting has been the rare exception to the more commonly understaffed ranks of conservation officers. Of much greater practical value in the effort to enforce game laws that hunters had called for and supported themselves were the vast majority of responsible sportsman in the hunting fraternity. In "The Hunter and the Law," Rutledge applauds the efforts of these dedicated individuals. Though tinged with his characteristic good humor, the sketch effectively depicts not only the change in the American landscape brought on by greater mobility and population growth but also suggests that the leading authors of southern sporting narratives had achieved a highly self-conscious awareness of their responsibility to the natural environment.

Set in the remotely rural county of Fulton in southeastern Pennsylvania, "The Hunter and the Law" opens with the author's injunction that, for hunters, observing the established rules and regulations is vitally important, primarily because they are necessary for preserving the existence of the sport itself. Since Fulton has been assigned but a single warden to patrol its vast acreage, the responsibility for enforcing the game laws falls largely on the hunters themselves, and Rutledge is not long in dramatizing their contribution. Arriving at the edge of the deer woods on opening day, the narrator finds a group of red-capped hunters circled around the carcass of an albino doe that had been killed only minutes before. Instead of the high good humor and congratulatory ribbing that normally follows a successful hunt, the "solemn ring" that the men had formed was marked by the sharpest resentment and outrage (113). It seems that a visiting hunter from out-of-state had illegally killed the hunters' "pet" that had lived on the nearby preserve (113). Without the proper license and while trespassing on the state reservation, the offender had not only killed a doe illegally but had taken an animal who had been given no reason to fear the human presence. Quite the contrary; for as one hunter explained, "She was our pet. . . . We seed her constant. I would just as soon shoot one of my little girls. We hoped she would breed, and we might have had a race of white deer in these mountains" (113). More importantly, the poacher had not been arrested by the local warden in whose custody he now reposed but had instead been surrounded by the hunters themselves. In the following passage, the gravity of this citizen's arrest transcends the dialect in which it appears:

> We were just getting ready for a drive . . . when we heard shootin' across the wire in the refuge. You see, we don't stand for that. So up we go, and across the wire, and we find this here poacher with this little white doe he had killed. He started to run, but he soon stopped, and it's a good thing he did. . . . Some of us had it on him, and he wouldn't have gone far. If he hadn't stopped himself, we'd have stopped him (113–14).

Though imaginatively transposed into the behavior of a plainspoken but resolute group of Pennsylvania sportsmen, this important scene reaffirms the strong emphasis on fair play that informs the southern sporting ethos. As Rutledge says, hunters are most often "put largely on their honor in the matter of observing the law" (126). Usually far removed from the presence of the local wardens and so seldom observed in their sport, responsible men obey the game laws not out of fear but from the deeper motives of self-respect and decency and to preserve the element of fair play that ensures the essence of a genuine hunt. There is also what Rutledge calls a "sense of wisdom" that operates, for abiding by the game laws is an important step toward preserving the sport itself. Like other nature writers of his time, Rutledge had come to view ethical conduct afield as an integral part of the larger, older ideal of personal honor. His long stay in the North had also brought with it an awareness that the improvements in firearms and transportation, coupled with the rapid growth in population, had made good sportsmanship more than simply a desirable refinement. He had learned, that is, that if the sport were to survive at all, the hunter must not only become a naturalist, keenly aware of the environment around him, but also an active force in conserving the land and its game.

In spite of the significant contribution that sportsmen had made in helping to impose upon themselves regulations governing sport hunting, and notwithstanding the pervasive emphasis on conservation, ethical sportsmanship, and the reverence for nature that had marked Rutledge's work to date, he still found it necessary to counter the growing sentiment that hunting is a barbarous pastime unsuited to the enlightened citizens of a modern and progressive America. In "Why I Taught My Boys to Be Hunters," Rutledge makes his strongest case for the value of sport hunting to the development of character and the strength of the nation. In doing so, he also reveals that while the sport and the landscape have changed, the values revered in the southern sporting narrative have remained largely intact since antebellum times. In addition, his emphasis on the value of the sport for establishing close ties among fathers and their sons places him squarely within the larger concerns of the southern renascence. With a high degree of consistency, scholars of southern literature have found an intense emphasis throughout the genre on the importance of family ties and concrete personal relationships. This, too, is the case with Rutledge, and in the present essay he reports that over the last twenty-five years, he has seldom been hunting without one or more of his sons along. Moreover, he argues that "few human relationships are closer than those established by a mutual contact with nature" and that if "more fathers were woodsmen, and would teach their sons to be likewise, most of the so-called father-and-son problems would vanish" (141). Bringing his sons up to be hunters was for Rutledge not simply a means for transmitting his southern heritage or of satisfying his own proclivities but also a means for instilling in his sons a sense of what full maturity should encompass. As he says, "I have a conviction that to be a sportsman is a mighty long step in the direction of being a man" (141). Finally, Rutledge admits that, just as importantly, he wished to ensure a lasting relationship between himself and his children, for "if a man brings up his sons to be hunters, they will never go away from him. Rather the passing years will only bring them closer" (141–42).

How is it, then, that Rutledge justifies training his sons as hunters to that portion of his audience that condemns the sport and its practice? First of all, he argues that for early teaching, the rod and gun are "better for boys than the saxophone and the fudge Sundae," primarily because the former can teach lessons invaluable for later manhood: "The hunter learns that reward comes from hard work; he learns from dealing with nature that a man must have a deep respect for the great natural laws," and he learns "in a far higher degree than any form of standardized athletics can give him, to play the game fairly" (142–43). Despite these laudable aims and practical considerations, he realized that critics of the sport would persist in ignoring everything about hunting but the killing of fish and game. At the bottom of their arguments Rutledge posits a fundamental and often willful ignorance of life in the wild. The most common examples concern the perennial questions—"How can you love nature and yet shoot a deer?" (142) and "How can you bear to teach those children to kill things?" (143). For what he calls the "parlor naturalists and lollypop sentimentalists" (143), Rutledge has little patience; he argues convincingly that it is "far less cruel to kill a wild deer than it is to poleax a defenseless ox in a stall. The ox has no chance; but the deer has about four chances out of five against even the good hunter" (143). Like Elliott and Hunter before him, Rutledge viewed life in the natural world as a constant struggle for survival, what William Faulkner would later call the "ancient and unremitting contest" (Faulkner, *Go Down, Moses,* 184), and by the very nature of this contest some of the participants must die. It is the reluctance on the part of those opposed to sport hunting to recognize and to accept this elemental verity that Rutledge would bring to the foreground and expose.

Ultimately, it is not in the thrill of sport hunting that Rutledge finds its true value but rather in its potential as a training ground for dealing positively with the pitfalls, problems, and complexities of modern life. Against the dangers of the "vicious and crazily stimulated joy[s]" pursued by what had come to be known as the lost generation (146), and against the kind of overly civilized sophistication that produces "little lisping men" (147) and "lazy effeminates" (147), characters reminiscent of T. S. Eliot's J. Alfred Prufrock, Rutledge posits the sport of hunting as a means to achieving a "sense of balance, a sanity, [and] a comprehension of the true values of life" (146). Perfectly compatible with the "deepest and most genuine love of nature" (144), the type of hunter-naturalist that Rutledge celebrates in his writing is well-suited for the rigors of modern existence. Instead of developing men "able to dance the Brazilian busybody or . . . to decide whether a lavender tie will match mauve socks" (147), the men that hunting's challenges would produce are well equipped for becoming useful members of their societies. Unlike sentimentalists who feared that hunting would develop an unwanted cruelty of character, Rutledge believed instead that it would "inculcate patience, demand discipline and iron nerve, and develop a sanity of spirit," virtues universally valuable to society at any period in history (149).

The wealth of natural and moral inspiration that Rutledge found in his sporting adventures proved an invaluable source of strength in his personal life. As a public personage in many different roles, he celebrated the sporting life as a suitable technique for moral development and environmental perception, and he continued the legacy of the scholar-sportsmen and hunter-naturalists before him by combining a challenging public career with a vigorous code of sportsmanship. He also represented, with but a very few exceptions, the end of an era where the roles of intellectual and sportsman could comfortably coexist. As more Americans migrated to urban environments, necessarily decreasing their direct contact with and understanding of the natural world, so, too, did the demand for scientific specialization discourage the academy's intellectuals from incorporating their outdoor interests into their professional lives (a distinguished exception is the work of University of Georgia professor James Kilgo, noted in chapter 5). In the South, however, the strong attachment to the land persisted in permeating the literary output of its writers, many of whom found a wealth of imagery and cultural metaphors exposed and foregrounded by the South's gradual move from an agricultural to an industrial society. For those raised in the rural South, this tendency was especially important, and the renascence as a whole can be viewed as a shift away from employing distinctively southern imagery and themes as the subjects of narrative focus and toward a more complex rendering that employs them artistically as metaphors for addressing larger societal concerns. In *Aleck Maury, Sportsman* (1934), Caroline Gordon presents the cultural and spiritual deracination of a modern southerner whose only regional inheritance is the traditions of the southern sporting code. While one might expect that a female author employing traditionally masculine imagery would approach the material from a distinctively feminist perspective, Gordon's heavy reliance on her father's spoken memoirs for the structure and the content of the novel completely masks her authorial gender. Though we find a shift in narrative focus from first-person accounts of sporting life to the more sophisticated stance of an objective, self-conscious artist, the values of Gordon's hero remain those of the educated southern sportsman. The important difference between Hunter's and Rutledge's accomplished but more nearly straightforward narratives and Gordon's novel has little, if anything, to do with political activism. What sets Gordon's work apart from the work of these earlier writers is that for the first time the southern sporting code is being used primarily as the imagistic foundation for a complex work by an intensely modern novelist.

Caroline Gordon (1895–1981) was born on Merry Mont Farm in Todd County, Kentucky, to James Morris and Nancy Meriwether Gordon. Merry Mont had been the Meriwether home for several generations, and through her mother Caroline inherited a vast family connection of Meriwethers, Barkers, and Fergusons and the sense of being enveloped within an extensive clan of relatives. Her father was a gifted if eccentric man, trained in the classical literary tradition by his parents and at the University of Virginia. When he first moved west to Kentucky to tutor at the Meriwether home in 1883, he brought with him his love for Greek and Roman literature and an insatiable fascination with the sports of the field. When not teaching classes in Latin translation or preaching for the local Church of Christ, J. M. Gordon pursued the field arts of hunting and fishing with passion and consummate skill. Despite his frequent absences, he had a profound impact on Gordon's development as a novelist, and it is his character and his passion for sport that served as the model for the hero of *Aleck Maury, Sportsman* (1934).

In a published letter to Sally Wood on June 6, 1933, Gordon sketched out the plan for the novel as she then saw it. Saying that she considered the project a "relaxation and a sort of labor of love," she planned originally to call it "Green Springs to White Oak" and to write it in collaboration with her father. From the first, Gordon envisioned the novel as a "history of a life dominated by a passion for fishing" that would include "a lot of detailed information" about the techniques and equipment of the sport. She also foresaw the ending: "chopped off arbitrarily at some place like White Oak, some place that he hopes is the spot so long sought for" (Wood, ed., *Southern Mandarins,* 146). By August 14, she could write to Sally that she had spent several days with her father where he was staying at a fishing lodge on the banks of the Caney Fork River in east Tennessee:

> I got back from Caney Fork yesterday, found I could do the work in two days and a half after all. We worked all morning then Dad fished till four o'clock, then we worked from dinner till bed time. In the night he was heard to yell

out: "Take this down." I shall model the book on the autobiography of Davy Crockett (150).

In an undated letter to Katherine Anne Porter reprinted in Waldron's *Close Connections,* Gordon commented further on the novel's composition:

> I wrote the book in a rather funny way. . . . I set him down in a very large chair . . . and said "Now, talk." He would say, "My Uncle James Morris had the finest pack of hounds in Eastern Virginia" and soon I'd have a chapter. I took seventy pages of notes the first whack, then went back to visit him one other time and did the whole book from those notes—a sort of mosaic, it is (Waldron, 132).

As Katherine Anne Porter would write in a letter to Gordon in 1934, the novel is distinguished by a "fine masculine prose" that was naturally to be expected when writing "with the sound of your father's voice, all the voices of your fore-fathers in your ears" (Waldron, 141). The novel is not, of course, a literal transcription of James Gordon's spoken memoirs but rather a selective and self-conscious rendering of this autobiographical material set within the framework of a Latin epic, most notably Virgil's *Aeneid*. Nevertheless, its fine reputation for the unerring accuracy with which the details of the southern sporting life are rendered is the direct result of J. M. Gordon's meticulous and passionate memories. As Nancylee Jonza points out in *The Underground Stream*, Gordon created a "fictionalized autobiography of her father's life" that inspired fan mail that "insisted that 'Caroline Gordon' had to be a pen name for a male author, because no woman could get all that fishing and hunting lore so straight" (Jonza, xii).

Owing partly to her father's commitment to escape the boredom of his personal and professional life, Gordon's family was constantly on the move. J. M. Gordon was always in search of different schools to teach in, more enlightened churches to preach for, and better places to hunt and fish. Despite the nomadic wanderings of her impoverished family, Caroline was always returned to Merry Mont Farm for the summers to stay with her grandmother Meriwether. It was during her early years and the long summer vacations at Merry Mont that she absorbed the details of the natural world she would use over and again in her fiction. As Ann Waldron reports in her biography, "Caroline learned the names of trees and plants and, more importantly, the look of leaves and bare branches with the light coming through them; she felt at home in the woods" (35). In fact, the forests of the Kentucky homestead where she spent so much of her youth provided what Waldron calls an "Arcadian incubator that nourished her love for the natural world and her liking [and tolerance] for eccentrics" (35). Without this early exposure to the rural landscape and the deep appreciation for the beauties of the natural world it engendered, Caroline Gordon would not have been able to render successfully the engaging natural imagery that we find throughout the text of *Aleck Maury*.

Like the heroic image of Aeneas's flight from the ruins of Troy that provides the mythical background for the novel, Aleck Maury is presented to us as a man whose cunning and constant alertness are his only real weapons. There remains, however, another important dimension to the professor's character. In flight from the responsibilities that would defeat his efforts to make every moment count, and committed to the rituals of sport as the pathway to the secret life that alone affords him release from despair over the incessant march of time, Maury completely escapes the pitfalls of materialism and practical ambition that plague his wife and associates. Gordon's frequent exposure to the writing and thought of many of the Fugitive poets who provided the moving spirit for the Agrarian manifesto of 1930 both influenced and contributed to her imaginative celebration of a character for whom the pursuit of material success represents a species of moral dehumanization directly at odds with the more important needs of the spiritual side of man. The complexity of the novel and its true source of power derive from the conflict between Aleck Maury's need to preserve the humanistic values of the old South as reflected in its code of sportsmanship and the ideal of progress to which the other characters with whom he must deal in mature life are committed. No doubt Gordon realized, as Radcliffe Squires argues in his commentary on the novel in *The Southern Review*, that "[Maury's] intense curiosity about natural phenomena, his painstaking observations of the habits of bream and quail, are, for him, in the nature of faith" (469). Like his real-life Agrarian counterparts, Professor Maury believes that the southerner had made a grave error in his capitulation to the tenets of an industrial ideal that celebrates material wealth as the only viable index of man's earthly salvation. As Louis D. Rubin writes in his introduction to the 1962 edition of *I'll Take My Stand*, "In place of beauty and truth [man] had erected a new ideal, Progress" (xii). For the Agrarians as well as for Aleck Maury, the American dream of progress was not only anathema to the humane traditions of the old South but was also diametrically opposed to developing ways for using "the fruits of economic progress, once achieved, as a means to the more spiritual side of a good, full and happy life" (Rubin, xxxiii). It is this type of life, a life spent in harmony with both nature and the spiritual needs of man, that Gordon's hero desires. However, for a character with these kinds of views set down in the modern South, conflict would be inevitable.

Had Caroline Gordon been unwilling to temper her "labor of love" with the kinds of conflicts and ironies that saved it from becoming a romanticized eulogy of her father's life, *Aleck Maury* would be little more than a pleasant recounting of sporting memoirs that reflect the cultural values of the old South. As the novel comes down to us, we have instead the story of a meticulous southern sportsman who must face the criticisms of a society that would require its men to pursue material progress and to subordinate their spiritual well-being to the dictates of the American dream. Instead of the fictionalized confessions of an irresponsible man with a Falstaffian appetite for sport, we find a modern version of the epic hero, though at times a comic one, who must live by his wits to avoid spiritual annihilation. In addition, his efforts to divert himself from the specter of various forms of death recalls Ortega's message about hunting. For Ortega, hunting and fishing are the only ways in which man can successfully reenter nature and so divert himself, entirely if temporarily, from the harsh realities of his mortal humanity. For Aleck Maury these realities exist on a number of different levels, and Gordon portrays his efforts to deal with them by escaping through sport to the values of an older, agrarian South.

Aleck Maury is in flight from the specter of his own annihilation, but he is also fleeing the ruin of the old South as represented by his father, a once proud man reduced by his faulty idealism, lack of enterprise, and massive self-indulgence into a decadent wastrel. The figures of Aleck's father, however, and Aleck himself, took shape within a complex cultural context. On one level, the wasteland imagery of the Reconstruction South and the pervasive decadence of its male inhabitants clearly informs the novel's tone of a threatened, tenuous existence. On another, the contemporary flourishing of high modernism and the southern literary renascence account for the novel's emphasis on the emotional pitfalls of spiritual deracination in a world where traditional icons of stability, morality, and strength have lost their meanings. As a type of potentially redemptive counterbalance to the psychological dangers these literary movements address, Gordon opposes the humanistic tenets of Agrarian thought in the form of the aristocratic, southern code of sportsmanship, the only remaining discipline wherein her culturally orphaned hero can actively reclaim his perspective on life as a harmonious and morally responsible extension of the natural world. While scholarly opinion differs on the extent to which Gordon subscribed to the Agrarian platform, James Rocks makes a convincing case for viewing her early novels and stories as attempts "to dramatize—indirectly to advance—the Agrarian world view" (Rocks, "Mind and Art," 67–68). Superimposed finally upon this web of complementary influences is Gordon's fascination with the life and times of the hero, for her the only proper focus of serious narrative inquiry. In key scenes that develop Aleck's desperate quest to survive the onslaught of modernity, Gordon often elevates the tenets of Agrarian thought into classically epic proportions.

While the novel is richly inlaid with detailed narratives of hunting and fishing that offer an aristocratic perspective on personal conduct, honor, and sportsmanship, the narrative complexities of the tale that Professor Maury is purported to tell also continues the commentary on southern culture with which we are here concerned. Well aware of the self-imposed alienation resulting from the intensity of his preoccupations with the struggles for physical and spiritual survival, and steeped in the classical traditions that figured prominently in the ideology of the old South, Aleck Maury uses his "sportsman's instinct for ritual as a barrier against the onslaught of time" (Brown, "'Old Red,'" 55). In much the same way that poetic form provided a stay against confusion for Robert Frost, the recurrent and comforting rituals of hunting and fishing provide Professor Maury with a means of dealing with chaos. During his lifelong flight from family ties, personal relationships, and geographic stability, he remains a uniquely representative, heroic figure of traditional man in the postbellum South who refuses to deny his cultural inheritance in a headlong quest for material gain. Without his loyalty to the sporting traditions he has inherited, Maury's life would have had little meaning for himself or his creator. As it is, Gordon's artistic rendering of her father's career provides a unique form of cultural commentary that dramatizes the life of a modern southerner—beset by loss, grief, and an uprooted cultural ethos, but wonderfully resilient in his efforts to maintain his dignity and humanistic values against the pressures of conformity and the threat of spiritual annihilation.

From the novel's opening pages, Gordon makes it clear that her hero will have to deal with loneliness in his struggle to fend off his dual adversaries of physical and spiritual destruction. The backdrop for Aleck's earliest memories posits a wasteland environment in which an isolated figure wanders aimlessly in the shadows of a ruined tradition. Aleck's father had quit his law practice in Charlottesville to live on six hundred acres that his wife had inherited from her father. Committed to a life of reading poetry and occasional gambling, Aleck's father gave him "the rudiments of a classical education," but otherwise "paid very little attention" to his children (Gordon, 4). The figure of Aleck's father is rendered in oppressively distant terms; for his son he was often no more than "a reverberating voice." The narrator frankly admits that he was a lonely child, and even the family home presents a vacant appearance, "not sinister, yet curiously blank." Amid these images of "a withdrawnness from which you could not escape," Aleck is recalled as he wanders "for hours among the huge oak trees that dotted the lawn." Even the ground is "barren, whitish soil with rocks outbreaking in it here and there," and "not a shrub breaks the stark outline of the house where it arises among the black trunks" (4–5).

It is a part of Gordon's artistry to have young Aleck begin his childhood recollections with the bleak and oppressive imagery of his father and his yard, for they contrast in sharp relief the emotional warmth and excitement he later describes in the private and homely landscape behind the Maury homestead. The servants' quarters are located here, and in one of them lives the black cook, Nancy, and her husband, Rafe. He is fond of young Aleck, and though seven feet tall, blind in one eye, and possessed of a fierce and savage countenance, Rafe takes time often to talk with young Aleck about his adventures afield. In contrast to Aleck's father, whose only contact with his son is to teach him Latin, at least as long as Aleck "came up to a certain level," Rafe's conversation is devoid of dry intellectuality and filled with his passion for hunting. Aleck remembers these talks with pleasure: "He had a special way of talking to me when no one else was by. It was the talk of one hunter to another, comments, mostly on the qualities of his dog, Ming" (7). Aleck's father may have given him life and an education, but it was the Negro Rafe who provided the beginnings of Aleck's lifelong passion for sport, a spiritual reawakening of his primitive identity as a hunter that would help sustain him for the rest of his life. Looking back from the perspective of years, Aleck puts the matter in no uncertain terms: "I think that life, the life of adventure that is compacted equally of peril and deep, secret excitement, began for me in that cabin when I was about eight years old" (7). This awakening is triggered by Aleck's first hunt with Rafe and his dog, Ming. With surprising adeptness and imagination, Rafe easily circumvents the family's objections to his taking the young boy out at night, and as the porch door closes behind them a curious change ensues. The tone of the Negro's voice begins to transform itself from that of a careful and patronizing servant to the voice of strength and command: "Get your cap," he orders Aleck, "Get your cap and come on now fore she change her mind" (10). The metamorphosis implied by the change in Rafe's voice continues to unfold when Ming, earlier described as "short-legged . . . lop-eared, and a little mournful of visage," strikes a hot trail and his voice rings out, "bold and challenging." Under the spell of the chase, Rafe's character continues to evolve, and he speaks to his dog in a "coaxing gentle voice that I had never heard from him before: "'Come on now . . . at's the boy . . . at's the baby' . . . and then suddenly as if addressing an unseen listener: '*Ain't* he tellun 'em?'" (13). At the tree we learn that Ming is in a "perfect frenzy, breaking his stand every now and then to bound convulsively as high as he could up the tree trunk." Before the shot that ends this first, long hunt, Aleck can see the opossum's eyes high above him. Until this point in the narrative, the transfigurations evoked by the excitement of the hunt have been reserved for Rafe and Ming, but now Aleck, too, transcends the barriers of his former existence:

> Then I saw the eyes, oval, golden. They regarded me steadily, or rather they regarded nothing. They glowed, and it was as if there were nothing in the world but whirling blackness and set in it those immense, those golden orbs.
>
> A long time they glowed. The gold became fire, whirled with the blackness. Blackness was splintered suddenly by gold. I think I put my hand up to shield my eyes (14).

The life of "deep, secret excitement" had begun for Aleck on the night of this long-ago hunt, and between that life and his everyday existence Gordon draws a sharp and deliberate contrast. Under his father's formally restrained tutelage, marked most notably by the "cool impatience, almost scorn" that crept into his voice when Aleck's translations were faulty, and subject daily to the chores and other restraints visited upon him by his older sisters, Aleck was bored and lonely. After he begins to hunt with Rafe and Ming on his infrequent escapes from the domestic regime at Oakleigh Farm, he can now partake of the kind of spiritual fulfillment and fascination with sport that makes his life worthwhile. In one sense, Aleck's indoctrination to the sports of the field will continue to be a form of escape, but their rituals will afford him the momentary, spiritual transformations that allow him to transcend the dehumanizing influences of the modern world.

In chapter 2, these rituals become increasingly formalized at Grassdale, the stately plantation where he is sent to live with his prosperous, fox-hunting uncle, James Morris. The loneliness, poverty, and spiritual barrenness of Aleck's former life are replaced by friendship, prosperity, and intensely fulfilling sporting activities. Hunting is pursued at Grassdale in the grand manner, and many of the tenets of the southern sporting code celebrated by Elliott, Hunter, and the early Simms are firmly in place. However, Aleck will later come to realize that he has only escaped from one type of unworkable tradition of decadent southern manhood into another. Instead of his father's total retreat into the life of the mind and the subsequent financial and emotional impoverishment, his uncle James's hearty appetites and nearly obsessive commitment to fox hunting lead ultimately to failure as well: in contrast to his robust and prosperous middle age, his final years are plagued by a debilitating obesity and a lack of attention to managing his property that nearly loses the plantation to debt. Gordon here is concerned with the extreme opposite ends of the intellectual spectrum: too little emphasis on intellectual development as opposed to too much. Both are potentially lethal, but at Grassdale plantation Aleck is at least afforded a first-hand introduction into the upper echelons of the southern sporting world.

In contrast to the financial and emotional privations of his father's home, Aleck finds at Grassdale a luxurious southern lifestyle and a close friend in the person of his cousin, Julian Morris, Uncle James's son and heir to both his father's fortune and his passion for hunting. It is during his years at the Morris plantation that Aleck learns to ride to the hounds, to fish with the fly, and to accept the "democracy of sport" that permeates the great hunt breakfasts in the plantation dining room. It is here, too, that he learns of hunting's dangers, and on his first trip out is thrown from his horse and knocked senseless when his head strikes a large rock. More comprehensively than at any other point in his sporting career, Aleck is enveloped by the rituals of serious hunting that at Oakleigh he could only imagine. Though his aunt Victoria kept him strictly at work on his lessons during the mornings, the masculine life of the plantation revolved solely around sport; and hunting, especially fox hunting, was pursued in the grand manner befitting a man of Uncle James's prerogatives. It is fair to say that in the person and deportment of Uncle James, already Aleck's youthful ideal of what a well-bred and full-blooded Virginia gentleman should be, we are presented with a character whose pride in his horsemanship and his pack of splendid hounds are shown to be the true sources of joy in his life. Uncle James is also portrayed in his role as leader, not only as the owner of the largest plantation and the richest man in the community but as he who is responsible for enforcing the code of ethics that governs the communal rituals of fox hunting. In two complementary scenes, Uncle James is called on to exercise this authority, and in so doing exhibits the reverence for fair play that consistently informs the southern sporting code. As deeply committed to the rules of the chase as Aleck's father is to the rules of Latin grammar, Uncle James's conduct shows that the sporting rituals he observes, and on occasion must enforce, stem from deeper convictions than a penchant for surface propriety.

By the end of the first scene, the men, horses, and dogs have thoroughly exhausted themselves in a day-long chase after a single fox. Unable to reach the safety of the river, the fox runs into a wide expanse of lowland thickets, "doubling and turning for all he was worth" (43). The chase now becomes a grueling test of endurance, and the riders follow in what Aleck remembers as "the hardest riding I have ever done in my life" (43). This was the time when "the culls fell out," but Aleck, Uncle James, and the best of the foxhounds persevere. For there to be survivors, and for this properly to emulate a genuine struggle, there must also be victims, and not a few of the riders and their horses are forced to stop from injuries and sheer exhaustion. Just at sundown the fox is finally run to earth in one of the most dramatic scenes in the history of the genre:

> By the time we boys got there, half a dozen hard-breathing men sat their horses in a semicircle about the fallen pine. The fox lay crouched, perfectly still. His lips drawn back showed his white teeth, his lolling tongue. His eyes, glassed with weariness, stared straight ahead. He might have been alone in the thicket.
>
> Suddenly he raised his head, a quiver ran along his heaving flanks. He staggered up and tongue still lolling, ran a few paces. The dogs rose too. But the three of them had fallen before he sank to the ground. He got up again. This

> time his bush was trailing the ground. But he made it, past the end of the pine and was staggering on towards a cedar stump that rose not twenty feet away. The Mag pup and Old Rattler rose too. The third dog lay still. The fox ran twenty paces before he sank to the ground, tongue lolling out. Something like an ejaculation broke from one of the men.
>
> Uncle James had turned and was looking about the circle. He drew a pistol from his pocket, rested it across the pommel of his saddle. "I'll shoot the first man who says a word," he said. His eyes went back to the fox. He was staggering up again. This time he could only make a few paces. Old Rattler lay perfectly still. Only his sobbing breaths told that he was still alive. I saw the Mag bitch's eyes roll sideways in her head, toward the fox. She got up, trembling, staggered forward and fell across him, slavering, but too weak to bite.
>
> Uncle James stood up in his stirrups. He shouted:
>
> "Boys, go home . . . go home quicker than hell can scorch a feather" (44–45).

The boys do go home, and they return with a wagon and mattress on which the dogs and the fox, all well massaged with liniment, are carried ceremoniously back to Grassdale. What makes this long scene so important to understanding the meaning of the sport for Aleck and his friends is the hunters' response to the courage and persistence involved in this type of primitive struggle. Uncle James Morris, well aware of the archetypal nature of the scene unfolding before him, even draws his revolver to underscore the importance of not disturbing the final moments of this ritual confrontation with death. In it he clearly recognizes the metaphorical embodiment of the duty, courage, and persistence upon which human survival often depends. And here we hit upon a key point, for in this carefully orchestrated scene the chase is shown to be an important and indigenous ceremony through which the sportsmen can acknowledge the primordial link between the difficulties of their own lives and the struggles inherent in the natural world. The hours of hard riding, the exhaustion of the dogs, and the gameness of their prey exist for them as a species of tribute to the qualities and virtues they live by and admire. In this classic sporting tableau, Gordon provides a rare insight into the interconnectedness of life and sport in the South.

During the second of these consecutive, paired scenes, Aleck introduces Old Red, the fox who, like Old Ben in "The Bear," has established a longstanding reputation among the local sportsmen. He, too, is pursued with the keenest relish by Aleck and his friends, but the circumstances surrounding his death show that even Uncle James's authority is not proof against the erosion of traditional values in the new, postbellum South. As Aleck tells us, Old Red "loved the chase as much as the men and the dogs did," but on the day of his final run his long career is cut short by a breech of conduct that does not go unpunished. By this point in the narrative, Old Whiskey, the fountainhead and patriarch of the famous Grassdale pack, has aged to the point where he cannot keep up for the twenty-mile race to Peters Mountain that marks the highlight of Old Red's familiar course. Instead, he "adapted himself to his failing powers" by waiting until the dogs and the fox returned and trying to ambush Old Red when he slipped through a break in the fence. The boys knew this, and so did Uncle James, but he always ordered Aleck and Julian to hold Old Whiskey until the fox could get away. After a forty-plus-mile run even the fox was growing tired, but Old Whiskey, still the fastest dog in the county for a short run, had been all this time resting in the shade. We never learn exactly why Aleck and Julian disobey Uncle James's orders and release Old Whiskey on the fox, who is hardly a match for the swift and rested hound. All we are told is that the fox was killed and that Aleck experienced "a queer feeling" when he saw Old Red's brush held up because "[i]t didn't seem possible that he'd never give us another race" (47). Uncle James is livid with rage at their blatant indiscretion. His authority has been challenged, the ritual has been desecrated, and the code of sportsmanship by which he lived has been abridged. He thrashes the boys soundly in what Aleck remembers as "the worst licking either of us ever had in our lives" (48). And no wonder, for the rituals of sport were for Uncle James, as they would soon become for Aleck, far more than a pleasant and manly diversion. They represented instead a way to escape into a world where courage, endurance, and fair play were still revered and where the appreciation of truth and beauty still took precedence over the quest for material gain. Nevertheless, like the dry intellectuality of Mr. Maury's escapist immersion in the world of classical literature, Gordon makes it clear that the unbridled passion for masculine sport at Grassdale represents an abandonment of the serious, realistic, and practical life of the here and now. Both are forms of escape that look back to the past for order, stability, and heroism and as such provide delight for the conservative, traditional, and educated mind. Practiced immoderately, however, both of these two formal rituals, classical study and the sports of the field, lead inevitably to stultification and decay, and it is no accident that Aleck's father must live in poverty, nor that Uncle James, finally grown too fat to ride, dies with the plantation's affairs heavily in debt. James

Rocks is correct in arguing that Caroline Gordon "desires her novel to be a dialectic," and one lesson she seems always ready to teach is that to live in the past is to die (Rocks, 5).

Aleck, however, is not allowed the apparently ruinous luxury of devoting his early maturity either to study or to sport but must instead make his own perilous way in the new South, a place where the ravages of progress and materialism are steadily taking their toll on the gracious traditions in which he was raised. Chapters 3 and 4 take Aleck through his first days at Merry Point Farm, the home of Mr. Douglas Fayerlee on the Kentucky border in Tennessee, and the tutoring position that is expanded to headmaster of the local family school. It is at Merry Point that Aleck meets Molly Fayerlee, his future wife, and where his love for hunting and fishing brings him into comic conflict with the more practical and ambitious members of the vast family connection. On the whole, Aleck (now Professor Maury) adapts himself well to his role in the agrarian lifestyle at Merry Point Farm, but long before he becomes a formal member of the family he divines Mr. Fayerlee's practical attitude toward spending one's time in the pursuit of fish and game. Following a week of helping Mr. Fayerlee during a late winter storm that coincides with the births of Merry Point's lambs, a situation demanding grueling stints of enforced labor that begin at two o'clock in the morning and end well after dark, the spring arrives suddenly and with it Aleck's craving to go fishing. Now free to spend his Saturdays as he likes, he rises promptly at 3:30 A.M. for the long ride by horseback to his favorite stream. When he arrives at the barn to saddle his horse, hardly expecting anyone else on the farm to be awake, Mr. Fayerlee is already there organizing the day's work. He tells Aleck that he always rises this early, and that "the hands are always in the field by four o'clock" (97). This kind of life and its relentless hours leave little time for sport or, for that matter, much of anything else. This Aleck knows from his recent experience, and he replies that, excepting when he "had something on hand . . . [he] didn't believe [he] could do it every morning to save [his] neck." Riding away from the barn with his rod and gear, he imagines Mr. Fayerlee's thoughts: "Doubtless he regarded me as one of the most thoughtless young fools he had ever known. I remember thinking as I rode off that I would not have changed places with him for all the money in the world" (97). Even Mr. Fayerlee's wife, the "kind, motherly woman" towards whom Aleck's heart had warmed upon his arrival at Merry Point, is as uncomprehending of Aleck's passion as her husband. One evening she upbraids Aleck for his lack of perception and enterprise after he had failed to see a burning tobacco barn in clear sight of the Woodstock pond where he had been fishing: "I don't see how you could have failed to see it sitting there all afternoon doing nothing" (98). Thinking back on their talk and recalling his rejoinder that "a man who is fishing doesn't have a moment to himself," Aleck pinpoints his recurring dilemma: "People . . . think that a man goes fishing to kill time. They do not realize that every day of good sport is one of unremitting, exhausting effort" (98). The Fayerlees' attitude was apparently common, for in an excerpted quotation from *Forest and Stream*, an unidentified contributor makes much the same point: "a man who went gunnin' or fishin' lost caste among respectable people just about in the same way that one did who got drunk" (Reiger, 25).

Despite the pressures of his more practical associates, Aleck is formally accepted into the family when he marries his student, Molly Fayerlee. The hunting and fishing are good around Merry Point and he soon acquires a setter named Gyges ("after the mythical hero who could disappear at will") and a fine, fourteen-gauge English double manufactured by the prestigious London firm of W. W. Greener. Settled into his role as what Jerry A. Herndon calls one of the "ornaments" rather than one of the leaders of this agrarian society, Aleck proves to be a responsible teacher, an attentive husband, and a loving father, in time (Herndon, "Tragic Sense," 205). It is the occasion of the birth of his first child, however, that provides the first clear insight into how hunting and the rituals of the southern sporting code function for him within the larger scheme of his emotional existence. As Molly's time draws near, Aleck abandons all sport to be near his expectant wife. As he tells us, it hadn't occurred to him that he would be of little use "when the time came," but duty bound and anxious, he abandons both hunting and fishing to be within easy call. Determined, persistent, and genuinely concerned for his wife, Aleck cannot but notice the effects that his self-enforced abstinence are beginning to have on his constitution:

> There are times in every man's life when he does not seem to be living, when every faculty is held in suspension while he waits for events to shape themselves. It was like that with me, those last few weeks. I could not follow any of my usual pursuits. I could not even think with my own mind. I could only wait and wish it were over (117).

Fortunately for Aleck, Mrs. Fayerlee, perhaps realizing the strain he is under, tells him, "Go on . . . get your gun . . ." and orders him into the field.

Out with his setter, Gy, Aleck begins to revive emotionally as he practices the familiar rituals. Their quail hunt is successful, but more important for Aleck's peace of mind are the reassuring continuities that serve to reaffirm his perspective as part of the larger world of nature and eternity. With deliberate attention to the details that ground the scene in the concrete particulars of the hunt, Gordon provides a series of prescribed rites, really a form of sporting liturgy, which custom and habit have combined into a comforting ritual. First of all, the fourteen-gauge Greener is loaded: ". . . the work of a few seconds. The caps were on, pressed down, and the gun at half-cock." Next, Gy begins to wind the quail, "walking skip-legged," and by his familiar movements and manner Aleck "knew" that Gy had the scent of game. With characteristic good form, Gy "never" lowers his head and, "as so often happened," catches one of the quail as they erupt from the broomstraw. The setter is so delicate a retriever that his bird escapes when Aleck reaches for him, but we learn again that "this had happened many times." From the way the covey flies, primarily the distance and the set of the birds' wings, Aleck "knew" they would light and go on feeding. However, he doesn't bother to mark their landing because "Gy would do that. He was unfailing." The next point comes soon after, "As . . . expected," and Gy surprises his master by retrieving a bird he thought he'd missed. But even this "surprise" is familiar. Aleck has seen him perform similarly "many a time," and yet "it always surprised him" that the setter could tell that a bird that flew off normally had actually been hit (118–20).

The upshot of the afternoon is that Aleck is so relieved by the familiar rituals that his mind drifts back to his first walk around the fields with Mr. Fayerlee, ten years before. As he says, it seemed like a long time in one way, in another "a period not to be measured by time" (121). He thinks of his family, of his older sister now married with children, and about a letter from his old friend Julian Morris that he'd always meant to answer. He is so diverted from his cares and responsibilities by the familiar routines and his subsequent reentry into the natural world that, "for a moment," he is completely baffled by the Merry Point bell that has begun to ring in the distance. It announces, of course, that his son is now being born.

As Aleck will realize much later in life when Molly's death leaves him temporarily numbed to the pleasures of sport, the "delight" by which he had lived was something he'd first known looking up into the opossum's eyes on that long ago hunt with Rafe and Ming. Suffering from grief and unable to enjoy even the fishing that had come to be his only pleasure, Aleck can look back on his sporting life with a coldly critical eye. His meditations reveal that now he can appreciate the extent of the "almost transfiguring excitement" sport affords him, and with this particular insight he touches upon a point that resonates throughout the length of the novel. Aleck Maury, sportsman and scholar, had long ago discovered a way to transform himself. As he had earlier told his daughter, Sarah, who asked him why he liked to hunt so much, "I have a better time when I'm hunting than any other time" (130). Once again, the reentry into the natural world proves to be what Ortega claims, the "supreme diversion" from the human condition, and this diversion, temporary though it may be, is why hunting is "such a great delight for man" (Ortega, 59). Within the Agrarian and modernist contexts of the novel's composition, however, there are other, more complex implications.

As portrayed by his creator, Aleck Maury represents a character involved in continual flight, and this apparent escapism is the hallmark of his character, whether in the novel or in the group of related stories in which he appears. As Robert Penn Warren argues in his introduction to *The Collected Stories of Caroline Gordon* (1980), Maury is in "perpetual flight from all that might bind him—from love, from the practical, vain, professional, and ambitious world. He is in flight from all that would deny him the deep aesthetic texture of life and of nature, and their interrelation" (xiii). The important point is not, however, that Professor Maury, a southerner with "only the memory of a civilization to perpetuate" (Brown, "Achievement," 284), is in flight from the emotional brutalization brought on by the new ideals of progress and industrialization, the twin banes of the Agrarian theorists, nor that he seeks to escape the fragmentation of modern uncertainty where traditional icons and institutions have failed. Instead, the relevance of his particular kind of flight to the study of the southern sporting narrative lies in its direction—toward a closer communion with the natural world and the feelings of wholeness and unity that his meticulous involvement evokes. That what becomes a near obsession with sport proves an inadequate substitute for the communal faith and shared values of an older, agrarian South is not at issue. The point is, rather, that in the course of his quest to make the most of his time, he pursues the very essence of the Agrarian ideal. In his introduction to the 1991 edition of *I'll Take My Stand*, Rubin succinctly identifies the world that Aleck Maury pursues. Rubin calls it simply "the Southern tradition: . . . the good society, the community of individuals, the security and definition that come when men cease to wage an unrelenting war with nature and enjoy their leisure and their human dignity" (xx). It is toward this traditional, communal vision that Aleck Maury is in flight, but he finds his existence threatened and himself trapped by his own mortality and a postbellum society that has begun to worship the American ideal of material and social progress. As Caroline Gordon says in "Cock-Crow," death is the hero's only true opponent, and the physical and emotional varieties of this inevitably victorious adversary are what provide Aleck Maury both the occasion and the focus of his struggle.

Because Aleck's faith is not in the American dream of material progress but rather in the non-acquisitive rewards of spiritual wholeness achieved through his communion with nature, it is thematically consistent that his one capitulation to the solicitations of progress and material wealth is fraught with disaster and grief. Near the end of chapter 4, Aleck, Molly, and their two children have been living at Merry Point for ten years. While there were certain drawbacks to the arrangement, Aleck tells us that he "would have been contented to stay at Merry Point the rest of my life if fortune had not decreed otherwise" (132). Gordon's choice of words here is especially significant, for instead of "fate" or "luck" or any number of words she might have chosen to suggest the element of chance that brought about the invitation for Aleck to take over the small seminary in Mississippi, she deliberately selected "fortune," a term that can mean destiny as well as wealth. Molly's mother and old Aunt Frances are strongly opposed to the idea of her move with Aleck and the children to the proffered job, and Gordon's obvious respect for Mrs. Fayerlee's strength of character and good judgement serve to validate her arguments. There is considerable foreshadowing of disasters to come in the matriarch's warnings, and on their first night away Molly finds that Aunt Frances has tied a rabbit's foot around Dick's neck with a greasy string. But there are two compelling reasons that combine to cause Aleck and his wife to abandon their comfortable life at Merry Point. First, the offer Aleck has been made is "so attractive financially" that he believes he cannot refuse. As for Molly, she is ambitious to get her children away from her mother's supervision and to establish herself in a matriarchy of her own. The increase in Aleck's salary and the chance for Molly to elevate herself to the mistress of her own household constitute upwardly mobile forms of "progress," but both the professor and his wife will pay dearly for their worldly advancement.

Their troubles begin on the trip west when the Maurys stop at Cairo on their steamboat ride down the Mississippi and where Aleck rents rooms at The

Marshall House, the only respectable establishment he can find that also has accommodations for his gifted setter, Gy. But the next morning he discovers that Gy has been stolen; the dog is never seen again. During a later stop at Memphis, Aleck visits an old hunting friend of his, William Mason. Though highly successful as a businessman, Mason's sporting life has diminished to three days of shooting in the last five years. All he really has left of his sportsman's identity is a pointer named Trecho, the "most magnificent" of the breed Aleck has ever seen, who paces impatiently about the efficient office or stares mournfully out the window. The image of the "lordly . . . snow white" pointer whose magnificent strength and beauty are trapped within a purely materialistic value system that stifles his heroic potential is yet another of Gordon's metaphorical indictments of the American dream, serving both to foreground and to intensify Mason's spiritual poverty. Even the view from Mason's rooms suggests the emotional sterility that his full capitulation to the goddess of success has cost him, and we learn that as he looks out daily on "an expanse of brick wall, not even a leaf broke its monotony" (137). Meditating silently on the lifeless boredom of the monotonous view, Aleck wonders "how a man could endure to look on it day after day" (137).

Still brooding over Gy's loss and the image of Mason and Trecho trapped within their prison of worldly success, Aleck arrives at Oakland with his family. It is here that they meet Harry Morrow, the efficient, ambitious, and forward-looking presidential assistant whose administrative ability will make the machinery of the small college run "as if on greased wheels" (143). Studiously indulgent of his superior's sporting interests, though regarding them as a weakness, Harry proves an able administrator and soon develops a genuine liking for the school's new president. For Molly, however, the polish of Harry's efficiency and industry are only a facade for his ruthless ambition. Though never satisfied with her husband's penchant for putting sport ahead of his academic career, she recoils at what she sees lurking beneath Harry's pleasant professional manner. As she says, "I believe he'd step over his grandmother's dead body to get anything he wanted" (144).

Despite Molly's early misgivings regarding the extent to which Harry's ambitions could drive him, Maury's tenure at Oakland is marked most tragically by the drowning death of his fifteen-year-old son, Dick. Though Aleck suffers grievously from the loss, he is able to deal realistically with the drowning, but for Molly it signals the beginning of a lifelong retreat into an uncontrollable grief punctuated by wild fits of hysterical sobbing. Aleck finds that quite often he must "tend her as if she were a child," and he comes to realize that her mind is "distraught," unbalanced enough to bring on the delusion that because he has been able to go on with the realities of living, he does not feel the debilitating grief that Molly believes to be the only adequate response. Reminiscent of the dramatic situation in Frost's "Home Burial," Molly's delusions place a barrier between herself and her husband that nothing can remove. What both Molly and the wife in Frost's famous poem lack is a method of placing their grief within some larger context that will provide a realistic perspective for their loss and divert their minds from the horrors of physical death.

For a time, Aleck, too, is powerless to act, and once again he imposes upon himself a strictly disciplined abstinence from all sport. Having come to feel that Molly's resentment over his supposed lack of grief ("I must have appeared perfectly recovered" [161]) has caused her to shun his company, but unwilling to be out of earshot should the "paroxysms of grief" come on her again, he sits brooding alone in his study throughout the long autumn afternoons. When he can endure it no longer, he turns to the familiar rituals of the hunt as a way of coping with the chronic depression that has come to plague him. Unlike his more vulnerable wife, Aleck has long ago learned the therapeutic values of a brisk outing afield. Years later, Havilah Babcock would explain the phenomenon in his classic sporting essay, "My Health Is Better in November":

> After a day-long tramp behind a brace of ambitious dogs, a man doesn't need an appetizer when he sits down to dinner. Nor does he require a lullaby to put him to sleep. And it's a hardy neurosis indeed that will outlast a few busy and sparkling days afield . . .
>
> Farmers seldom have nervous break-downs. They haven't time. People who lead a brisk outdoor existence don't go in for neuroses, psychoses, and other expensive and fashionable complaints. For a stirring day in the field purges the mind (Babcock, *Health,* 282–83).

Though delivered with a tinge of self-derision, Babcock's comments have particular relevance for Professor Maury's situation. As he takes down his gun, calls his dog from his bed beneath the live oak, and cautiously makes his way through the hedge and into the field, he finds solace and respite in the familiar and reassuring rituals of the reentry into the natural world. In this important scene, Gordon has succeeded in capturing the delight Aleck has lived for. The carefully direct and simple images are provided without commentary, and their artistic juxtaposition allows them to evoke metaphorically the spiritual transformation that Maury's literal movements from the civilized chaos of his home to the freedom of the field afford. At home in his study, the "dusty faded room" where he suffers the anxiety of "waiting for something, I did not know what," his fears prey upon him relentlessly. And we have learned that, in another wing of the rambling old house, Molly is similarly closeted. However, when Aleck moves across and through the barriers of civilization suggested first by the door, then the shrubbery, and then the hedge, that symbolically map his psychological progress, he reenters a natural world where he can divert his mind from its civilized fears. To the feelings of helplessness and grief that bring on his wife's delusions, Aleck opposes the concrete particulars of the chase. At least temporarily, he is dealing again with the solid and natural realities involved in the primordial rituals of the hunt. When he returns later that evening, he is a far different man from the tangle of fears and anxieties that had earlier walked out the side door. Instead of an anxiety-ridden invalid debilitated by grief and uncertainty, we see instead a man who can begin drafting the correspondence that will soon establish him as headmaster of his own school back in Gloversville, Tennessee. Aleck Maury has regained his perspective on life and his ability to deal productively with its hardships. As Ortega would explain it, hunting is shown here to be both the supreme diversion from the human condition as well as an invaluable exercise in spiritual regeneration, a positive shift in perspective that allows man to deal with the complexity of civilized pressures that threaten to destroy him.

Aleck Maury will continue to retreat into the naturally ordered and compelling world of nature and sport throughout the course of his fictional career: by fishing the Black River during his tenure at Rodman College; through his experiments as a fish culturist back in Tennessee; and finally as he escapes in the novel's closing lines from his daughter and her husband to the banks of the Caney Fork. His life is indeed the history of a man engaged in an epic flight, but unlike the classical heroes whose mythic careers lend resonance to his adventures, Aleck Maury's commitment is only to his own survival. As Louise Cowan observes in her analysis of the novel and the stories that cluster about it, Professor Maury is "finally lost in his commitment to a private inner voice that, in the end, calls him to no communal quest, gives him no chance of regaining

Ithaca or founding the new Troy, and leaves him in retreat . . ." (29). Maury is isolated and alone; the trajectory of his career is increasingly private and marked rarely by a desire to save anyone but himself. As such, he represents the decline of the scholar-sportsman as a genuinely heroic figure who not only takes reasonable account of his fellows but whose career and concerns become directed more and more toward those outside himself. In contrast, Alexander Hunter's concern for the game and the land allowed him to move beyond the relatively narrow concerns of sporting etiquette to a leading role in drafting his state's first game conservation laws. Following the lead of Theodore Roosevelt and the hunter-naturalists, Archibald Rutledge employed his considerable narrative skill to promote conservation and the virtues of the chase as modes of environmental awareness and character development appropriate for the moral and ecological health of the nation. For Aleck Maury, however, isolated by the breakdown of traditional southern values, the cultural destruction of the war, and the postbellum drive for material progress, sport becomes much more than a metaphorical expression of regional identity. For this desperate and alienated modern sportsman, hunting and fishing become the single forms of successful escape into the humane and orderly values of the antebellum South.

CHAPTER FOUR

The End of the Southern Wilderness

William Faulkner's *Go Down, Moses*

William Faulkner brought to the genre of the southern sporting narrative an unprecedented artistry, an endless fascination with the culture of his native land, and an epic determination to examine in his fiction the broadest possible range of the southern experience. In *Go Down, Moses*, he blends the major themes of the scholar-sportsmen who preceded him into a dramatic rendering of the end of the southern wilderness. Its final passing lights up for a moment the ancient contours of its character, and Faulkner follows these primordial lineaments in his searching inquiry into the complex relationships between the postbellum southerner and his cultural and natural inheritance. The life history of Isaac McCaslin is therefore historic as well as imaginative, and his conflicts with himself and his society are presented through a series of moral dilemmas that establish his identity as a civilized man who has gained an authentic rapport with the prehistoric rhythms of the remaining southern wilderness. By allowing his idealistic hero to achieve a genuine spiritual communion with nature through the ancient rituals of the hunt, and by pitting the ideals of the prelapsarian innocence he rediscovers against the cultural and moral imperatives of his civilized society, Faulkner reveals important insights into the metaphysical underpinnings of the southern sporting code.

What Isaac seeks is to purge himself of moral culpability by fully embracing his Paleolithic vocation as a hunter. By adopting this pose of Edenic innocence and relinquishing his paternal inheritance, he hopes to transcend his identity as a fallen and civilized man and to reclaim for himself and his society an irretrievable moral purity. What he ultimately discovers is that the moral culpability he bears as an integral and organic part of the fallen society into which he was born categorically denies him the freedom he desires. Nevertheless, the direction and trajectory of Isaac's epic journey into the inner sanctuaries of the wilderness reveal much about the spiritual longings of the aristocratic southern sportsman in the Reconstruction South. In much the same way that Alexander Hunter found in the practice and etiquette of southern field sports a way to escape temporarily from the painful realities of the war and its aftermath, Isaac looks to the pagan rituals of the wilderness hunt as a way to escape the burden of guilt he feels he has inherited. But unlike Hunter, Isaac is portrayed as a character so consumed with the sense of his own familial guilt that nothing less than a permanent escape into the moral purity of man's prehistoric identity has for him any appeal or relevance.

Though Faulkner was himself a devoted and accomplished sportsman, one who had personally hunted the last of the Mississippi Delta wilderness and witnessed its final demise, he felt it necessary to go back in "The Bear" to a time that predated his own birth. By so doing, he was able to set Isaac's encounter with the wilderness at a crucial point in the southern past that would provide the historically dramatic circumstances on which he would draw for his narrative development. In the character of Isaac McCaslin, he created a unique type of cultural metaphor for the tortured consciousness of the aristocratic southern sportsman as he was pressured to accept the spiritually bankrupt condition of postbellum society. Of course, a part of his cultural inheritance could be preserved but only those beliefs, values, and institutions that would be useful as practical tools for surviving the onslaught of modernity and the death of the wilderness. In *Go Down, Moses*, Faulkner uses Isaac's ill-fated quest to argue for the need to adapt to the South's radically altered material circumstances through a kind of conceptual evolution that involves the acceptance of loss and a willingness to change.

At the Nagano Seminar in 1955, Faulkner was asked if he, like Rousseau, believed "we should return to nature to recover our whole and proper humanity." His response makes it clear that he did not: "I don't hold to the idea of a return. . . . once the advancement stops then it [civilization] dies. It's got to go forward and we have got to take along with us all the rubbish of our mistakes and errors. . . . We must take the trouble and sin along with us, and we must cure that trouble and sin as we go" (Jeliffe, *Faulkner,* 77–78). Although the Nagano Seminar was held thirteen years after the publication of *Go Down, Moses*, Faulkner seems to have changed his mind very little about this particular point, for the story of Isaac McCaslin's inadequate responses to progress and to change, both in his role as sportsman and as heir to the culture of the southern plantation, argues against attempting to return to the kind of Edenic perfection that can only exist in the realm of ideas and abstractions. Indeed, it is man's misplaced reliance on abstractions, especially in their guise as stereotypes, that Faulkner posits as the South's true enemies, and even Isaac falls prey to their undeniable appeal. Ironically, he views himself as the opponent of abstractions and stereotypes, for the repudiation of his inheritance is fostered by his outrage over Carothers McCaslin's abuse of his slaves, an abuse in which Old Carothers ignored their humanity, not to mention his own paternal and moral responsibilities, and treated them simply as another part of his purely inanimate property. Instead of trying to "cure" this burden of inherited sin and guilt with the virtues he has learned and the power he stands to inherit, Isaac himself will only retreat into what he sees as a prelapsarian innocence, content to let the rest of the world take care of itself as best it can. All he can ultimately accomplish is to arrest his own development in a total self-effacement that borders on suicide, a self-defeating denial of life that only frees him from the duties of leadership and the rigors of command. As Roth Edmonds says to him in "Delta Autumn," "I suppose the question to ask you is, where have you been all the time you were dead?" (329). By implying the ultimate failure of Isaac's relinquishment and denial, Faulkner reveals the enormous and tragic gulf between what Isaac intends and what he actually achieves. At the end of "Delta Autumn," the futility of his gift of the silver-bound hunting horn to the child of Roth's mistress as a symbol of the wilderness virtues he would pass on carries the metaphorical burden of his wasted life. For all practical purposes, a hunting horn would be useless in the urban North where he encourages the woman to take refuge, just as Isaac's retreat from the difficult responsibilities of managing the plantation and helping to provide for the future development of his region proves ultimately to be a costly and a futile fiasco. As Roth's comments suggest, Isaac's admittedly noble gesture of relinquishing his birthright in hopes of removing the curse of guilt and shame from the land results in a denial of life, and even he is unable to escape the stereotypical racial attitudes most prominently portrayed in the novel by the deputy at the end of "Pantaloon in Black." Isaac neither makes any significant change in his society nor leaves a son or follower to carry on the values and goals in which he believes. Instead, the very magnitude of his misdirected altruism causes him to be regarded by his fellows as more of a weakling and a coward than a saint. As Cleanth Brooks observes, "Isaac's own sense of the guilt incurred by his family and by his whole community in the matter of black chattel slavery recommends to the same reader a man who, on other counts, might possibly be regarded as weak and impractically idealistic" (Brooks, *Yoknapatawpha Country,* 254).

As a balance to Isaac's failures and weaknesses, Faulkner presents us with a very different side of this otherwise admirable character for whom he had obvious compassion. If Isaac fails to deal rationally with the problems of civilized change, his failures are not those of indifference or greed, and his anguish over the loss of the wilderness reveals the mind of a sensitive man wracked by grief and despair. Faulkner is concerned in *Go Down, Moses* with portraying Isaac's struggle to accept the realities of progress and to deal realistically with the morally and financially bankrupt state of the postbellum South. One of the reasons that he cannot is that he seeks to escape their thorny problems by cultivating his appreciation of the beauty and innocence of the natural world through a deeply profound engagement with its rituals. To give Isaac's dilemma the power and tragedy necessary for artistic success, Faulkner captures for his readers details of the scenes and scenery that have caused his hero to cling passionately to his hopes for restoring the lost Eden. In his fictional rendering of the end of the southern wilderness and the formal society of hunters that it fostered, he is able to preserve a part of the southern past that he knew would otherwise be forgotten and lost.

In his commentary on the composition of *Flags in the Dust (Sartoris),* Richard Gray argues that Faulkner had "applied himself to an enterprise that seemed to involve not only recovery and reinvention but also resistance to the pressures of time" (Gray, *Life of William Faulkner,* 127). In Gray's view, Faulkner intended for his audience to feel compassion for a southern ethos and way of life that had irrevocably passed. In an interview at the University of Virginia in 1958, Faulkner commented on this intent in regard to his treatment of the disappearing wilderness in *Go Down*, *Moses*:

> What the writer's asking is compassion, understanding, that change must alter, must happen, and change is going to alter what was. . . . It's to have compassion for the anguish that the wilderness itself may have felt by being ruthlessly destroyed by axes, by men who simply wanted to make the earth grow something they could sell for a profit, which brought into it a condition based on an evil like human bondage. It's not to choose sides at all—just to compassionate the good splendid things which change must destroy, the splendid fine things which are a part of man's past too, part of man's heritage too, but they were obsolete and had to go. But that's no need to not feel compassion for them simply because they were obsolete (Gwynn and Blotner, eds., *Faulkner in the University,* 276).

In *Go Down, Moses,* especially in "The Old People" and "The Bear," Faulkner goes to great lengths to portray for his readers the beauty of the Delta wilderness and the powerful if unspoken sense of reverence that his sportsmen feel for the natural world and the game they pursue. One is again reminded of Faulkner's comments concerning his portrayal of southern society in *Flags in the Dust (Sartoris)*: "nothing served, but that I try by main strength to recreate between the covers of a book the world . . . I was already preparing to lose and regret" (Gray, 127). One clear implication of this acknowledgment is that Faulkner realized the impossibility of preserving intact the traditional values of the old South in the face of the modern world, at least in their original forms, and part of his plan was to endow his familial and regional past with a permanence it could not otherwise possess. Although he succeeded, even the archetypal elements of southern culture and history he portrayed chronicle the inevitable decadence of his conquered society as it entered the modern age.

In *Go Down, Moses*, Faulkner returns to his artistic commentary on the impossibility of preserving traditional southern values in the modern world, and he again is concerned with the failure of the hereditary leadership to accept its communal responsibilities in favor of an ultimately self-defeating personal quest. The destruction of the wilderness in which Isaac learns to hunt is symbolic of the ruinous moral corruption that he believes his ancestors have brought to the land, and though ultimately futile, his efforts to recreate the lost Eden often cast him in a favorable and sympathetic light. Because of his many positive qualities, a major source of the novel's complexity and tension stems from the fact that Isaac is afforded so many virtues that one is tempted to grant him the blameless sainthood to which he aspires. His courage, humility, and selflessness permeate his conduct both in and out of the woods, and his love for the game and appreciation for nature emerge as solid values worthy of emulation. In light of his many virtues and his strict adherence to the finest traditions of the southern sporting code, Isaac appears at first to be the highest possible refinement of the aristocratic southern sportsman. His failures, however, argue ultimately that the perfection to which he aspires is not merely unobtainable but undesirable as well. As the leading cultural representative that Faulkner chose to examine in *Go Down, Moses*, Isaac is afforded a complexity of characterization that aims at a searching scrutiny of the aristocratic southern sportsman, both in his relationship to the natural world and to his society at large. He therefore chose to portray Isaac as a dedicated hunter and woodsman, for only by coupling the insights of a self-conscious sportsman to those of a postbellum southerner painfully aware of the burden and weight of history could he hope to approach the comprehensiveness of the southern drama at which he aimed. To the genre of the southern sporting narrative and the code of behavior it endorses, the characterization of Isaac McCaslin brings not only emphasis on the courage, fair play, and noblesse oblige of his literary predecessors but also a historical consciousness that allows his instincts as a sportsman to resonate within the ample chambers of southern history. Unlike Aleck Maury, whose only concern is himself and the present diminishment of time, Isaac takes full account of the past and its relevance for both the present and the future. Tragically, he fails to comprehend the futility of trying to serve his society, the wilderness, and himself by retreating into dreams of restoring a lost Eden. As a result, his overly refined, passive, and dysfunctional attempts to restore a lost innocence prove of little value in helping either the land or the people to whom he is devoted.

That Isaac's efforts are doomed to failure and himself to a celibate and childless poverty not at all diminishes his stature as a sportsman who draws strength and spiritual regeneration through his encounters with the natural world. Though his circumspective view of history sets him apart from Aleck Maury's obsession with the present, Isaac, too, seems only fully alive when in the woods. But despite their similarities and their shared reverence for the rituals of the chase, there nevertheless remains a distinctive and characteristic difference between Faulkner's hero and Gordon's errant professor. On the one hand, Aleck Maury has nothing left of the southern past but the memory of a proud sporting tradition, and it is only through the sports of the field that he can reclaim any part of his vanishing heritage. On the other, Isaac McCaslin is born heir to a working plantation and its moral and economic responsibilities. By relinquishing his inheritance in favor of a permanent return to the rituals of the wilderness, he attempts a cultural, no less than a moral, capitulation. He has no use for the exploitative traditions and practical conventionalities of his family and his society, but the teachings of Sam Fathers, couched as they are in a particular type of romanticized moral purity, inspire him to pursue his ill-fated and impossible course. And so it happens that the impractically idealistic code of moral conduct that Isaac adopts is not learned within the context of the fallen and compromised world of civilization but rather in the untainted innocence of nature. In this mystical and prehistoric realm, the virtues of honor, courage, and justice can manifest themselves in the graceful perfection of unblemished form. The strong appeal of their perfect moral rightness proves irresistible to Isaac's tortured mind, and he wants desperately to impose their

Edenic imperatives onto his postlapsarian world. His dreams, of course, can never come true, for the working dynamics of his flawed society will not support the tremendous burdens of moral perfection that he would impose upon them. In fact, Isaac's substitution of Sam's heritage for his own is both stupid and blind. Sam's ancestor is Ikkemotubbe, the most frighteningly amoral figure in the book. The "Sam Fathers set me free" speech shows how the guilt Isaac feels has blinded him to the a basic truth about the world: namely, that no race, time, or place is the sole repository of either *good* or *evil.*

Another reason that Isaac fails is that while he rejects the exploitative traditions to which he is heir, he refuses to make any practical, realistic efforts to amend them. All he is willing to do in this regard is to attempt to escape them and their attendant burden of guilt. For him, hunting becomes much more than a diversion, a pleasure, or a training ground for the development of character as it was for hunter-naturalists like Archibald Rutledge and Theodore Roosevelt. It becomes instead a self-perpetuating and ritualistic affirmation of the innocence to which he would return. Unlike Boon Caudill in A. B. Guthrie's *The Big Sky* (1947), a pioneer and hunter of the American West who laments the destruction of the wilderness without accepting his role in helping to bring it about, Isaac is only too willing to shoulder his responsibility for the desecration of the southern Eden. Unfortunately for himself and his society, he will not give up his impossible dream of recreating the past as the vanished paradise he envisions it to have been. He attempts instead a permanent return to nature and feels truly alive only during the two weeks in November when he can return to the big woods and reenact the ritual of the hunt, a vehicle for his reentry into nature and for reclaiming the innocence he desires. As Lynn Levins suggests in her study of Faulkner's use of Christian mythology, the wilderness represents for Isaac a chance to return to a state of "pristine moral innocence" (Levins, *Faulkner's Heroic Design,* 80).

Those parts of *Go Down, Moses* in which Faulkner most directly portrays Isaac's dilemma in terms of his role as an aristocratic southern sportsman are "The Old People," "Delta Autumn," and, most prominently, "The Bear." Because "The Bear" affords Isaac his fullest development, and because it is here that Faulkner is able to bring together and address many of the elements of southern sportsmanship that Elliott and Rutledge had earlier engaged, the present focus will be the scenes and events of this often anthologized section. The first published version of what was to become the fifth section of *Go*

Down, Moses was a story entitled "Lion" that appeared in *Harper's Monthly Magazine* in December 1935. In it we find many of the major characters: Boon Hogganbeck, Major de Spain, and, of course, Lion and Old Ben. This early version, however, is narrated in the first person by an anonymous youth, and it begins with his and Boon's trip to Memphis to buy more whiskey, the journey that opens the third section of "The Bear" in *Go Down, Moses.* Isaac McCaslin appears only briefly as Uncle Ike, already an old man who is afforded second place to Major de Spain in terms of his hunting savvy. In "Lion," Jefferson is just twenty miles away, but the narrator thinks about his stand as a place "where no axe or plow had left a scar, which looked exactly as it had when the first Indian crept into it and looked around, arrow poised and ready" (Utley et al., eds., *Bear,* 141). There is no mention of Sam Fathers or any suggestion of a sacred wood desecrated by greed and progress, and the emphasis is placed on the great dog, Lion, and how his passing even more than Old Ben's causes the still intact wilderness to lose some of its former grandeur.

By mid-December 1941, Faulkner had revised "The Bear" considerably for its inclusion in *Go Down, Moses* and had submitted his final revisions to Saxe Commins at Random House. This is the version that appeared as the fifth of the novel's seven chapters and includes the long genealogical section that became part 4. Most notable for Isaac's explanation of why he feels compelled to relinquish the plantation to his cousin McCaslin Edmonds (the alleged miscegenation and incest Ike believes he has discovered in the plantation's ledgers), this section would at first seem to have little relevance to the themes of the southern sporting narrative. Even the beginning seems to suggest that the narrator would have us leave the forest behind and begin now to concentrate on the world of the civilized South: "then he was twenty-one. He could say it, himself and his cousin juxtaposed not against the wilderness but against the tamed land which was to have been his inheritance" (243). Moreover, Faulkner himself clearly stated section 4's irrelevance to "The Bear" as a short story. When questioned about it in an interview at the University of Virginia, he made it clear that part 4 does not belong when "The Bear" is read as a separate hunting story. Responding to the question "Why did you put Part V after Part IV?," Faulkner replied: "That story [part 4] was part of a novel. . . . It doesn't belong with the short story. The way to read that is to skip that when you come to it" (Gwynn and Blotner, 273). In both the truncated version clearly designed for the consumption of public readerships, which appeared in the *Saturday*

Evening Post just two days before the publication of *Go Down, Moses* (May 9, 1942), as well as in the much longer version of "The Bear" that appeared in *Big Woods* in 1955 and that includes four of the five sections from the earlier novel, part 4 is omitted.

It may at first seem appropriate to select the *Big Woods* version for analysis, especially since this volume collects only Faulkner's stories about hunting, but to do so would be to ignore an important part of the conflict between Isaac's civilized and wilderness experiences. Though the fourth section of "The Bear" deals very little with hunting and sportsmanship, it reveals the manifestation of the philosophical underpinnings for Isaac's relinquishment that had been formed in the big woods under the tutelage of Sam Fathers. It also reminds us that the pristine varieties of courage, justice, and noblesse oblige that both demand and enable Isaac's repudiation are not the products of his civilized world but exist only in the prehistoric realm of the morally untainted wilderness. As Isaac says to his cousin McCaslin in the course of his lengthy explanation, "I am free. . . . Yes, Sam Fathers set me free" (285–86). Isaac, of course, wants desperately to believe it, but the important point here is that the fictional Isaac McCaslin, unlike the actual plantation owner William Elliott, totally and willfully abandons his worldly responsibilities in favor of an attempt to return to the pristine moral innocence of the southern Eden. While in *Carolina Sports* Elliott clearly reveals his belief in the therapeutic value of a temporary reentry into the natural world afforded by hunting, he also spends an entire chapter ("A Business Day at Chee-Ha") portraying how returning too often to the pleasures of the field can be ruinous to the sportsman who ignores his civilized responsibilities. And here again we run hard up against Isaac's tragic flaw. He is unable and unwilling to acknowledge the difference between the kinds of moral and religious imperatives that govern the innocent, natural world and their secularized counterparts in his flawed and fallen civilization. What he discovers is that he cannot escape his inherited, civilized responsibilities by reverting to what he sees as the rituals of innocence, nor can he escape the guilt that he feels is part and parcel of the plantation he stood to inherit. He finds that he cannot go backward in time, nor can he escape his cultural identity no matter how religiously he follows the code of sportsmanship he has learned. On one level, Isaac wishes to perpetuate the ritual of the hunt for the sake of the spiritual solace it brings him, not because he has faith that the rituals have any greater redemptive power. What he in fact desires is the kind of moral perfection that exists only in mystical regions such as the Christian concepts of Heaven or Eden before the Fall.

It is not primarily to Christianity, however, that Isaac turns for moral support to help him justify and endure his relinquishment of the plantation and the subsequent loss of his fortune and his wife but to an older form of pagan ritual first fully articulated by the English anthropologist Sir James Frazer. In the story of Isaac McCaslin that we find in *Go Down, Moses*, Faulkner adapts and incorporates his reading of the first section of Frazer's *The Golden Bough: A Study in Magic and Religion* (1923). According to Carvel Collins, Faulkner read Sherwood Anderson's copy of the one-volume edition of Frazer's book while staying with Anderson in his New Orleans apartment in 1925 (Brylowski, *Faulkner's Olympian Laugh,* 84). In Frazer's first chapter, "The King of the Wood," he describes the ancient myth of the succession to the priesthood of Diana at Aricia near the modern village of Nemi, Italy. Frazer believed this myth formed one of the cornerstones of ancient mythology and religion and openly acknowledges that the object of his book is "to offer a fairly probable explanation of the priesthood at Nemi" (Frazer, 2). According to Frazer, the fundamental elements of the succession are these:

> In this sacred grove there grew a certain tree round which at any time of day, and probably far into the night, a grim figure might be seen to prowl. In his hand he carried a drawn sword, and he kept peering warily about him as if at every instant he expected to be set upon by an enemy. He was a priest and a murderer; and the man for whom he looked was sooner or later to murder him and hold the priesthood in his stead. Such was the rule of the sanctuary. A candidate for the priesthood could only succeed to office by slaying the priest, and having slain him, he retained office till he was himself slain by a stronger or a craftier (Frazer, 1).

With the imaginative license of the novelist, Faulkner adapted this mythical tradition into the story of Isaac McCaslin in *Go Down, Moses*. There were, however, certain necessary changes. Though the succession continues to require the death of the current priest, that death need not be a violent one at the hands of the successor, and the relations between the priest and his heir could now remain entirely amicable. Moreover, the sacred wood over which he presides is no longer a stable geographic entity that can be identified by consulting a map. It is instead dependent on the priest's own choosing as the proper place for the rites of the priesthood to be performed. For example, the first priest to appear in the present time of the novel is a Chickasaw Indian named Jobaker. In the following passage Faulkner describes what becomes the familiar and Spartan seclusion of the priest's hermitage:

> He called himself Jobaker, as if it were one word. Nobody knew his history at all. He was a hermit, living in a foul little shack at the forks of the creek five miles from the plantation and about that far from any other habitation. He was a market hunter and fisherman and he consorted with nobody, black or white; no negro would even cross his path and no man dared approach his hut except Sam (164).

It would appear that during the time of Jobaker's novitiate and succession, the "forks of the creek five miles from the plantation" was considered an adequate and proper ground for the residence of the priest. However, the changing times since Jobaker's ascension have brought civilization too close to his residence for it to remain so. When Jobaker dies, Sam burns the shrine (Jobaker's hut) and presumably the dead priest along with it, for "nobody ever found Jobaker's grave" (166). The morning after the Negro possum hunters have seen the blaze and Sam has fired at them from beyond the shadows, he makes a shockingly unprecedented appearance at the McCaslin plantation house. So far as Isaac remembers, Sam had disdained coming nearer the big house than the plantation's blacksmith shop, nor had he ever courted McCaslin's favor through the "ready and easy mirth which negroes sustain between themselves and white men" (164). Instead, though Sam lived among and occasionally consorted with the plantation's Negroes, his deportment and mien had always seemed to Isaac austere and aloof: "In the boy's eyes at least it was Sam Fathers, the Negro, who bore himself not only toward his cousin McCaslin and Major de Spain but toward all white men, with gravity and dignity and without servility . . ." (164). Nevertheless, when Sam enters the room where Isaac and his cousin are having breakfast, his demeanor on this occasion seems strangely different, like that of a man feeling the weight of a new and formal responsibility that has tempered his customary pride and reserve.

Entering the room "just far enough for the door to close behind him," Sam addresses his hosts without actually seeing them: "the Indian face above the nigger clothes, looking at something over their heads or at something not even in the room" (168). Sam appears distracted, nearly entranced: "'I want to go,' he said. 'I want to go to the Big Bottom to live'" (166). When McCaslin asks how he means to get away from Isaac, Sam does not respond. He only repeats what is phrased as a request but now seems more desperate: "'I want to go,' he said. 'Let me go.'" McCaslin quietly agrees, almost as if he understands that a man of Sam's reserve and pride would never have come to the plantation house with this or any other request unless he felt the goad of some deeply compelling need. Asked when he will leave, Sam replies in the language of a man with no time for the perfunctory niceties of the plantation breakfast room: "'I'm going now,' Sam said. He went out. And that was all." In short, Sam's words and demeanor reflect his need, as the newly ascended priest of the sacred wood, to abandon his customary reserve and to act in conformity with his inferior status in the civilized world of the plantation. What he sees that morning lies beyond and above Isaac's and McCaslin's world; it is "over their heads . . . not even in the room." What Sam is called to do is to discharge his official responsibilities as the newly ascended priest, duties to him far more important than maintaining intact the aloof dignity he has heretofore believed his royal blood required.

Like all of Faulkner's most admirable characters Sam is responsible and duty bound, and a further obligation of his new office is to prepare and train his replacement, a need made even more compelling in view of Sam's advancing age. In fact, Sam has already begun long before Jobaker's death, and "The Old People" shows the steps by which Sam begins to groom Isaac to succeed him as priest. The training begins early and requires most of Sam's time and energy, even though he has always been a privileged character and had never done any more work as plantation blacksmith than what suited him. We learn that he abandons most of what work and consorting with anyone he did as soon as Isaac "got big enough to walk alone from the house to the blacksmith-shop and then to carry a gun" (163). The first stages of Isaac's indoctrination begin in the settled country around the plantation home, and Sam makes a point of teaching his charge the basics of woodcraft, safe gun handling, and the care of the game he kills: "He taught the boy the woods, to hunt, when to shoot and when not to shoot, when to kill and when not to kill, and better, what to do with it afterward" (164). Not surprisingly, the steps in Isaac's early training are entirely consistent with the code of southern sportsmanship.

By the time of Jobaker's death and Sam's move to the Big Bottom, Isaac is nine, only one year away from the time McCaslin has promised him he can go with them to the Big Bottom. Appropriately, Sam has finished the initial stages of Isaac's training the summer before. As Sam and Isaac listen to the mellow tones of a foxhound under the "high, fierce August stars," Sam reveals his satisfaction with his student's progress and development. "I done taught you all there is of this settled country. . . . You can hunt it good as I can now. You are ready for the Big Bottom now, for bear and deer. Hunter's meat." Sam continues: "Next year you will be ten. You will write your age in two numbers and you will be ready to become a man" (167). Of course, nothing could suit young Isaac better, for he has suffered bitterly each November as they begin to load the wagon for the annual hunting trip to the Big Bottom of the Tallahatchie:

> But before the wagon was even loaded the boy would find that he could watch no longer. He would go away, running almost, to stand behind the corner where he could not see the wagon and nobody could see him, not crying, holding himself rigid except for the trembling, whispering to himself: "Soon now. Soon now. Just three more years (or two more or one more) and I will be ten. Then Cass said I can go" (163).

After Jobaker's death, Isaac can accept Sam's decision to move alone to the Big Bottom "without any wrench," for he believed that "the exigencies of his maturing, of that for which Sam had been training him all his life some day to dedicate himself, required it" (167). Though it may appear that Isaac's understanding is preternaturally precocious, he nevertheless is portrayed as a young man eager not only to take part in the mature game of the adult woodsmen and hunters, but also to transcend his "novitiate," both as a boy and potential priest. As Cleanth Brooks has argued, "the boy is trying to learn how to become a man" (Brooks, 250). The dual paths of the priesthood for which Isaac is being trained and the manhood that he desires run on a parallel course, and Faulkner, well aware of the profound intensity of the southern sportsman's engagement with the natural world, tells the story of Isaac's maturation in terms that argue for the close relationship of the code of southern sportsmanship with the code of southern manhood. Both the civilized and the natural versions of maturity require training, discipline, and sacrifice, and Isaac must endure and master them all. He is an exemplary student of both his civilized culture and the wilderness, but he fails to recognize the fundamental differences between the two. One of the major reasons that he cannot is that he has been able to reenter the natural world through his role as hunter on such a deeply profound level and at such an early, impressionable age that the intensity of his wilderness experience has no balancing counterpart in the civilized world of the plantation. Indeed, Faulkner makes a point of underscoring the thoroughness of Isaac's early development in the skills of the wilderness:

> He was thirteen then. He had killed his buck and Sam Fathers had marked his face with the hot blood, and in the next November he killed a bear. But before that accolade he had become as competent in the woods as many grown men with the same experience. By now he was a better woodsman that most grown men with more. There was no territory within twenty-five miles of the camp that he did not know. . . (201).

For those unfamiliar with the role of hunting in human history or without experience in a rural environment where the chase exists as an integral part of the culture, Isaac may appear to be a complex but entirely fictional vehicle for developing Faulkner's ideas—a character that could not possibly have anything like a real-life counterpart. To some scholars of the modern, urban South, it may indeed seem that Isaac's identification with the world of nature not only is a pure fiction but that no one born into the civilized world of nineteenth-century America could ever regain the kind of instinctual relationship with his natural surroundings that Isaac is able to develop. But notwithstanding the seeming plausibility of these reasonable doubts, the hereditary intensity of Isaac's perfect rapport with the wilderness and its rituals argue against these very kinds of faulty misperceptions. It is rather the case that his development as a hunter is based solidly on a complex of psychic and biological realities that reach far back into mankind's primordial past.

Appearing in 1942, the same year that saw the first publication of "The Bear" and *Go Down, Moses*, Jose Ortega y Gasset's *Meditations on Hunting* identifies several of these historical realities. Most importantly he reminds us that for the earliest form of humanity, hunting was the "first occupation" and that in order to survive man had to "dedicate himself wholly to hunting" (118). As Ortega claims, "Hunting was, then, the first *form of life* that man adopted, and this means—it should be fundamentally understood—that *man's being consisted first in being a hunter*" (118). In modern times, men who hunt enjoy it as a sport, a diversion from their civilized, human condition and a chance to return to their hereditary and original vocation, but the hunting instinct remains as one of the "*permanent availabilities in man*" (134). As Ortega reminds us, "It has always been at man's disposal to escape from the present to that pristine form of being a man." Under Sam's tutelage in what remains of the natural southern landscape, Isaac is provided with the perfect imaginative opportunity to reclaim this part of his identity. That he can do so is due in part to the skill and dedication of his mentor, but though his development as a hunter is guided by a semi-mythical figure who desires above all that the priesthood he occupies be properly filled and perpetuated, Isaac brings with him his Paleolithic identity as hunter. Ortega concludes: "'Natural' man is always there, under the changeable historical man. We call him and he comes—a little sleepy, benumbed, without his lost form of instinctive hunter, but, after all, still alive. 'Natural' man is first 'pre-historic man'—the hunter" (134).

Without the existence of this kind of prehistoric inheritance—this kind of "permanent availability"—the story of Isaac's rapid and thorough metamorphosis may place a great, perhaps even an unbearable burden upon sophisticated, urban readers in terms of suspending their disbelief. However, if we accept man's ability at all periods of modern history to succeed through hunting in "annihilating all historical evolution, in separating himself from the present, and in renewing the primitive situation" (135), Isaac's development is entirely credible. In Ortega's words, "The hunter is, at one and the same time, a man of today and one of ten thousand years ago. In hunting, the long process of universal history coils up and bites its own tail." While Ortega would be quick to point out that hunting is not an "exclusively human" occupation, the widespread survival in modern man of this primordial, inherited set of behaviors is presented in *Go Down, Moses* as not only a permanent availability but as a permanent reality as well. Moreover, we learn that Faulkner's young sportsman begins his training in how to reclaim his Paleolithic identity as soon as he is old enough to walk from the plantation house to the blacksmith shop where Sam is waiting. From simply listening to Sam and Jobaker talk about the old hunts, Isaac begins to move through the successive stages of his development.

Because this ongoing process of initiation figures prominently in the thematic structure of the novel, it is fitting that "The Old People" opens with a major step in Isaac's maturation that signals an important turning point in the boy's life. In a scene repeated yearly in southern hunting camps to the present day, Isaac is marked as a hunter after he has killed his first deer: "Sam stooped and dipped his hands in the hot smoking blood and wiped them back and forth across the boy's face" (158). As priest of the sacred wood, the aging Sam Fathers has now formally consecrated the youth to his destiny, and in "The Bear" Faulkner frankly calls Isaac's early training in the Big Bottom his "novitiate to the true wilderness" (187). The term "novitiate" is the right one, for Isaac is being deliberately groomed for high office in a vanishing religious order. What seems strange about this particular novitiate is that the novice here experiences a recurring sense of *deja vu*. During his first two weeks in the Big Bottom, Isaac's impressions are not those of a visitor encountering some new and exotic landscape but rather of a traveler returning to his home:

> It seemed to him that at the age of ten he was witnessing his own birth. It was not even strange to him. He had experienced it all before, and not merely in dreams. He saw the camp . . . and he knew already how it was going to look. He helped in the rapid orderly disorder of their establishment in it and even his motions were familiar to him, foreknown (187–88).

These are hardly the reactions expected from a fledgling novitiate being introduced to alien forms of behavior and thought, but in order to understand the relevance of this unusual passage, we must return for a moment to Ortega's *Meditations*. In the passage below, Ortega explains why Isaac's seemingly unaccountable reactions could be entirely credible:

> When we leave the city and go up on the mountains it is astounding how naturally and rapidly we free ourselves from the worries, temper, and ways of the real person we were, and the savage man springs anew in us. . . . the strange thing is that, although Nature is not our native or habitual environment, when the hunt places us in it we have the impression of returning to our old homestead. The hunting ground is never something exotic that we are discovering for the first time, but on the contrary something known beforehand, where we might have always been, and the savage man who suddenly springs up in us does not present himself as an unknown, as a novelty, but as our most spontaneous, evident, and comfortable being (136).

For Ortega, Isaac's impressions would therefore appear quite natural and even expected. They would represent for him the normal reactions of a civilized being involved in the process of reassuming the most comfortable form of himself. The habits of mind and patterns of thought of the Paleolithic hunter had not been "tamed out of his blood," as McCaslin would have him believe, but only muted and obscured by the slow accretions of culture and society. When Isaac returns to his original vocation, he rekindles a part of himself.

As Isaac's apprenticeship intensifies, he moves away from the perceptual norms and moral conventionalities of what he comes to see as a corrupt and decadent society and toward a conception of the world that is more in keeping with his authentic and original identity. The view he adopts is prehistoric, but it is also prelapsarian, for the southern Eden before the Fall was a realm not only outside of time but outside of sin and death. As he reawakens his archetypal identity through his total immersion and intensive training in the pagan rituals of the wilderness, he also begins to regain a sense of the moral blamelessness that originally surrounded him. Inspired and compelled by this timeless vision of pastoral innocence, Isaac begins the impossible task of restoring to his region the unblemished moral purity his people have lost through their own rapaciousness and greed.

Because his efforts to restore the lost Eden are ultimately ineffectual, Isaac's personal quest is most profitably approached by examining the evolution of his thought as he moves through the stages of his novitiate. The progress of Isaac's development is largely defined in terms of his growing mastery of woodcraft and hunting, and as his prowess increases, so does his receptiveness to a sacramental view of nature and morality. Like the ideal student, Isaac is a willing and precocious apprentice. Faulkner tells us that he accepts his consecration willingly: "humbly and joyfully, with abnegation and with pride too" (159), but before the formal ceremony of drawing and being marked with the first worthy blood, he must first serve his "apprenticeship in the wood which would prove him worthy to be a hunter" (186). Sam has already coached Isaac in how to handle a gun and care for his game, but in the big woods he must also learn the twin virtues of humility and patience. The second year that Isaac goes to the Big Bottom he is eleven years old, but because he is still "alien" until he "had drawn honorably blood worthy of being drawn," his daily post is "one of the poorer stands of course" (169). Isaac's despair at the enforced patience he must learn is considerable: "I'll never get a shot. . . . I'll never kill one." But Sam reassures him: "Yes you will . . . you wait. You'll be a hunter. You'll be a man." Sam takes him to his stand every morning during the two weeks of his first year and on through the last day of his second year, until finally, on the last day of his third year, Isaac kills his first buck, proof positive not only of his approaching manhood but that he has shown to Sam's and the wilderness' satisfaction that he was "humble and enduring enough" (185).

There is another quality that Isaac must learn, however, without which the others can have no real value. That virtue is courage, and Isaac encounters it first in the young hound bitch that overtakes Old Ben during the race on the third morning of his first trip. He hears the dogs running that day, but on this morning they sound strangely different: "no ringing chorus strong and fast on a free scent but a moiling yapping an octave too high and with something more than indecision and even abjectness in it which he could not yet recognize . . . that echo of thin and almost human hysteria, abject, almost humanly grieving" (188). After Isaac and Sam return to the camp, the eleventh hound finally arrives near mid-afternoon, and Isaac and Tennie's Jim must hold "the passive and still trembling bitch while Sam daubed her tattered ear and raked shoulder with turpentine and axle-grease" (190). None of the relevance of the dog's courage to Isaac's development is lost on Sam, and he tacitly compares her action to the challenges that Isaac will soon have to face: "'Just like a man,' Sam said, 'Just like folks. Put off as long as she could having to be brave once so she could keep on calling herself a dog, and knowing beforehand what was going to happen when she done it'" (190–91). On the last morning of Isaac's first two weeks in the big woods, Old Ben passes close enough to his stand to observe him: "'I didn't see him,'" Isaac tells Sam. "'I know it,' Sam said, 'he done the looking.'" Even though Isaac had not seen or even heard the bear, he still felt the pressure of Old Ben's scrutiny: "He only heard the drumming of the woodpecker stop short off, and he knew the bear was looking at him . . . tasting in his saliva that taint of brass which he had smelled in the huddled dogs when he peered under the kitchen" (194). To Sam all this is foreknown, but instead of openly directing his student to confront the necessity of coming to terms with this newly recognized element—fear— he simply makes an offhand gesture: "Sam looked down at the bitch trembling faintly and steadily against the boy's leg" (195). Isaac has, as Sam believes, progressed to the point where the gesture is enough, for Isaac has "recognized fear" and silently accepts the challenge: "*So I will have to see him*, he thought, without dread or even hope. *I will have to look at him*" (196).

When the hunters return to the Big Bottom the following summer to celebrate General Compson's and Major de Spain's birthdays, Isaac sets out alone to see Old Ben. This part of his initiation provides an important part of Faulkner's commentary on Isaac's development as a man and as a hunter. It also continues a part of Faulkner's ongoing attempt to define the virtue of courage that he had begun in *Sartoris* (1929). In the earlier novel, Old Man Falls tells the now aging Bayard about his father's philosophy of courage:

> "Ever' now and then a feller has to walk up and spit in deestruction's face, sort of, fer his own good. He has to kind of put a aidge on hisself, like he'd hold his ax to the grindstone. . . . Ef a feller'll show his face to deestruction ever' now and then, deestruction'll leave 'im be 'twell his time comes. Deestruction likes to take a feller in the back."
>
> "What?" old Bayard said.
>
> Old man Falls rose and dusted his knees carefully.
>
> "Deestruction's like airy other coward," he roared. "Hit won't strike a feller that's a-lookin' hit in the eye lessen he pushes hit too clost. Your paw knowed that" (193).

In the wilderness too, it would seem, the same rules apply, and Sam's advice to Isaac is geared to help the boy deal successfully with what he knows he now must do: "Be scared. You can't help that. But don't be afraid. Ain't nothing in the woods going to hurt you if you don't corner it or it don't smell that you are afraid. A bear or a deer has got to be scared of a coward the same as a brave man has got to be" (198–99). Once again, Faulkner's young sportsman proves himself fully equal to the task. With a deliberate disregard for his safety and in a gesture that seems almost contemptuous of his own death, Isaac leaves his gun in camp long before daylight on the morning he will finally see Old Ben. This relinquishment of power is admirable, and it is well to remember that Isaac at this point in the narrative is only thirteen years old. He is, in fact, exactly what Faulkner implies: "a child, alien and lost in the green and soaring gloom of the markless wilderness" (199). Nevertheless, he has taught himself how to range alone with the compass, and he apparently accepts the inevitable encounter with his loneliness in the steaming summer woods: "green with gloom, if anything actually dimmer than they had been in November's gray dissolution, where even at noon the sun fell only in windless dappling upon the earth which never completely dried and which crawled with snakes—moccasins and water-snakes and rattlers, themselves the color of the dappled gloom so that he would not always see them until they moved" (197). Fairly struck by a mature moccasin or rattler, Isaac would have died just as surely as if Old Ben had mauled him. Nevertheless, he accepts the danger and proceeds unarmed to what he hopes is the long-awaited rendezvous. As Old Man Falls might have explained the scene, Isaac's journey that morning involves looking destruction squarely in the eye.

Nine hours out from camp Isaac pauses to reflect on his situation. He is unarmed, but now he understands that this gesture has not been enough: "Then he relinquished completely to it. It was the watch and the compass. He was still tainted. He removed the linked chain of the one and the looped throng of the other from his overalls and hung them on a bush and leaned the stick beside them and entered it" (199). Soon he is lost and after trying unsuccessfully to cross his backtrack pauses again. As Isaac is soon to discover, he has now reached the inner sanctuary of the sacred wood. In *The Golden Bough*, Frazer describes the "sacred grove and sanctuary of Diana Nemorensis, or Diana of the wood" as a "little woodland lake" with "calm water, lapped in a green hollow" in the "dappled shade of summer woods" (1–2). Isaac, too, finds himself in the "summer woods" lighted only by a "dappled gloom" and in pausing finds himself facing a kind of "woodland lake," described here as "a little swamp, a seepage of moisture somewhere between earth and water" (200). As he starts to sit down on the cypress log, he sees Old Ben's tracks in the soft earth, vanishing as they fill slowly with water, and he follows them into an opening where "the wilderness coalesced. It rushed, soundless, and solidified—the tree, the bush, the compass and the watch glinting where a ray of sunlight touched them. Then he saw the bear" (200).

Within the semi-mythical context of Isaac's novitiate, Old Ben can here be viewed as temporarily assuming Sam's role as teacher. On the page following Isaac's and Old Ben's encounter, Faulkner underlines the bear's role as teacher: "If Sam Fathers had been his mentor and the backyard rabbits and squirrels his kindergarten, then the wilderness the old bear ran was his college and the old male bear himself, so long unwifed and childless as to have become his own ungendered progenitor, was his alma mater" (201–2). As Isaac begins to enter the inner sanctuary of the sacred wood he discerns not the bear himself but rather his fresh but rapidly dissolving tracks. He responds, as any hunter would, by following them, but this scene has been specially staged for his further instruction. He has first of all had to cleanse himself of the taint of civilization by divesting himself not only of his gun but of his watch, which abstracts time and so destroys nature's cyclical endurability, and of his compass, which abstracts space much as the mapping of the wilderness or the "ruthless mile-wide parallelograms wrought by ditching and dyking machinery" (325). Purged and innocent, Isaac is now about to receive his final lesson, a lesson that applies both to the natural and the civilized complements of his life. By this point in the narrative, he has already shown the necessary patience, humility, and courage necessary for leadership in the natural priesthood, but Isaac forgets that he is also heir to the leadership of his civilized society. He also fails to realize that Old Ben, the "epitome and apotheosis of the old wild life," has deliberately led him back to his watch and his compass at the very same instant that he allows himself to be seen for an important reason. He has deliberately juxtaposed himself and the watch and compass in order to illustrate and to underscore the uncrossable gulf that now exists between fallen, civilized man and the uncorrupted natural world from which he evolved. Though Isaac has learned much and has freed himself from at least the external taints of civilization, he can never recover his original innocence, just as he can never regain the natural instincts required for survival in the wild. He is lost in the big woods without his compass and watch, and Old Ben, acting here as both teacher and host, must lead him back to the civilized instruments he needs to survive. Unfortunately for Isaac, he is so awed by what he has seen that he misinterprets his lesson. Having surrendered himself to the discipline and sacrifice necessary finally to see the bear, he mistakenly concludes that the self-abnegation his efforts required constitute the total pattern of moral behavior he is to follow. This particular species of relinquishment and passiveness appears to him as the surest path to restoring his own sense of innocence, and in later years he will attempt to impose this same sort of giving-up onto the personal and communal problems of his civilized world. The tragedy of Isaac's life is that he never realizes the nature of his mistake; he continues to develop the virtues of his class and future office with no thought but that through a passive self-abnegation he can return himself and his land to the kind of pristine moral innocence they have irrevocably lost.

One of the marks of Faulkner's artistry is that he is able to structure his story in such a way that the reader is faced with an interrelated complexity of events wherein Isaac's virtues cloud the issue of his moral culpability. Despite his misperceptions and failures, Isaac is portrayed as master of many of the virtues that both the wilderness and his society need: patience, humility, courage, and a profound respect for the lives of both their human and their animal inhabitants.

With these as the thematic and moral underpinnings of his character, it is only logical that he should develop as well the sense of noblesse oblige that is the hallmark of the aristocratic southern sportsman. We see it emerging first early in the second section of "The Bear" when he and Sam ambush Old Ben (202–3). Here, too, we see an early manifestation of Isaac's tragic flaw, a kind of passive aestheticism that emerges ever more prominently as he develops.

It is during the summer of Isaac's thirteenth year that he and Sam actually ambush Old Ben. By this time, Isaac has already killed his first deer and has developed moreover into a splendid woodsman and hunter to whom no territory within twenty-five miles of Major de Spain's camp is unknown. To this summer's birthday celebration in the big woods Isaac has brought a smallish dog whose diminutive size would seem to disqualify it for hunting bear. Faulkner describes its appearance and temperament succinctly: ". . . a mongrel, of the sort called fyce by negroes, a ratter, itself not much bigger than a rat and possessing that sort of courage which had long since stopped being bravery and had become foolhardiness" (202). In the scene depicting the ambush, the image of the little dog's reckless bravery serves as a dramatic intensifier that parallels the counterproductive and abstract quality of Isaac's own quest for moral expiation. When Old Ben arrives they release both the fyce and a brace of hounds, and the bear, probably "from surprise and amazement at the shrill and frantic uproar of the fyce," turns at bay against a large cypress (203). When Isaac realizes that the fyce actually intends to attack the bear himself, he throws away his gun and runs the dog down so close to the standing bear that it seems that he is directly beneath it. Miraculously, Old Ben harms neither Isaac nor the dog and simply runs back into the forest, followed by the baying hounds. Isaac has acted nobly, even courageously, but his selflessness has brought him no nearer to completing the ritual for which his has been trained. What Isaac must do is finally to consummate the ritual killing of Old Ben, of spilling back into the ground the blood that will fertilize the wilderness spirit and so foster new life. He cannot, or he will not, and his failure to kill the bear parallels his failure to accept the arduous task of dealing realistically with the imperfections of his society and the guilt attached to his material inheritance.

Walking up to where Isaac kneels holding the little dog who continues to "yap frantically, surging and straining . . . like a collection of live-wire springs," Sam is put out and flatly disgusted: "You've done seed him twice now, with a gun in your hands. . . . This time you couldn't have missed him." In other words, Sam is asking the more important question: "Why didn't you consummate the ritual for which I've been training you?" But Isaac has a ready rejoinder: "Neither could you. . . . You had the gun. Why didn't you shoot him?" (203). However, any attempt to resolve this dilemma must first take into account Cleanth Brooks's analysis of the scene. For Brooks, Isaac's failure to shoot Old Ben during any of the three opportunities afforded him is based on his reluctance to bring an end to the ritual: "the yearly pageant-rite of the old bear's furious immortality." As Brooks says, "If the reader . . . ascribes Ike's reluctance to humanitarian motives, he will have missed the point completely" (260). As usual Brooks is correct, and the relevance of his observation operates on a number of different levels. On the one hand, Isaac is indeed reluctant to take advantage of his several opportunities to kill Old Ben because he "does not want a great drama to end" (Brooks, 260). Above all he wants to avoid that "queer feeling" that the young Aleck Maury experienced after releasing the swift and rested hound that finally kills Old Red, the fox that had provided the means and the occasion for their escape into the mystical world of the hunt. In the sacramental view of nature Isaac has learned from Sam Fathers, the hunts for Old Ben are the chief rituals through which the elemental struggle for survival and the persistence, endurance, and courage they involve can be reenacted and manifest with superbly dramatic perfection. They represent for him a singular opportunity to escape into a world where the truth, beauty, and savage innocence he admires can continue to exist in their most nearly perfect forms. To kill Old Ben would be to destroy this world and to return Isaac permanently to an imperfect, fallen world where vice and greed can intrude unopposed upon the moral perfection he wants so desperately. Late in part 4 of "The Bear," McCaslin divines something of Isaac's unworkable aestheticism, and he punctuates his insights by reading Keats's "Ode on a Grecian Urn" to his young kinsman, reiterating the lines "She cannot fade, though thou hast not thy bliss/Forever wilt thou love, and she be fair" (230). This is, of course, exactly the kind of perpetual suspension that Isaac has come to desire: to continue to exist in a kind of imaginative rendering of the world where the realities of life are indefinitely suspended, arrested, and therefore negated by a brooding and perpetual longing for a state of imagined perfection.

While he often acts heroically, Isaac's tragic flaw is that he lacks the strength to accept his flawed inheritance and to use the power and wealth it would afford him to help reverse the human and natural exploitation he abhors. With fatal consistency, Isaac proves equally unable to accept his responsibility for consummating the potentially regenerative wilderness ritual he wishes indefinitely to suspend. As the heir to the pagan priesthood of the sacred wood, his role is to kill Old Ben, thereby spilling back into the earth the blood of the sacred bear and the wild immortal spirit it contains. This is Isaac's role and his alone, one of the sacred duties he must perform to complete his novitiate, but he will not because he knows that to do so would end the glimpses of heroic innocence on which he has come to depend. It is no accident that section 4 of "The Bear," in which Isaac discovers what he believes is Old Carothers's outrage and relinquishes his inheritance because of it, follows immediately on the heels of section 3, in which Sam, Old Ben, and Lion meet their deaths. They were, as Faulkner tells us in the opening lines of "The Bear," "taintless and incorruptible" (183). They represent an elite and impenetrable circle of innocence, and one reason for Isaac's failures is that he cannot accept his necessary and unalterable exclusion from it.

Despite Isaac's failure to accept his responsibilities in either the wild or the civilized world, Old Ben and the wilderness are already doomed, and Boon and the mongrel Lion must finish the drama themselves. Boon, however, is of the "plebeian" class and so unqualified to ascend to the priesthood. Though the sacred animal is technically sacrificed, the formal ritual is ineffective because it was not consummated by the proper authority. As a result, the sacred wood falls victim to the powers of progress and modernity, and the man who should have become its high priest and potentially its salvation is reduced to a childless, impoverished, and ineffectual life. This sort of moral falling off is Isaac's fate, but it remains a destiny that he chose for himself. He could have chosen quite a different path, but in the character of Boon, Faulkner created a literal giant whose limited intelligence restricts his development with a type of naturalistic doom. He is, almost, not even human and is cast in terms that emphasize the strongly animalistic side of his nature: "Boon was a mastiff . . . almost completely unratiocinative" (164), with "the mind of a child, the heart of a horse, and little hard shoe-button eyes without depth or meanness or generosity or viciousness or gentleness or anything else" (218). Unlike Isaac, who even at sixteen can reflect on the pride and humility that he has learned in the wilderness, Boon has no idea of the meaning of the great pageant in which he finds himself involved. He has, that is, none of the qualities of the southern aristocrat except a species of physical courage and his loyalty to McCaslin and

Major de Spain. Moreover, Faulkner makes a point of several times reiterating Boon's incompetence with a gun in order to underscore his lack of qualifications for leadership. He must finally kill Old Ben with his knife, no doubt a courageous gesture and motivated by a genuine regard for Lion's safety, but otherwise Boon is portrayed as "a slave to all the appetites" (164). Very nearly a stock character in the tradition of the wild and illiterate southern backwoodsman, he provides the perfect contrasting background for Isaac's overly nice aestheticism.

Lion, too, plays a major role in the annual pageant, and though non-human and so even less ratiocinative than Boon, his insensitivity to his masters forms a sharp contrast to the fidelity of other canine characters such as Aleck Maury's Gy or Alexander Hunter's Jessie. As we have seen, Hunter could wax eloquent about his faithful setter: "A man may sink into the gutter and kill the affections of all who are nearest to him, but his dog will cling to him through all" (Hunter, *Huntsman,* 245). But Lion is a very different kind of dog, and with good reason. He was not born into a civilized, human world where love and compassion exist but rather into the Darwinian world of nature where the necessities of survival complete the list of one's priorities. Lion is simply a natural force—pure energy—but descended from civilized, European stock that has reverted back to nature and whose strength has been harnessed to help conquer the wilderness. On one level, Lion resembles the American pioneers who opened the West for settlers, civilized beings who had temporarily to revert to savagery in order to be able to master both the elements and the Indians. Later, of course, some of these same pioneers helped to establish centers of civilization and revived their domestic identities, but Lion has had no experience in developing the loyalty of the mastiff and Airedale breeds that were his domestic ancestors. While his courage and great strength make the final consummation of the wilderness ritual possible, there is never any suggestion that Lion hunts Old Ben for anyone but himself.

One reason that Faulkner chose to portray Lion's lack of attachment to his human masters is that this emotional chasm served further to dramatize the progressively widening distance between civilized man and the natural world in which he hunts. This steadily increasing gulf is neither exclusively chronological nor necessarily geographical, though in "Delta Autumn" Isaac twice compares the thirty-mile trip of his youth to the two hundred miles he must now traverse to reach the remnants of the Delta bottom. The true nature of the distance in question here has rather to do with the changes in man's perceptions of the hunt, logical reactions to the inverse ratio of hunting's predominance in his modern, day-to-day activities. As a minor example, the history and evolution of these perceptual changes is suggested by the dramatic content and sequential arrangement of those sections in *Go Down, Moses* that are primarily concerned with hunting: "Was," "The Old People," "The Bear," and "Delta Autumn." In "Was," hunting is so thoroughly a part of Uncle Buck's and Uncle Buddy's lives that they keep both fox and foxhounds in their home. Granted that both the mock hunts for the tame fox and later for Tomey's Turl are laced with irony and humor, the language and imagery of the chase is the vehicle not only of narrative development but also for dramatic articulation. After Uncle Buck has accidentally tried to get into Miss Sophonsiba's bed, Mr. Hubert explains his view of Uncle Buck's moral dilemma in a metaphor about hunting:

> You come into bear-country of your own free will and accord. All right; you were a grown man and you knew it was bear-country and you knew the way back out like you knew the way in and you had your chance to take it. But no. You had to crawl into the den and lay down by the bear. And whether you did or didn't know the bear was in it don't make any difference (21–22).

In both "The Old People" and "The Bear," the situation is greatly altered. The plantation owners and other aristocrats continue to hunt, but now their sport is confined to two weeks in November and they must travel overland by wagon for thirty miles to reach the sprawling tract of virgin timber owned by Major de Spain. Most revealing in this regard is the story of young Isaac's formalized acculturation into the rites of the hunt, a part of his initiation into adulthood that is no longer a matter of simply absorbing the customs and practices of his culture but that now requires a master hunter whose biological ancestry and life's experiences have little or nothing to do with Isaac's own heritage. Isaac's training in the rituals of the hunt are delegated, as it were, to Sam Fathers, but even Sam is an aristocrat by birth, the son of a Chickasaw chief. In the remaining wilderness he may quite rightly be regarded as the high priest of a vanishing order that maintained a sacramental devotion to nature, but in the civilized world of the plantation he is an alien, if privileged, underling. If his duties as priest of the sacred wood require him to train his novitiate to succeed him, his role as the plantation's venatic schoolmaster is to acculturate young Isaac into an important aspect of the rites and practices of an elite and powerful group: General Compson, Major de Spain, and McCaslin Edmonds—all wealthy and influential men for whom hunting had become an expression of their power and prerogatives. It is into this elite, decidedly aristocratic group that Isaac is being acculturated, and Sam is allowed to initiate his young charge into how to acquit himself properly as one of its future members. That Isaac repudiates, or as he says, "relinquishes," his membership in the service of a personal quest for moral purity is not McCaslin's fault, nor is it Sam's, nor even Old Carothers's. Isaac alone must bear the responsibility for his failures and his weakness, and the celibate, impoverished, and wasted life he leads argues that he stoically endured the moral culpability of his decision.

The story of Isaac McCaslin may seem at first to occupy a literary realm so far removed from William Elliott's *Carolina Sports* that only the most strained comparisons could be made between them. It is true that William Elliott's antebellum hunting stories lack the sophistication of Faulkner's artistry, and perhaps some, but certainly not all, of Faulkner's more somber tones can be traced directly to the tragic, intervening events of 1861–65. It may also be observed that unlike Elliott, Faulkner had to leave his accustomed surroundings and employments to hunt with the "right" group, while many of Elliott's tales are set within the environs and the day-to-day existence of his life as a plantation owner. Both men, however, looked to hunting as what Ortega would call a "vacation from the human condition," and both authors' narratives celebrate hunting as a ritual reenactment that afforded them and their fictional characters a means of keeping in touch with the traditions and virtues of the past. Moreover, both Faulkner and Elliott were well aware that those who hunted ethically invoked upon their actions the same kinds of moral imperatives that the southern aristocrat revered in his civilized life. In fact, whether examining the sport of antebellum plantation owners like Major Bulmer in *The Golden Christmas*, professional hunters like Mike Baynam in *The Cub of the Panther*, or postbellum hunter-naturalists like Archibald Rutledge, one easily discerns a definite and clearly articulated moral element in the major southern sporting narratives since 1846. Even Gordon's Professor Maury is clearly concerned with the importance of ethical behavior afield as he seeks his escape into the moral blamelessness of the southern Eden. It is therefore not surprising that in the very zenith of the genre in *Go Down, Moses*, the archetypal representation of the southern sporting hero should err on the side of excessive moral aestheticism.

Like his real and fictional predecessors, Isaac McCaslin valued the rituals of the hunt as a way to escape the flawed and fallen society of which he found himself a part. Unfortunately for Isaac and the wilderness to which he was devoted, he chose to pursue a pattern of self-indulgent denial and retreat that in the end proved fatal for both himself and the pagan priesthood he had sworn to serve. Ike's sense of guilt blinds him, and his moral imperceptiveness includes his failure to understand that Sam's heritage (through Doom and Ikkemotubbe) is as tainted as his own. Ike is too much a Rousseau, a guilt-obsessed "liberal" type, and as such is totally out of touch with the reality that there are no noble "savages" and that wilderness has never been perfect nor Edenic. He fails to learn what his southern sporting ancestors all know—that man (flawed and violent and savage) is only an extension of nature (flawed and violent and savage). He has the southern understanding of sin, but without the southern understanding of redemption. In a very important way, the great southern theme *is* redemption. Faulkner's work demonstrates it at every turn, but Ike is blinded by his guilt and therefore oblivious to it. In this regard he is quite remarkably un-southern, as he is in his abstractionist belief in an earthly, man-willed utopia.

CHAPTER FIVE

Whither the Tradition

Samuel Derieux, Havilah Babcock, and James Kilgo

The literature that has grown out of the life and times of southern society has evolved within a cultural framework whose recognizable identity has remained largely intact despite a broad range of different situations and changed circumstances. Beginning with the time when antebellum regional defensiveness permeated the work of even the finest southern authors, continuing through the inflated rhetoric and sentimental feeling of the bitter years of Reconstruction, and transcending the period when pioneering southern modernists like John Crowe Ransom embraced the objective techniques present in the serious literature of their time, southern writing has consistently been marked by a sense of historical identity, a feeling of community, an emphasis on the specific and the concrete, and a conviction that man is involved in a struggle for survival different only in particulars from his most primitive beginnings. With surprising continuity, this mode of viewing one's identity and experience in terms of the region's natural and cultural history is a strikingly stable element and one of the most enduring qualities of distinctively southern writing.

That southern writers have exhibited a tendency to see the present in terms of the past does not mean that they have ignored the realities of the present, nor that in addressing contemporary issues they have failed to reflect in their writing the particular ideals of moral conduct prevailing at the time. This last, of course, can be said of writers of all times and genres, and the success with which the moral dilemmas of a writer's own milieu are identified, explored, and portrayed remain the measure of his or her stature as an artist. In the southern sporting narrative, the moral element looms large. It may be expressed in imagery that at first seems designed merely for entertainment, but the careful reader will find sharp, decidedly rhetorical divisions between the positive and the negative portrayals of both character and event. The narrative treatment of these important elements constitutes the ways in which the South's sporting writers articulate and explore their moral concerns, both in supporting and celebrating their most cherished beliefs and in ridiculing conduct of which they heartily disapprove. It is, moreover, not surprising that writers as varied as William Elliott, Caroline Gordon, and William Faulkner would choose to express themselves imaginatively in terms of southern sporting imagery, especially in view of its indigenous position in the traditions of the South, traditions that lie at the very center of the southern imaginative vision. But then all great literature has a serious moral dimension. Indeed, it is the very presence or absence of this dimension that primarily differentiates serious from merely humorous or sentimental writing. In one way or another, serious literature seeks to illuminate, identify, and deal imaginatively with moral dilemmas, and the artistry with which an author portrays those problems of good and evil is the evaluative mark of his particular kind of genius. Granted that some authors are more skillful than others in portraying the great problems of mankind, it is nevertheless the impact of the author's life experiences on his thought that remains the determining factor in how he will define the particular moral problems he chooses for his work and in how he decides to depict them. What authors have always been unable to escape is the cultural milieu in which they live. They may celebrate it, criticize it, or simply analyze it, but use it they must, no matter how favorable of, critical of, or indifferent to their surroundings they are.

This is especially true for southern writers, and even a casual look into the genre of southern literature reveals the strong presence of the natural environment as a powerful force in the southerner's life and literature. As scholars of southern writing have long ago learned, the southerner's attachment to the land and his natural surroundings forms one of the hallmarks of southern fiction, both now and in the past. Even with the dramatic demographic changes of recent years, this primitive relationship can be perpetuated and reaffirmed through the rituals of the hunt, and it is through these rituals that the southern scholar-sportsmen examined in this study have succeeded in keeping in touch with the traditions and the values of their cultural heritage. Because these customary sports formed such a large and important part of southern life for much of its history, it is not surprising that southern authors would incorporate these important practices into their fiction nor that they would attempt to express the moral dilemmas they faced, or the societal infirmities they observed, in terms of traditional pastimes and employments. Though long freed from the necessity of relying on hunting and fishing for survival, many educated southerners who were also sportsmen continued to find in the pursuits and etiquette of the field a reaffirmation of the virtues they revered, virtues that were defined by the conservative society to which they belonged as the proper and necessary ideals of the ruling class. On another level, the hunt is portrayed time and again as providing an invaluable type of respite from the tedium and deracination of modern existence, what Ortega has called a "vacation from the human condition." Nevertheless, as the story of Isaac McCaslin tragically reveals, that vacation was never designed to become permanent.

Since its first publication in book form in 1942, the moral complexities portrayed in "The Bear" have been largely taken over by profound and formal literary criticism. It is here that the story and Faulkner's other tales about hunting primarily are situated, in the professional literary canon of the modern academy. In addition, however, the four-part version of Faulkner's famous story that so often appears in literary anthologies has simultaneously been widely read and appreciated by non-literary audiences more oriented toward the sporting ethos and narrative excitement of this classic tale of southern hunting. At one and the same time, "The Bear" is read and studied by professional critics whose primary interest lies in its position within the Faulkner canon and what its themes and artistry reveal about the development of his thought, and also by a devoted following of general readers more interested in its value as a matchless sporting yarn. By positioning "The Bear" as the lead story in *Big Woods* (1955), the publishers at Random House formally situated the story within the subgenre of the southern sporting narrative, publicly acknowledging the existence of the lucrative market of sportsmen and naturalists eager to pay for a volume of stories by the famous author that was chiefly concerned with hunting. In effect, "The Bear" was thereby afforded a type of dual identity within two overlapping literary canons, though writing about hunting in the South appeared to some scholars as a much more limited tradition. Perhaps so, but by the time that *Big Woods* first appeared, the overlapping subgenre of the southern sporting narrative had been kept vigorously alive by the southern scholar-sportsmen Archibald Rutledge (1883–1973) and Samuel Derieux (1881–1922), and the tradition continues to survive in the books and stories by more nearly contemporary writers such as Havilah Babcock (1898–1964) and James Kilgo (b. 1941).

While the mutually beneficial integration of moral and environmental responsibility reached its zenith of harmony and complementary development within the world of antebellum plantation society, this ideal blending of elevated principle and ecological reverence permeates the writing of southern sporting writers of all generations. Samuel Derieux had been born in Richmond, Virginia, in 1881, only sixteen years after the southern surrender at Appomattox Courthouse. He studied at Wofford College in Spartanburg, South Carolina, from 1897 to 1899, and completed his bachelor of arts degree at Richmond College in Virginia in 1904. Following two years of graduate study at Johns Hopkins in Baltimore, he finished his master of arts degree at the University of Chicago in 1910. After a series of assistant professorships in English at his alma mater in Richmond (1910–11), Missouri State Normal School (1911–13), and Wake Forest College (1915–17), he accepted a position on the editorial staff of *The American Magazine* in New York where he served until his death in 1922. As he looked back on his early life from the mature perspective of years as a magazine editor in New York, it must have seemed to him that the world in which he lived had undergone a massive reworking during the course of his professional career. Although he had spent his boyhood in the woods and streams of the rural South, by the time he wrote the series of articles for *The American Magazine* that were collected in *Animal Personalities* (1923), the reality of plantation life had largely vanished from the world that he knew as a boy. He nevertheless shared with his famous contemporary Archibald Rutledge the ennobling influence of an austere southern upbringing, and the summers he spent on his grandfather's South Carolina plantation remained for him a powerful imaginative influence. His life, like Rutledge's, had been tempered and enriched by the sporting traditions and etiquette of the South. They gave him the opportunity to have vital interactions with the land and its game, as well as a wealth of practical experience that taught him to understand himself and his fellows as logical extensions of the nature that surrounded them. Not surprisingly, he found ample justification for this belief in the human traits of the wild and domestic animals that formed such an important part of his life. As his wife wrote in the preface to the 1923 edition, Derieux's ability to allow us to see ourselves in the animals he describes is "the most striking quality in everything he wrote" (xvii).

Man's close kinship with the natural world was clearly self-evident to this traditional-minded southern author, and many of his sketches in *Animal Personalities* suggest how closely the reactions of his animal characters parallel the human condition under similar circumstances. Like many another southern writer both past and present, Derieux harbored an uneasy, nearly instinctive distrust of the city as a hotbed of vice, corruption, and discontent. If we consider the psychological trajectory of his collection as a whole, this apprehension becomes apparent in the marked contrasts between the rural dwellers with which it begins and that of the urbanites with which it ends. For the animals who live in the famed Bronx Zoo in Derieux's final section, "Visits to the Park" (197–279), boredom, unprovoked viciousness, and insanity are commonplace. Compared to the balanced lives of the rural inhabitants with which the book begins, the contrasts in the tenor of their lives could hardly be more pronounced.

The early rural sketches focus primarily on bird dogs, pointers and setters who are either undergoing their training or hunting with their masters as finished performers in the field. There is very little in the way of dissatisfaction or of tragedy here, and most of the stories deal with a kind of canine bildungsroman of how wild-eyed young pups in their youthful exuberance come to accept responsibility for upholding a similar variety of the codes of duty, diligence, loyalty, and honor that their masters revere. Derieux's writing here is impeccable. In his figurative portrayal of the finished dog's character, his faithful depictions of his well-bred charges quietly echo the aristocratic values to which he was heir. The dogs are taught to develop a "habit of obedience" and along with the business of their life's work receive training in "morals and manners" as well (2). The pups are broke of stealing and taught not "to molest the property of others," for "a thieving dog . . . is a reproach to his master. It means, as it means so often in the case of children, that master or mistress, father or mother . . . is careless, lazy, or inefficient" (10). Clearly, the behavior of a dog, for Derieux, gives away the character of his master. In contrast, the well-trained dog is the reflection of a balanced, judicious home life. As Derieux concludes, "I have never known a first-class bird dog who did not have for a master or trainer a patient, just-minded, considerate man. . . . In fact, all the really first-class bird dogs I have known were well mannered" (10–18). Not content to leave so important a topic in the realm of abstraction, Derieux is at pains to articulate some of the finished dog's virtues. The well-trained dog, on command, "should come in and trot at his master's heels" (16). Moreover, he "should be trained not to be greedy about food" and "be broken of a tendency to jump up on people, thereby muddying their clothes." If the dog is allowed to come into the house, he should not "come bolting into the room . . . but walk in quietly, with just a grateful look up at the kind host or hostess" (17). Almost as if he anticipated the reactions of those who believe that a dog subjected to these exacting requirements would be little more than a broken-spirited, mechanical performer whose entire life is a terrified tedium of command and response, Derieux reveals his understanding of canine, as well as human, nature: "Self control, whether coming from within, as with a man, or being imposed from without, as with a dog or a child, does not take away from initiative, but adds to it. I do not think it an accident or coincidence that the gentle-mannered bird dogs I have known were all aggressive in the field and courageous in the presence of danger or insult" (18).

In the rural settings for these excerpts from "Hie On!," the leading story in the opening section titled "My Friends of the Field," Derieux's passion for his topic is evenly tempered by an earthy realism that firmly grounds his subject in the actual facts of its existence. While the kind of hierarchical and structured—even regimented—life that his opening sketches suggest are free from romantic digression into the beauties of a lost civilization and culture, they argue strongly for the particular values of a distinctively southern, nobly austere, and highly disciplined approach to life that celebrates the very practical benefits of such a philosophy. In the sketches from "My Friends of the Field" and "Around the House and Barn," Derieux never tries to lead his readers outside the realm of practicality, moral or otherwise. Indeed, in "Mister Crow," he celebrates the manifest practicality in the crow's "good hard common sense in meeting life as it is" (168). Coarse, unlovely, and without distinction or beauty, the crow continues to thrive in spite of man's attempts to annihilate him, primarily by his wariness to man's approach and his shrewd common sense. In contrast, the bobwhite partridge, who possesses both beauty and the extraordinary gifts of camouflage and speed, is perishing because of his impracticality in sitting tight before the dog who has "seen" him with his nose and in waiting for the man whose shotgun can overcome his swiftness. The rules that govern survival seem always to be in favor of a realistic and practical approach to life, and whatever an animal's gifts, he plays the game for survival with an intensity of involvement that leaves little time for boredom, wastefulness, or brooding. Totally absorbed in their efforts to meet the exacting requirements of the always lethal contest for survival, the behavior of animals in their natural state is consistently governed by an instinctively practical approach to life that appraises each situation in terms of whether it presents an asset or a liability to survival.

In sharp contrast, the sketches in "Visits to the Park" reveal a setting where the natural order of things is sadly askew. In the descriptions of his visits to the famous New York Zoological Park, Derieux presents a far different situation, an artificial and controlled circumstance where the natural world has been captured and turned on its head. In the earlier stories, the animals had either been trained to observe the discipline that would help them to live in harmony with man, as with the pointers or setters, or else examined in their practical adaptations to the business of life in the wild. With the rare exception of the canine degenerate whose passion for killing chickens becomes an obsession, the animals are never unreasonably vicious nor do they ever appear crazed or perversely malicious. But at the "Park," things are different. These quietly alarming sketches portray animals suffering metaphorical reflections of the modernist ennui present in the crowded city that surrounds them. In "Animal Brainstorms" (248–64), Prufrock's moral angst and desperation of boredom and hopelessness confront the reader in abundance.

In captivity, removed from any usefulness to themselves or to their captors, and in the heart of a thriving metropolis, mental aberrations arise in the zoo's inmates that Derieux describes with the matter-of-fact understatement that he has maintained throughout. Is he insensitive to what he sees? By no means, for his very pose of nonchalance beckons us to think about the neuroses he describes and asks us to compare them to the human condition. Like other southern authors then and now, he is skeptical of the effects of urban life on the mind and morals of its inhabitants, though never does he go so far as to say so. What he does, instead, is to present his finely crafted observations with a deliberate objectivity that conceals his narrative intent nearly to perfection. Indeed, it is the very perfection of his narrative camouflage that alerts the careful reader to Derieux's true message. Unobtrusively, as if to assure his readers that the animals in the park are as normal and predictable as they are anywhere else, he begins by citing examples of the zoo's "hell raisers," which posit perfectly believable reasons for their outbursts of violence and rage. There is Mom, for example, the American bison who wrecked her pen and hospitalized her keepers in what she supposed was her necessary defense of the calf they were trying to rescue from a bog. And there is Stanley, the male elk who, during the rage of mating season, attacked his keeper and would have killed him on the spot if a fellow worker had not managed to attract the elk's attention. Later, however, Stanley goes inexplicably insane and, "seized with a sudden rage, rushed

’round and ’round the corral until he dropped, struck dead by thundering apoplexy . . .” (254). Then we learn about the elephant, Gunda, whose unexplainable dislike of her stable boy escalates to include the entire human race, and she finally has to be shot. And there is the male zebra named Bob, who during the beginning years of his captivity had remained comparatively gentle. One day, however, he began to “paw and snap at the keeper, to cry aloud at sight of any human being—shrill yells full of menace” (255). In an attempt to measure the danger he actually posed, the keepers tried an experiment. A keeper’s uniform was skillfully stuffed, provided with a painted cabbage for a head, a wig, and a keeper’s hat and boots. Propped in a natural position with a pitchfork in its hand, the dummy was placed in the empty corral adjacent to the zebra’s iron-doored stall. It is a well-established fact that even the most aggressive wild animals stalk their prey before charging, looking for any type of advantage that might present itself, but when the door leading to the corral was opened for the zebra to see the dummy, his reaction was instantaneous: “[He] let out a cry of rage that could be heard all over the zoo and charged straight at the figure” (256). In the following passage, Derieux captures the savagery of the assault:

> When Bob reached the dummy he reared up and struck it with his breast. The figure went over and Bob fell on his knees above it. First, he jerked off the legs, tossing them into the air, then the body and the head; meanwhile the Park echoed with his cries of triumph and rage. . . . his rage was so great that he knew nothing (256).

After the exhibition with the dummy, the zebra was watched and handled with the utmost care, and not even the bravest keeper would enter his stall or corral. As all came to know, “To enter where Bob is means death” (257). And so it is with others of the wild captives, a lengthy list that includes not only the great bears and tigers we expect to demand the utmost in vigilance on the part of their handlers but also normally nonaggressive animals that confinement has maddened to the point of lethal insanity. There is Ki, the wild ass, who came near killing his keeper after years of docility, and the nameless white-tailed gnu who came to believe that men in uniform were responsible for his misery. Around the throngs of people who visited the park daily, he was normally calm, but if in the crowd he should catch so much as a glimpse of a man in any sort of uniform, he went berserk in what Derieux calls a "noble and devastating rage. . . . You would think he would break [his legs] the way he rushes, stops, wheels about, springs into the air, bucks, kicks, and cavorts. Then he gets down on his knees and begins to rear at any imaginary enemy who he seems to think he has knocked down" (261). Clearly the "brainstorms" in the story's title have a meaning quite different from the common connotation. The animals Derieux describes here are insane, and for their insanity Derieux offers no plausible explanation. But in the background, hovering darkly above and around the animals themselves, is the specter of the city, an unnatural, artificial, and forced confinement of humanity where even animals deteriorate into their most savage and mindless instincts.

Professor of English at the University of South Carolina from 1927 until his death in 1964 and chairman of the department from 1939 until 1962, Havilah Babcock published over one hundred stories about hunting and fishing in the South, many of which were collected into five published volumes: *My Health Is Better in November* (1947), *Tales of Quails 'n Such* (1951), *I Don't Want to Shoot an Elephant* (1958), *Jaybirds Go To Hell on Friday* (1964), and posthumously, *The Best of Babcock* (1974). In addition, he also brought out the short novel *The Education of Pretty Boy* in 1960 and left unpublished at his death the complete manuscript of another full-length novel ("The Affair at King's Elbow") as well as several other unfinished, working manuscripts. The tales that Babcock tells of his own hunting and fishing adventures are rendered with considerable artistry that far exceeds in length and narrative complexity the vignettes of magazine humorists such as Corey Ford, a sporting columnist whose work often appeared contemporarily with Babcock's in the pages of *Field and Stream.* His stories of the sports of the field continue in the narrative tradition of couching moral admonitions in the disarming guise of often hilarious sporting anecdotes, and his concern for the ethical conduct of the sportsman in both the field and society was the natural outgrowth of his career. As president of both the South Carolina Wildlife Federation and the South Carolina Fish and Game Association, as well as national director of The Izaak Walton League, Babcock was a leading supporter of enlightened conservation practices designed to ensure the survival and propagation of the fish and game he loved so well. Not surprisingly for such a dedicated advocate of the morally uplifting virtues of the sports of the field, the last story published during his lifetime carried the title "When a Man's Thoughts Are Pure."

If Faulkner's stories of hunting in the South are considered by literary critics as only tangentially a part of the subgenre of the southern sporting narrative, the writing of Havilah Babcock easily occupies a mainstream position within this smaller corpus that includes such widely divergent southern authors as Andrew Lytle ("The Guide," 1945), Robert Ruark (*The Old Man and the Boy*, 1957), and Franklin Burroughs (*Billy Watson's Croker Sack*, 1991). With Babcock we move away from the realm of the accepted canon of literary art and toward a type of imaginative writing that aims primarily at the fictive recreation of the educated southerner's encounter with the natural world through the field arts of hunting and fishing. This is not at all to suggest that the world of classical myth or the thorny moral dilemmas of contemporary society are left entirely behind, nor that through his sketches Babcock attempted to create a mystical utopia divorced wholly from the society in which he lived. On the contrary, his work is as solidly grounded in the culture and customs of his society as it is in the natural life of the streams and fields he describes. Though he labored patiently at his craft with an eye toward faithfully and forcefully reproducing the South he had known, his writing more nearly resembles that of Rutledge and Gordon in its celebration of both the objects and the ethos of southern sporting life. In metaphorical language drawn directly from the performing fine arts of the field, Babcock's writing continues the tradition of codifying an educated, aristocratic, and decidedly southern view of nature, society, and man's proper role within them.

Blended carefully but unmistakably into this unspoken code are celebrations of the courage, honor, and noblesse oblige of the southern social elite, virtues he expressed imaginatively in the sportsmanship and respect for the land and the game that form the distinguishing hallmarks of the southern sporting hero. Perhaps most importantly for understanding the strong cultural and historical dimension of the southern sporting narrative is Babcock's recurring argument for viewing southern sports and sportsmen, and the traditions they represent, as the logical outgrowths of a culture for whom the natural world remains a profound and enduring presence. In what is commonly considered his most articulate apologia, "My Health Is Better in November," Babcock positions himself and his fellow sportsmen squarely within the tradition of the southerner's inherited and inherent attachment to the land:

> We are children of the earth. When they try to civilize and regiment us, we fret and fume. Our colons become spastic, our pancreatic juices become unhappy,

> and our old chronic ailments go to work on us. We are not unlike the Titans, the earthborn giants of mythology, who were invincible in battle only as long as their feet were planted on the good earth (Babcock, *Health,* 284).

Perhaps without consciously realizing that he had done so, Professor Babcock has here identified one of the major, unifying themes of both the sporting narrative and the larger corpus of southern literature of which it forms a part. Like the Titans to whom he refers, the strong tradition of erudite southerners who have continued to portray the sporting life of their region is firmly grounded in both the climate and the culture they depict. Theirs is an intensely localized, never a globalized, perspective on the human condition, and the moral dilemmas they portray are worked out within the concrete particulars of the southern experience. The emphasis they place on enduring personal relationships, the influence of geography, and the natural cycles of death and rebirth are manifest in their refusal to allow the permanent importance of moral responsibility to become obscured, and thereby minimized, by fashionable trends that define actual human experience in terms of the abstract, arbitrary agenda of political correctness. This penchant for looking beneath and spurning the surface gloss of overly intellectualized, allegedly all-encompassing theories of human and environmental morality and of focusing instead on the practical dynamics of the southern experience is nowhere more evident than in the work of the South's finest sporting writers. Instead of retreating before the seemingly inevitable forward march of theory, their penchant for steadfastly celebrating the perceptible, specific, and practical virtues of southern sportsmanship has intensified in recent years.

One notable example of this enduring tradition is the writing of James Kilgo, Distinguished Professor of English at the University of Georgia in Athens, whose *Deep Enough for Ivorybills* (1988) draws heavily on the realities of the traditional southern life in his collection of stories about modern southern sportsmen. In *Deep Enough for Ivorybills*, he presents a sort of "autobiographical narrative" that portrays the southern sporting heritage in its true light: a complex system of established behavioral imperatives through which its participants learn both the dynamics of their culture and its abiding close relationship to the realities of the natural world (Kibler, *Contemporary Authors,* 248). For Kilgo, the craft of hunting is much less a means of masculine self-expression than it is a vehicle for celebrating his kinship with his family, with his fellows, and with the teeming life in the woods and rivers that surround them. The loosely connected narratives reveal as well that the rituals of the hunt provide him with the kind of solid cultural framework that intelligent writers have always required for serious thought and meaningful articulation. In his highly successful attempt to portray his experiences afield with what he calls "the aesthetic and moral sensitivity one usually expects from serious nature writing," Kilgo believes that his work should serve "to blur if not to obliterate the barrier between 'nature writing' and 'outdoor writing'" (Kibler, 249). These labels for him are simply "a nuisance . . . of use mainly to critics, scholars, and booksellers" unwilling to credit sporting narratives with the serious moral dimension they often possess. Kilgo's writing never descends into the easy rhetoric of second-hand environmentalists, what Archibald Rutledge called the "parlor naturalists," whose starry-eyed euphoria over an imaginary utopia of a serene natural world passes as current to a generation whose life's experience has given them little opportunity to understand either the dynamics of the traditional southern landscape or its ongoing reality of evolutionary cause and effect. His work instead focuses faithfully on the southern literary penchant for the concrete, the specific, and the particular, and his narrative concern with the evolution of the land he hunts emphasizes his belief in the importance of the weight of history to the southern view of the world.

Like many of his literary forebears, Kilgo views the southern experience as very much a story about a large and extended family. He understands how important family ties would be to the traditional-minded characters he portrays, and he uses this motif successfully as a means of achieving the strong sense of organic unity for which his writing is justly known. In his celebration of the communal importance of southern sporting life in acculturating its novitiates into the values of their society, Kilgo focuses on the important roles of the many father figures who appear prominently throughout the text. By imaginatively rendering the positive roles that hunting and fishing play in defining, solidifying, and interpreting their relationships with their sons, Kilgo shows us that the southern sporting tradition is both an educational curriculum and a medium through which its participants can communicate their affectionate regard for each other. By the end of the collection, the narrator has evolved from the youth whose father had taught him to love the natural world into the full maturity of adulthood where he transmits his sporting heritage and its code of conduct to his only son. *Deep Enough for Ivorybills* is, therefore, very much of a family story, one that is intimately bound up with southern ideals of tradition, brotherhood, honor, and morality and with Kilgo's belief, like Rutledge's, that the process of becoming a true sportsman involves an increasing awareness of one's place within the broad fabric of southern society and the moral obligations that one's position demands.

In his commentary on Kilgo's book in *Contemporary Southern Authors*, Hugh Ruppersburg also recognizes that Kilgo's narrator "discovers that the hunt . . . serves as a vehicle toward affirmation of the importance of kinship with his family and his fellows" (220), and one might easily extend that kinship to include a primal, ancestral relationship with the natural world as well. What Kilgo shows us time and again throughout the pages of his collection is a classic, distinctively southern tableau in which the sportsman, the game he pursues, the natural world in which they exist, and the social fabric of his society are bound up intimately in an interwoven system of moral conduct that places a premium on enduring human relationships and environmental responsibility. The hunt is therefore much more than a mere sport or pastime. It is instead a complex, ceremonial link between and among all of these important elements.

As Kilgo maps out his narrator's growing appreciation for the beauty and intelligence of the game he pursues and allows him to think self-consciously about the quality of the relationships that grow out of the shared rigors of the hunt, he discovers a common ground upon which he and his fellow sportsmen can express their reverence for the natural world in an unabashed freemasonry of genuine affection. This is the first virtue of the sporting tradition as it comes down to us through Kilgo's sketches, and it is no accident that his book begins with a scene of the youthful narrator fishing with his father and ends with the image of a red bandanna tied to a giant oak on the hunting club, a gesture of affectionate regard for a deceased member they all had loved. While Kilgo allows his persona to look beyond the pageant of the hunt and to envision his place in the larger history and evolution of his region, his major contributions to the genre in *Deep Enough for Ivorybills* are his portrayals of how the gift of sporting fellowship is intimately interwoven into the most basic fabric of traditional southern society. To his father, to his son, and to his hunting companions, such as Jack Bass and Billy Claypoole, Kilgo's narrator is clearly devoted in the same kinds of concrete personal relationships we find between young Bayard Sartoris and Ringo in *The Unvanquished* or Isaac McCaslin and Sam Fathers in *Go Down, Moses*. Like Sam, Kilgo's narrator is finally involved in trying to hand down the noble traditions of southern sportsmanship, and in

"Peace in the Valley," the closing story in his collection, he wonders whether his son John will continue to hunt as he grows older. He could, of course, simply "outgrow it," and that, of course, is up to him. If he does, however, Kilgo fears that he will never find an activity "that would afford him companionship with such good men as I had known or occasion for establishing a bond with the son that he might have" (185). As Rutledge said in *An American Hunter*, few relationships are closer than those that are formed "through a mutual contact with nature" (141). For the men and boys who inhabit the fictional world of Kilgo's narratives, nothing could be nearer the truth.

Though the South has undergone dramatic, even cataclysmic changes since the time when William Elliott wrote about the pleasures of field and stream on his antebellum plantation, the southern imagination has continued to draw heavily on the imagery of the natural southern landscape as a way of grounding its literature in the concrete realities of the southern experience. In much the same way that the legends of the Civil War and the antebellum plantation remain enduring touchstones for dramatically articulating distinctively southern themes, the natural imagery and dramatic potentialities of the southern sporting narrative remain important staples in the repertoire of writers who continue to tell their particular versions of the story of the South.

BIBLIOGRAPHY

Aiken, David. Introduction to *The Golden Christmas: A Chronicle of St. John's, Berkeley,* by William Gilmore Simms. North Charleston, S.C.: Fletcher and Fletcher Publishing, 1994.

Alford, Terry. "Alexander Hunter and the Bessie Hale Story." *Alexandria History* 8 (1990): 5–15.

Alger, Horatio. *Ragged Dick; or, Street Life in New York with the Bootblacks*. Boston: Loring, 1868.

Alther, Thomas L. "The American Hunter-Naturalist and the Development of the Code of Sportsmanship." *Journal of Sport History* 5 (1978): 7–21.

Babcock, Havilah. *My Health Is Better in November*. 1947. Reprint, Columbia: University of South Carolina Press, 1985.

Bodie, Idella. *A Hunt for Life's Extras: The Story of Archibald Rutledge*. Orangeburg, S.C.: Sandlapper Publishing Company, 1980.

Boschung, Herbert T., et al. *The Audubon Society Field Guide to North American Fishes, Whales, and Dolphins*. S.v. "red drum." New York: Alfred A. Knopf, 1983.

Brooks, Cleanth. *William Faulkner: The Yoknapatawpha Country*. New Haven, Conn.: Yale University Press, 1963.

Brown, Ashley. "The Achievement of Caroline Gordon." *Southern Humanities Review* 2 (1968): 279–90.

———. "Caroline Gordon's 'Old Red.'" *The Southern Quarterly* 28 (1990): 53–62.

Brylowski, Walter. *Faulkner's Olympian Laugh: Myth in the Novels*. Detroit, Mich.: Wayne State University Press, 1968.

Burroughs, Franklin. *Billy Watson's Croker Sack*. New York: W. W. Norton, 1991.

Burroughs, John. "The Literary Treatment of Nature." In *Ways of Nature*. Vol. 12 of *The Riverby Edition of the Works of John Burroughs,* 191–208. New York: Russell and Russell, 1968. This article was first published in 1905.

Camp, Raymond R., James B. Trefethen, and Leonard Miracle, eds. *The New Hunter's Encyclopedia.* 3d ed. Harrisburg, Penn.: The Stackpole Company, 1966.

Carey, F. G. Review of *Carolina Sports by Land and Water*, by William Elliott. *North American Review,* October 1846, 316–34.

Couch, William T. *Culture in the South*. Chapel Hill: University of North Carolina Press, 1934.

Cowan, Louise. "Aleck Maury, Epic Hero and Pilgrim." In *The Short Fiction of Caroline Gordon: A Critical Symposium,* edited by Thomas H. Landess, 7–32. Dallas, Tex.: University of Dallas Press, 1972.

Davidson, Donald. Introduction to vol. 1 of *The Letters of William Gilmore Simms,* edited by Mary C. Simms Oliphant, Alfred Taylor Odell, and T. C. Duncan Eaves, xxxi–lviii. Columbia: University of South Carolina Press, 1952.

De Bow, James D. B. "Periodicals of the Month—What They Discuss, Etc." *De Bow's Review of the Southern and Western States* 9 (July 1850): 124–28.

De Kay, James E. *Zoology of New York*. 5 vols. Albany, N.Y.: Carroll and Cook, 1842.

De Retz, Cardinal Jean Francois Paul de Gondi. *Memoirs of the Cardinal De Retz: Containing the Particulars of His Own Life, With the Most Secret Transactions of the French Court during the Administration of Cardinal Mazarin and the Civil Wars.* 4 vols. Philadelphia: Edward Earle, 1817.

Derieux, Samuel Arthur. *Animal Personalities*. Garden City, N.Y.: Doubleday, Page and Company, 1923. Not all of Derieux's contributions to *The American Magazine* were collected in either *Animal Personalities* or in his earlier novella, *Frank of Freedom Hill*. A survey of original issues from 1917 to 1924 identified seven uncollected stories and sketches.

———. *Frank of Freedom Hill*. Garden City, N.Y.: Doubleday, Page, and Company, 1922.

Dickson, Bruce. "Hunting: Dimensions of Antebellum Southern Culture." *Mississippi Quarterly* 30 (spring 1977): 259–81.

Donovan, Gerald. "Irish Folklore Influences on Simms's 'Sharp Snaffles' and 'Bald-Head Bill Bauldy.'" In *William Gilmore Simms and the American Frontier*, edited by John Caldwell Guilds and Caroline Collins, 192–206. Athens: University of Georgia Press, 1997.

Edens, Janice L. "The *Southern Review*." In *American Literary Magazines: The Eighteenth and Nineteenth Centuries,* edited by Edward E. Chielens, 404–9. New York: Greenwood Press, 1986.

Elliott, William. *Address Delivered by Special Request before the St. Paul's Agricultural Society, May, 1850.* Charleston, S.C.: Press of Walker and James, 1850.

———. *Address to the People of St. Helena Parish.* Charleston, S.C.: Charleston Press, 1832.

———. *The Anniversary Address of the State Agricultural Society, Delivered in the Hall of the House of Representatives, November 30, 1848.* Columbia, S.C.: John G. Bowman, 1848.

———. *Carolina Sports by Land and Water; Including Incidents of Devil-Fishing, Wild-Cat, Deer and Bear Hunting, Etc.* Charleston, S.C.: Burges and James, 1846.

———. *Fiesco; A Tragedy.* New York: Trehern and Williamson, 1850.

———. *The Letters of Agricola*. Greenville, S.C.: Office of the *Southern Patriot*, 1852.

———. "On the Cultivation and High Prices of Sea-Island Cotton." *Southern Agriculturist* 2 (April 1828): 151–63.

———. "On the Cultivation of Male Cotton." *Southern Agriculturist* 2 (August 1829): 352–55.

———. Review of *Anne of Geierstein; or, The Maiden of the Mist*, by Sir Walter Scott. *Southern Review,* November 1829, 498–522.

———. Review of *The Works of Ben Jonson*, edited by William Gifford. *Southern Review,* August 1830, 91–116.

———. "A Trip to Cuba." Parts 1–6. *Russell's Magazine* 2 (October 1857): 59–63; 2 (November 1857): 116–23; 2 (December 1857): 235–39; 2 (January 1858): 322–27; 2 (February 1858): 439–45; 3 (April 1858): 60–69.

Faulkner, William. *Big Woods*. New York: Random House, 1955.

———. *Flags in the Dust*. Edited and with an introduction by Douglas Day. New York: Random House, 1973. An uncut version of *Sartoris.*

———. *Go Down, Moses*. 1942. Reprint, New York: Vintage Books, 1990.

———. "Lion: A Story." *Harper's Monthly Magazine,* December 1935, 67–77. Reprinted in *Bear, Man, and God,* ed. Francis Lee Utley, Lynn Z. Bloom, and Arthur F. Kinney (New York: Random House, 1964), 132–49.

———. *Sartoris*. New York: Harcourt and Brace, 1929.

Fraistat, Rose Ann C. *Caroline Gordon as Novelist and Woman of Letters*. Baton Rouge: Louisiana State University Press, 1984.

Franklin, Benjamin. *Autobiography*. 1791. Reprint, edited by Leonard W. Labaree et al., New Haven, Conn.: Yale University Press, 1964.

Frazer, Sir James. *The Golden Bough: A Study in Magic and Religion*. New York: The Macmillan Company, 1923.

Frost, Robert. "Home Burial." In *The Poetry of Robert Frost,* edited by Edward Connery Lathem, 51–55. New York: Henry Holt and Company, 1979.

Gladden, George. Review of *The Huntsman in the South*, by Alexander Hunter. *The Bookman,* August 1908, 609.

Gordon, Caroline. *Aleck Maury, Sportsman*. 1934. Reprint, edited by Matthew J. Bruccoli, Carbondale: Southern Illinois University Press, 1980.

———. "Cock-Crow." *The Southern Review,* n.s., 1 (1965): 554–69.

———. "Old Red." In *The Collected Stories of Caroline Gordon.* New York: Farrar, Straus, and Giroux, 1981. This story was first published in 1933.

Gray, Richard. *The Life of William Faulkner: A Critical Biography*. Cambridge, Mass.: Blackwell Publishers, 1996.

A Guide to the Famous Hunting and Fishing Grounds of Virginia, North Carolina, South Carolina, and Georgia, Traversed by the Seaboard Air Line, With a Synopsis of the Game Laws of Those States. Richmond, Va.: A. Hoen and Company, 1898.

Guilds, John Caldwell. *Simms: A Literary Life.* Fayetteville: University of Arkansas Press, 1992.

Guthrie, A. B. *The Big Sky*. New York: William Stone, 1947.

Gwynn, Frederick L. and Joseph Blotner, eds. *Faulkner in the University: Class Conferences at the University of Virginia, 1957–1958.* Charlottesville: University of Virginia Press, 1959.

Halls, Lowell K. *White-tailed Deer: Ecology and Management*. Harrisburg, Penn.: Stackpole Books, 1984.

Haliburton, T. C., ed. *Traits of American Humor: By Native Americans*. 3 vols. London: Colburn and Company, 1852.

Harris, George Washington. *Sut Lovingood: Yarns Spun by a "Nat'ral Born Durn'd Fool*." New York: Dick and Fitzgerald, 1867.

Haviland, William A. *Human Evolution and Prehistory*. 4th ed. New York: Harcourt Brace College Publishers, 1997.

Hemingway, Ernest. "Big Two-Hearted River." In *The Nick Adams Stories,* 177–99. New York: Charles Scribner's Sons, 1972.

Herndon, Jerry A. "Aleck Maury's Tragic Sense of Life," *The University of Mississippi Studies in English,* n.s., 5 (1987): 203–14.

Hubbell, Jay B. *The South in American Literature, 1607–1900.* Durham, N.C.: Duke University Press, 1954.

Hunter, Alexander. "Booth and Bessie Hale." *The Occasional,* June 1908. In "Alexander Hunter and the Bessie Hale Story," *Alexandria History* 8 (1990): 5–15. Terry Alford asserts that no copies of this issue of *The Occasional* have survived.

———. "The Club Houses of Currituck Sound." *Harper's Weekly* 36 (1892): 253–55.

———. *The Huntsman in the South.* New York: Neal Publishing Company, 1908.

———. *Johnny Reb and Billy Yank*. New York: Neal Publishing Company, 1905.

———. *The Women of the Debatable Land*. Washington, D.C.: Cobden Publishing Company, 1912.

Hunting and Fishing in the South: A Book Descriptive of the Best Localities in the South for Various Kinds of Game and Fish. The Game Laws of Virginia, North Carolina,

South Carolina, Kentucky, Georgia, Florida, Alabama, Tennessee, and Mississippi—the States Penetrated by the Southern Railway. Washington, D.C.: Southern Railway Company, 1904.

Jeliffe, Robert A., ed. *Faulkner at Nagano*. Tokyo: Kenkyusha Ltd., 1956.

Jones, Louis Pinckney. "William Elliott: South Carolina Nonconformist." *Journal of Southern History* 17 (August 1951): 361–81.

Jonza, Nancylee Novell. *The Underground Stream: The Life and Art of Caroline Gordon*. Athens: University of Georgia Press, 1995.

Kibler, James E., Jr. "James Kilgo." In *Contemporary Authors*. Vol. 127. Detroit, Mich.: Gale Research Company, 1989.

———. "Not-So-Intellectual Imperialism." *Mississippi Quarterly* 48 (spring 1995): 337–42. Review of William Elliott's *Carolina Sports by Land and Water* with a new introduction by Theodore Rosengarten.

———. "Simms's Indebtedness to Folk Tradition." *Southern Literary Journal* 4 (1972): 55–68.

———. "William Elliott III." In *Dictionary of Literary Biography*. Vol. 3. Detroit, Mich.: Gale Research Company, 1979.

Kilgo, James. *Deep Enough for Ivorybills*. Chapel Hill, N.C.: Algonquin Books of Chapel Hill, 1988.

Kreyling, Michael. *Figures of the Hero in Southern Narrative*. Baton Rouge: Louisiana State University Press, 1987.

Levins, Lynn. *Faulkner's Heroic Design: The Yoknapatawpha Novels*. Athens: University of Georgia Press, 1976.

Lytle, Andrew. "The Guide." *Sewanee Review* 53 (1945): 363–87.

———. "Caroline Gordon and the Historical Image." *Sewanee Review* 57 (1949). Reprinted in *Southerners and Europeans: Essays in a Time of Disorder*, edited by Louis P. Simpson, 78–99. Baton Rouge: Louisiana State University Press, 1988.

Marks, Stuart. *Southern Hunting in Black and White*. Princeton, N.J.: Princeton University Press, 1991.

Marshall, Ian. "The American Dreams of Sam Snaffles." *Southern Literary Journal* 17 (1986): 97–107.

Meriwether, James B. "Simms's 'Sharp Snaffles' and 'Bald-Head Bill Bauldy': Two Views of Men—and of Women." *South Carolina Review* 16, (1984): 66–71.

Mott, Frank L. *A History of American Magazines, 1741–1850.* New York: D. Appleton, 1930.

Nelson, Richard K. *Heart and Blood: Living with Deer in America*. New York: Alfred A. Knopf, 1997.

———. *Hunters of the Northern Ice*. Chicago: University of Chicago Press, 1969.

———. *Make Prayers to the Raven: A Koyukon View of the Northern Forest*. Chicago: University of Chicago Press, 1983.

———. *Shadow of the Hunter: Stories of Eskimo Life*. Chicago: University of Chicago Press, 1980.

O'Brien, Michael. *A Character of Hugh Legaré*. Knoxville: University of Tennessee Press, 1985.

Ortega y Gasset, José. *Meditations on Hunting*. Translated by Howard B. Wescott. New York: Scribner, 1972.

Owens, Loulie Latimer. "Guide to the Archibald Hamilton Rutledge Papers: 1860–1970." Columbia, S.C.: South Caroliniana Library Manuscripts Division, 1972–74.

Page, Thomas Nelson. *In Ole Virginia*. 1887. Reprint, Nashville, Tenn.: J. S. Sanders and Company, 1991.

Paulding, James Kirke. *Westward Ho! A Tale*. 2 vols. New York: J. and J. Harper, 1832.

Ransom, John Crowe et al. *I'll Take My Stand: The South and the Agrarian Tradition*. 1930. Reprint, New York: Harper and Row Publishers, 1962.

Redfield, Robert. *The Primitive World and Its Transformations*. Ithaca, N.Y.: Cornell University Press, 1953.

Rhea, Linda. *Hugh Swinton Legaré, A Charleston Intellectual.* Chapel Hill: University of North Carolina Press, 1934.

Reiger, John F. *American Sportsmen and the Origins of Conservation*. New York: Winchester Press, 1975.

Rocks, James E. "The Mind and Art of Caroline Gordon." *Mississippi Quarterly* 21 (1967–68): 1–28.

Roosevelt, Theodore. "A Hunter Naturalist in Europe and Africa." In *Literary Essays*. Vol. 12 of *The National Edition of the Works of Theodore Roosevelt,* edited by Hermann Hagedorn, 368–76. New York: Charles Scribner's Sons, 1924–27. This essay was first published in 1911.

———. *Hunting Trips of a Ranchman*. In *Hunting Trips of a Ranchman and Ranch Life and the Hunting Trail*. Vol. 1 of *The National Edition of the Works of Theodore Roosevelt,* edited by Hermann Hagedorn. New York: Charles Scribner's Sons, 1924–27. This work was first published in 1885.

———. "The Master of the Game." In *Literary Essays*. Vol. 12 of *The National Edition of the Works of Theodore Roosevelt*, edited by Hermann Hagedorn, 347–54. New York: Charles Scribner's Sons, 1924–27. This work was first published in 1904.

———. "Nature-Fakers." In *Through the Brazilian Wilderness and Papers on Natural History*. Vol. 5 of *The National Edition of the Works of Theodore Roosevelt,* edited by Hermann Hagedorn, 375–83. New York: Charles Scribner's Sons, 1924–27. This work was first published in 1907.

———. *Outdoor Pastimes of an American Hunter*. In *Outdoor Pastimes of an American Hunter 2 and A Book Lover's Holiday in the Open*. Vol. 3 of *The National Edition of the Works of Theodore Roosevelt,* edited by Hermann Hagedorn. New York: Charles Scribner's Sons, 1924–27. This work was first published in 1905.

———. *The Wilderness Hunter*. In *The Wilderness Hunter and Outdoor Pastimes of an American Hunter 1*. Vol. 2 of *The National Edition of the Works of Theodore Roosevelt*, edited by Hermann Hagedorn. New York: Charles Scribner's Sons, 1924–27. This work was first published in 1893.

Rosengarten, Theodore. Introduction to *Carolina Sports by Land and Water,* by William Elliott, ix–xliii. Columbia, S.C.: University of South Carolina Press, 1994.

Ruark, Robert. *The Old Man and the Boy*. New York: Henry Holt and Company, 1957.

Rubin, Louis D., Jr. Introduction to *I'll Take My Stand: The South and the Agrarian Tradition,* by Twelve Southerners, vi–viii. New York: Harper and Row Publishers, 1962. The Twelve Southerners are, of course, John Crowe Ransom and his co-authors.

———. *William Elliott Shoots a Bear: Essays on the Southern Literary Imagination*. Baton Rouge: Louisiana State University Press, 1975.

Ruppersburg, Hugh. "James Kilgo." *Contemporary Southern Writers*, edited by Roger Matuz. Detroit, Mich.: St. James Press, 1999.

Rutledge, Archibald. *An American Hunter.* New York: Frederick A. Stokes Company, 1937.

———. *Children of Swamp and Wood*. Garden City, N.Y.: Doubleday, Page and Company, 1927.

———. *My Colonel and His Lady*. New York: The Bobbs-Merril Company, 1937.

———. *Plantation Game Trails*. Boston: Houghton Mifflin Company, 1921.

Rutledge, Irvine. *We Called Him Flintlock*. Columbia, S.C.: R. L. Bryan Company, 1974.

Scafidel, Beverly. "William Elliott, Planter and Politician: New Evidence from the Charleston Newspapers, 1831–1856." In *South Carolina Journals and Journalists,* edited by James B. Meriwether, 109–19. Spartanburg, S.C.: The Reprint Company, 1974.

———. "The Letters of William Elliott." 3 vols. Ph.D. diss., University of South Carolina, 1978.

Shepard, Paul. *The Tender Carnivore and the Sacred Game*. New York: Scribner, 1973.

Shillingsburg, Miriam Jones. Afterword to *The Cub of the Panther: A Hunter Legend of the "Old North State,"* by William Gilmore Simms. Fayetteville: University of Arkansas Press, 1997.

———. "An Edition of William Gilmore Simms's *The Cub of the Panther*." Ph.D. diss., University of South Carolina, 1969.

———. "From Notes to Novel: Simms's Creative Method." *Southern Literary Journal* 5 (1972): 89–107.

———. "Simms's Last Novel, *The Cub of the Panther*." *Southern Literary Journal* 17 (1985): 108–19.

Simms, William Gilmore. "'Bald-Head Bill Bauldy'; and How He Went through the Flurriday Campaign!—A Legend of the Hunter's Camp." In *Stories and Tales,* edited by John Caldwell Guilds, et al., 466–521. Vol. 5 of *The Writings of William Gilmore Simms, Centennial Edition*. Columbia: University of South Carolina Press, 1974.

———. *The Cub of the Panther: A Hunter Legend of the "Old North State."* 1869. Reprint, edited by Miriam Jones Shillingsburg, Fayetteville: University of Arkansas Press, 1997. Parenthetical references to page numbers refer to this edition of the novel.

———. *The Cassique of Kiawah: A Colonial Romance*. 1859. Reprint, Gainesville, Ga.: The Magnolia Press, 1989.

———. *Eutaw: A Sequel to The Forayers, or, The Raid of the Dog-Days. A Tale of the Revolution.* 1856. Reprint, Spartanburg, S.C.: The Reprint Company, 1976.

———. *The Forayers: or, The Raid of the Dog-Days*. 1855. Reprint, Spartanburg, S.C.: The Reprint Company, 1976.

———. *The Golden Christmas: A Chronicle of St. John's, Berkeley*. 1852. Reprint, North Charleston, S.C.: Fletcher and Fletcher Publishing, 1994.

———. "How Sharp Snaffles Got His Capital and Wife." In *Stories and Tales,* edited by John Caldwell Guilds et al., 421–65. Vol. 5 of *The Writings of William Gilmore Simms, Centennial Edition*. Columbia: University of South Carolina Press, 1974. This story was first published in 1870.

———. *Katherine Walton: or, the Rebel of Dorchester: An Historical Romance of the Revolution in Carolina*. 1851. Reprint, Spartanburg, S.C.: The Reprint Company, 1976.

———. *The Letters of William Gilmore Simms*, edited by Mary C. Simms Oliphant, Alfred Taylor Odell, and T. C. Duncan Eaves. 6 vols. Columbia, S.C.: University of South Carolina Press, 1952–82. Parenthetical references to individual letters provide volume and page numbers in this collection.

———. *Views and Reviews in American Literature, History and Fiction*. First series. 1845. Cambridge, Mass.: Harvard University Press, Belknap Press, 1962.

———. *Voltmeier or the Mountain Men,* edited by James B. Meriwether. Vol. 1 of *The Writing of William Gilmore Simms, Centennial Edition*. Columbia: University of South Carolina Press, 1969. This work was first published in 1869.

———. *Woodcraft or Hawks about the Dovecote*. 1854. Reprint, Spartanburg, S.C.: The Reprint Company, 1976. Reprint of *The Sword and the Distaff.*

[Simms, William Gilmore?]. Review of *Carolina Sports by Land and Water*, by William Elliott. *Southern Quarterly Review,* July 1847, 67–90.

Skardon, B. N. "William Elliott: Planter-Writer of Ante-Bellum South Carolina." Master's thesis, University of Georgia, 1964.

Squires, Radcliffe. "The Underground Stream: A Note on Caroline Gordon's Fiction." *The Southern Review* n.s., 7 (1971): 467–79.

Utley, Francis Lee, Lynn Z. Bloom, and Arthur F. Kinney, eds. *Bear, Man, and God.* New York: Random House, 1964.

Watson, Charles S. "Simms and the Beginnings of Local Color." *Mississippi Quarterly* 35 (1981–82): 25–39.

Waldron, Ann. *Close Connections: Caroline Gordon and the Southern Renaissance*. New York: G. P. Putnam's Sons, 1987.

Warren, Robert Penn. Introduction to *The Collected Stories of Caroline Gordon*, ix–xiii. New York: Farrar, Straus, Giroux, 1981.

Wauchope, George Armstrong. "William Elliott (1788–1863)." Vol. 4 of *Library of Southern Literature,* edited by Edwin Anderson Alderman and Joel Chandler Harris. Atlanta: The Martin and Hoyt Company, 1909.

Welsh, John R. "Southern Literary Magazines 4: An Early Pioneer: Legare's *Southern Review*." *Southern Literary Journal* 3 (1971): 80–97.

Wheeler, Mary Bray and Genon Hickerson Neblett. *Hidden Glory: The Life and Times of Hampton Plantation, Legend of the South Santee*. Nashville, Tenn.: Rutledge Hill Press, 1983.

Who Was Who in America. Vol. 1, 1897–1942. S.v. "Derieux, Samuel Arthur." Chicago: A. N. Marquis Co., 1943.

Wimsatt, Mary Ann. *The Major Fiction of William Gilmore Simms*. Baton Rouge: Louisiana State University Press, 1989.

Wood, Sally, ed. *The Southern Mandarins: Letters of Caroline Gordon to Sally Wood, 1924–1937*. Baton Rouge: Louisiana State University Press, 1984.

Woodell, Harold. "Archibald Rutledge." In *Southern Writers: A Biographical Dictionary,* edited by Robert Bain, Joseph M. Flora, and Louis D. Rubin Jr. Baton Rouge: Louisiana State University Press, 1979.

INDEX